THE CRITERION;

OR THE

TEST OF TALK ABOUT FAMILIAR THINGS.

A Series of Essays.

BY

HENRY T. TUCKERMAN.

Our knowledge is real only so far as there is a conformity between our ideas and the reality of things; but what shall be the Criterion? — LOCKE.

——— the flowery walk
Of letters, genial table talk,
Or deep dispute and graceful jest.
TENNYSON.

NEW YORK:
PUBLISHED BY HURD AND HOUGHTON.
BOSTON: E. P. DUTTON AND COMPANY.
1866.

RIVERSIDE, CAMBRIDGE:
STEREOTYPED AND PRINTED BY
H. O. HOUGHTON AND COMPANY.

CONTENTS.

INNS.

> Whoe'er has travelled life's dull round,
> Whate'er his fortunes may have been,
> Must sigh to think how oft he 's found
> Life's warmest welcome at an inn.
>
> SHENSTONE.

HE old, legitimate, delightful idea of an Inn is becoming obsolete; like so many other traditional blessings, it has been sacrificed to the genius of locomotion. The rapidity with which distance is consumed obviates the need that so long existed of by-way retreats and halting-places. A hearty meal or a few hours' sleep, caught between the arrival of the trains, is all the railway traveller requires; and the modern habit of moving in caravans has infinitely lessened the romantic probabilities and comfortable realities of a journey: the rural alehouse and picturesque hostel now exist chiefly in the domain of memory; crowds, haste, and ostentation triumph here over privacy and rational enjoyment, as in nearly all the arrangements of modern society. Old Walton would discover now but few of the secluded inns that refreshed him on his piscatorial excursions; the ancient ballads on the wall have given place to French paper; the scent of lavender no longer makes the linen fragrant; instead of the crackle of the open wood-fire, we have the dingy coal-smoke, and exhalations of a stove; and green

blinds usurp the place of the snowy curtains. Not only these material details, but the social character of the inn, is sadly changed. Few hosts can find time to gossip; the clubs have withdrawn the wits; the excitement of a stage-coach arrival is no more; and a poet might travel a thousand leagues without finding a romantic "maid of the inn," such as Southey has immortalized. Jollity, freedom, and comfort are no longer inevitably associated with the name; the world has become a vast procession that scorns to linger on its route, and has almost forgotten how to enjoy. Thanks, however, to the conservative spell of literature, we can yet appreciate, in imagination, at least, the good old English inn. Goldsmith's Village Alehouse has daguerreotyped its humble species, while Dr. Johnson's evenings at the Mitre keep vivid the charm of its metropolitan fame. Indeed, it is quite impossible to imagine what British authors would have done without the solace and inspiration of the inn. Addison fled thither from domestic annoyance; Dryden's chair at Will's was an oracular throne; when hard pressed, Steele and Savage sought refuge in a tavern and wrote pamphlets for a dinner; Farquhar found there his best comic material; Sterne opens his "Sentimental Journey" with his landlord, Monsieur Dessein, Calais, and his inn-yard; Shenstone confessed he found "life's warmest welcome at an inn;" Sheridan's convivial brilliancy shone there with peculiar lustre; Hazlitt relished Congreve anew reading him in the shady windows of a village inn after a long walk; even an old Almanac, or Annual Register, will acquire an interest under such circumstances; and a dog-eared copy of the "Seasons" found in such a place induced Coleridge to exclaim, "This is fame!"

while Byron exulted when informed that a well-thumbed volume of the "English Bards" had been seen soon after its publication, at a little hostel in Albany. Elia's quaint anecdote of the Quakers when they all eat supper without paying for it, and Irving's "Stout Gentleman," are incidents which could only have been suggested by a country inn; and as to the novelists, from Smollett and Fielding to Scott and Dickens, the most characteristic scenes occur on this vantage-ground, where the strict unities of life are temporarily discarded, and its zest miraculously quickened by fatigue, hunger, a kind of infinite possibility of events, a singular mood of adventure and pastime, nowhere else in civilized lands so readily induced. It is, therefore, by instinct that these enchanting chroniclers lead us thither, from old Chaucer to our own Longfellow. Gil Blas acquired his first lesson in a knowledge of the world, by his encounter with the parasite at the inn of Panafleur; and Don Quixote's enthusiasm always reaches a climax at these places of way-side sojourn. The Black Bull, at Islington, is said to have been Sir Walter Raleigh's mansion; Dolly's Chop-House is dear to authors for the sake of Goldsmith and his friends, who used to go there on their way to and from Paternoster Row. At the Salutation and Cat, Smithfield, Coleridge and Lamb held memorable converse; and Steele often dated his "Tatlers" from the Trumpet. How appropriate for Voltaire to have lodged, in London, at the White Peruke! Spenser died at an inn in King Street, Westminster, on his return from Ireland. At the Red Horse, Stratford, is the "Irving room," precious to the American traveller; and how renowned have sweet Anne Page and jolly Falstaff made the very name of the Garter Inn! In the East a monastery, in the Desert a tent, on the Nile a boat, a *hacienda* in South America, a kiosk in Turkey, a *caffé* in Italy, but in Britain an inn, is the pilgrim's home, and one not less characteristic. The subject as suggestive of the philosophy of civilization is worth investigation.

In England and in towns of Anglo-Saxon origin, where the economies of life have a natural sway, we find inns representative; in London, especially, a glance at the parlor-wall reveals the class to whose convenience the tavern is dedicated: in one the portraits of actors, in another scenes in the ring and on the race-course, here the countenance of a leading merchant, and there a military effigy, suggest the vocation of those who chiefly frequent the inn; nor are local features less certain to find recognition: a view of the nearest nobleman's estate, or his portrait, ornaments the sitting-room; and the observant eye can always discover an historical hint at these public resorts. Heywood the dramatist aptly specified this representative character of inns:—

"The gentry to the King's Head,
The nobles to the Crown,
The knights unto the Golden Fleece,
And to the Plough the clown;
The churchman to the Mitre,
The shepherd to the Star,
The gardener hies him to the Rose,
To the Drum the man of war;
To the Feathers, ladies, you; the Globe
The seamen do not scorn,
The usurer to the Devil, and
The townsman to the Horn;
The huntsman to the White Hart,
To the Ship the merchants go,
But you that do the Muses love
The sign called River Po;

> The bankrupt to the World's End,
> The fool to the Fortune hie,
> Unto the Mouth the oyster-wife,
> The fiddler to the Pie,
> . . . .
> The drunkard to the Vine,
> The beggar to the Bush, then meet
> And with Sir Humphrey dine."

Inn-signs are indeed historical landmarks: in the Middle Ages the Cross-Keys, the Three Kings, and St. Francis, abounded; the Puritans substituted for Angel and Lady, the Soldier and Citizen; the Saracen's Head was a device of the Crusades; and before, the Coach and Horses was the sign of the Packhorse, indicative of the days of equestrian travel. Many current anecdotes attest the virtue of an old, and the hazards of a new inn-sign; as when the loyal host substituted the head of George the Fourth for the ancient ass, which latter effigy being successfully adopted by a neighboring innkeeper, his discomfited rival had inscribed under the royal effigy, "This is the real ass." Thackeray cites an inn-sign as illustrative of Scotch egotism: "In Cupar-Fife," he writes, "there 's a little inn called the 'Battle of Waterloo,' and what do you think the sign is? The 'Battle of Waterloo' is *one* broad Scotchman laying about him with a broadsword."

The coffee-room of the best class of English inns, carpeted and curtained, the dark rich hue of the old mahogany, the ancient plate, the four-post bed, the sirloin or mutton joint, the tea, muffins, Cheshire and Stilton, the ale, the coal-fire, and the "Times," form an epitome of England; and it is only requisite to ponder well the associations and history of each of these items, to arrive at what is essential in English history and character. The impassable divisions of society are shown in the difference between the "commercial" and the "coffee-room;" the time-worn aspect of the furniture is eloquent of conservatism; the richness of the meats and strength of the ale explain the bone and sinew of the race; the tea is fragrant with Cowper's memory and suggestive of East India conquests; the cheese proclaims a thrifty agriculture, the bed and draperies comfort, the coal-fire manufactures; while the "Times" is the chart of English enterprise, division of labor, wealth, self-esteem, politics, trade, court-life, "inaccessibility to ideas," and bullyism.

The national subserviency to rank is as plainly evinced by the plates on chamber-doors, at the provincial inns, setting forth that therein on a memorable night slept a certain scion of nobility. And from the visitor at the great house of a neighborhood, when sojourning at the inn thereof, is expected a double fee. As an instance of the inappropriate, of that stolid insensibility to taste and tact which belongs to the nation, consider the English waiter. His costume is that of a clergyman or a gentleman dressed for company, and in ridiculous contrast with his menial obeisance; perhaps it is the self-importance nourished by this costume which renders him such a machine, incapable of an idea beyond the routine of handing a dish and receiving a sixpence.

Old Hobson, whose name is proverbially familiar, went with his wain from Cambridge to the Ball Inn, Bishopsgate Street, London. Clement's Inn was the scene of that memorable dialogue between Shallow and Sir John; at the Cock in Bond Street, Sir Charles

Sedley got scandalously drunk. Will's Coffee-House was formerly called the Rose; hence the line, —

"Supper and friends expect me at the Rose."

Button's, so long frequented by the wits of Queen Anne's time, was kept by a former servant of Lady Warwick; and there the author of Cato fraternized with Garth, Armstrong, and other contemporary writers. Ben Jonson held his club at the Devil Tavern, and Shakspeare and Beaumont used to meet him at the Mermaid; the same inn is spoken of by Pope, and Swift writes Stella of his dinner there. Beaumont thus reveals to Ben Jonson their convivial talk: —

What things have we seen
Done at the Mermaid! heard words that have been
So nimble and so full of subtle fire,
As if that every one from whom they came
Had meant to put his whole wit in a jest,
And had resolved to live a fool the rest
Of his dull life.

The author of "Peter Wilkins" resided for a time at Clifford's Inn, and Dr. Johnson frequented all the taverns in Fleet Street. Old Slaughter's coffee-house in St. Martin's Lane was the favorite resort of Hogarth; the house where Jeremy Taylor was born is now an inn; and Prior's uncle kept an inn in London, where the poet was seen, when a boy, reading Horace. This incident is made use of by Johnson in his "Lives of the Poets" in a very caustic manner; for after relating it, he observes of Prior, that "in his private relaxations he revived the tavern, and in his amorous pedantry he exhibited the college."

There is no city in Europe where an imaginative mood can be so indefinitely prolonged as at Venice;

and, in the early summer, the traveller, after gliding about all day in a gondola, and thinking of Barbarossa, Faliero, Titian, and the creations of Shakspeare, Otway, Byron, and Cooper, at evening, from under the arches of St. Mark's Square, watches the picturesque, and sometimes mysterious, figures, and then, between moss-grown palaces and over lone canals, returns to his *locanda* to find its aspect perfectly in accordance with his reverie; at least such was my experience at the Golden Lion. The immense *salle-à-manger* was dimly lighted, and the table for two or three guests set in a corner and half-surrounded by a screen; when I raised my eyes from my first dinner there, they fell on a large painting of the Death of Seneca, a print of which had been familiar to my childhood; and thus memory was ever invoked in Venice, and her dissolving views reflected in the mirror of the mind, unbroken by the interruptions from passing life that elsewhere render them so brief. The mere fact of disembarking at the weedy steps, the utter silence of the canal, invaded only by the plash of the gondolier's oar or his warning cry at the angle, the tessellated pavement and quaintly carved furniture of the bedroom, and a certain noiseless step and secretive gravity observable in the attendants, render the Venetian inn memorable and distinct in reminiscence, and in perfect harmony with the place and its associations.

During the late revolutionary era in Europe, the inn-tables of Germany afforded the most reliable index of political opinion; the free discussion which was there indulged brought out every variety of sentiment and theory, as it included all classes, with a due sprinkling of foreigners. From the old novel to the new farce, indeed, the extremes of public opinion and the average tone of manners, the laughable *contre-temps* and the delightful adventure, are made to reveal themselves at inns, so that political sects and all vocations are identified with them. To Rip Van Winkle, the most astonishing change he discovered in his native village, after his long nap, was the substitution of Washington's likeness for that of King George on the tavern sign.

The dark staircase, rising from the mule-stable of a *posada*, the bare chambers, wool-knotted mattresses, odor of garlic, and vegetables swimming in oil, are items of the Spanish inn not likely to be forgotten by the epicurean traveller. But good beds and excellent chocolate are to be found at the most uninviting Spanish inns; and the imaginative traveller enjoys the privilege of sojourning at the very one where Don Quixote was knighted. In highly civilized lands, inns have not only a national, but a professional character; the sign, the pictures on the wall, and the company, have a certain individuality, — marine in sailors' inns, pugilistic in sporting ones, and picturesque in those haunted by artists; the lines of demarcation are as visible as those which separate newspapers and shops; in the grand division of labor that signalizes modern life, the inn also has thus become an organ and a symbol. Even their mottoes and symbols give traditional suggestions or emblazon phases of opinion; natural history has been exhausted in supplying effigies; mythology has yielded up all her deities and institutions; heroes and localities are kept fresh in the traveller's imagination by their association with "creature comforts." Thus he dreams of Cromwell at the Tumble-down Dick, and of the Stuarts at the King Charles in the Oak, the days of chivalry at the Star and Garter or the Croix de Malta, of brilliant campaigns at the Wagram and Montmorency, of woman's love at the Petrarch and Laura, and of man's at the Freemason's Tavern.*

My host at Ravenna had been Byron's purveyor during the poet's residence there; and he was never weary of descanting upon his character and the incidents of his sojourn; in fact, upon discovering my interest in the subject, he forgot the landlord in the *cicerone*, and gave no small part of a day to accompanying me to the haunts of the bard. Our first visit was to the Guiccioli Palace, and here he described his lordship's dinners with the precision and enthusiasm of an antiquarian certifying a document or medal; then he took me to the Pine Forest, and pointed out the track where Byron used to wheel his horse at full gallop, and discharge his pistol at a bottle placed on a stump, — exercises prepar-

* "A recent London paper advertises a genuine *thesaurus* of ancient tavern signs and other curiosities at auction, collected during a long life by some curious antiquary. The catalogue covered an extensive and unique collection for a history of ancient and modern inns, taverns and coffee-houses in town and country, (numbering upwards of 850 signs,) formed with unwearied diligence and vast outlay during a lifetime, and illustrated with upwards of 2500 of ancient and modern engravings, comprising topographical and antiquarian subjects, early views of London, caricatures, humorous and satirical subjects, portraits of celebrities whose names have been adopted as signs, characters remarkable for their eccentricities, actors and actresses, others illustrating ancient sports and pastimes, etchings, wood-cuts, and numerous others, plain and colored, many of great rarity; also 415 drawings in water-colors, sepia, and pen and ink, and numerous copies from scarce engravings and old paintings; together with extensive antiquarian, local, and biographical notices (both printed and in MS.) on signs and their origin, merriments and witticisms in prose and verse, tales, traditions, legends, and remarkable incidents, singular inscriptions on tap-room windows and walls, anecdotes of landlords, guests, visitors, writers, etc."

atory to his Grecian campaign. At a particular flagstone, in the main street, my guide suddenly paused; "Signore," said he, "just as milord had reached this spot one evening, he heard the report of a musket, and saw an officer fall a few rods in advance; dismounting, he rushed to his side, and found him to be a familiar acquaintance, an agent of the government, who had thus become the victim to private vengeance. Byron had him conveyed to his own apartment and placed on a bed, where in half an hour he expired. This event made a deep impression on his mind; he was dispirited for a week, and wrote a description of death from a shot, which you will find in his poems, derived from this scene." With such local anecdotes my Byronic host entertained me so well, that the departed bard ever since has seemed to live in my remembrance rather than my fancy.

Whoever has eaten trout caught in the Anio at the little inn at Tivoli, or been detained by stress of weather in that of Albano, will not forget the evidences the walls of both exhibit that rollicking artists have felt at home there. Such heads and landscapes, caricatures, and grotesque animals as are there improvised, baffle description.

A well is the inn of the desert. "The dragoman usually looks out for some place of shelter," says the author of "Over the Lebanon to Balbec;" "the shadow of a ruin or the covering of a grove of fig-trees is the most common, and, if possible, near a well or stream. The first of all considerations is to reach a spot where you can get water; so that, throughout the East, the well answers to the old English 'Half-way House,' and roadside 'Accommodation for Man and Beast,' which gave their cheerful welcome to the 'Tally Ho' and 'Red Rover' that flourished before this age of iron."

The pedestrian in Wales sometimes encounters a snug and beautifully situated hostel, (perhaps the Angler's Rest,) where five minutes beside the parlor-fire, and a chat with the landlady or her pretty daughter, gives him so complete a home feeling that it is with painful reluctance he again straps on his knapsack; at liberty to muse by the ever-singing tea-kettle, if the weather is unpropitious, stroll out in view of a noble mountain or a fairy lake in the warm sunset, or hear the news from the last wayfarer in the travellers' room; and there is thus mingled a sense of personal independence, comfort, and solitude, which is rarely experienced even in the most favored domain of hospitality. An equally winsome but more romantic charm holds the roaming artist who stops at Albano or Volterra, where the dreamy *campagna* or Etruscan ruins alternate with groups of sunburnt *contadini*, lighted up by the charcoal's glow in a way to fascinate Salvator, before his contented gaze; his portfolio fills up with miraculous rapidity; and the still life is agreeably varied by the scenic costumes and figures which grace the vintage or a *festa*. Some humble Champollion could easily add to the curiosities of literature by a volume gleaned among inn inscriptions, — from the marble tablet announcing the sojourn of a royal personage, to the rude caricature on the whitewashed wall and the sentimental couplet on the window-pane; to say nothing of the albums which enshrine so many tributes to Etna and the White Mountains, — the heirlooms of Abbaté, the famous *padrone* of Catania, and Crawford of the Notch.

Sicily is famous for the absence of inns and the intolerable discomfort of those that do exist; but mine host of Catania was the prince of landlords; a fine specimen of manly beauty, and with the manners of a gentleman, he seemed to think his guests entitled to all the courtesy which should follow an invitation; he made formal calls upon them, and gave sage advice as to the best way to pass the time; fitted them out with hospitable skill, and experienced counsels, for the ascent of Etna, and brought home choice game from his hunting excursions, as a present to the "stranger within his gates;" his discourse, too, was of the most bland and entertaining description; he was "a fellow of infinite wit, of most excellent fancy;" and these ministrations derived a memorable charm from a certain gracefulness and winsome cordiality; no wonder his scrap-book is filled with eulogiums, and that the traveller in Sicily, by the mere force of contrast, records in hyperboles the merits of the Corona d' Oro. Alas for the mutability of inns and their worthy hosts! Abbaté was killed by an accidental shot, during an *émeute* in Catania in 1848.

The waxed floor, light curtains, and gay paper of a Parisian bedroom, however cheerful, are the reverse of snug; but in the provincial inns of the Continent, with less of comfort there is often more historical interest than in those of England; the stone staircases and floors, and the scanty furniture are forlorn; and the exuberance of the host's civility is often in ludicrous contrast with the poverty of his larder. An hour or two in the dreary *salle-à-manger* of a provincial French inn on a rainy day is the acme of a *voyageur's* depression. The *restaurant* and *café* have superseded the French inns of whose gastronomic renown and scenes of intrigue and violence we read in Dumas' historical novels; romance and tragedy, the convivial and the culinary associations, are equally prominent. "Suburban *cabarets*," observes a popular writer, "were long dangerous rendezvous for Parisians;" before and during the Grand-Monarque's reign the French taverns were representative, the army, court, men of letters, and even ecclesiastics having their favorite haunt: Molière went to the Croix de Lorraine, and Racine to the Mouton Blanc; the actors met at Les Deux Faisants; one of the last of the old-school Parisian landladies—she who kept the Maison Rouge—is celebrated in Béranger's Madame Gregoire; Ravaillac went from a tavern to assassinate Henry the Fourth; and fashionable orgies were carried on in the Temple Cellars. It is not uncommon to find ourselves in a friar's dormitory, the large hotels in the minor towns having frequently been erected as convents; and in Italy, such an inn as that of Terracina, with its legends of banditti and its romantic site, the waves of the Mediterranean moaning under its lofty windows, infallibly recalls Mrs. Radcliffe. In the cities many of the hotels are palaces, where noble families have dwelt for centuries, and about them are perceptible the traces of decayed magnificence and the spell of traditional glory and crime. To an imaginative traveller these fanciful attractions often compensate for the absence of substantial merit, and there is something mysterious and winsome in the obsolete architecture and fallen grandeur of these edifices; — huge shadows glide along the high cornices, the mouldy frescoes look as if they had witnessed strange vicissitudes, and the imagination readily wanders through a series of wonderful experiences of which these old *palazzi* have been the scene. Here, as elsewhere in the land, it is the romantic element, the charm of antiquity, that is the redeeming feature. For picturesque beauty of situation, neatness, and rural comfort, some of the inns of Switzerland are the most delightful on the Continent, inviting the stranger to linger amid the clear, fresh, and glorious landscape, and relish the sweet butter, white bread, and unrivalled honey and eggs, served so neatly every morning by a fair mountaineer with snowy cap and gay bodice.

I am a lover of the woods, and sometimes cross the bay, with a friend, to Long Island, and pass a few hours in the strip of forest that protected our fugitive army at the Battle of Flatbush; there are devious and shadowy paths intersecting it, and in spring and autumn the wild flowers, radiant leaves, and balmy stillness cheer the mind and senses fresh from the dust and bustle of the city. Often after one of these woodland excursions we have emerged upon a quiet road, with farm-houses at long intervals, and orchards and grain-fields adjacent, and followed its course to a village, whose gable-roofed domicile and ancient graveyard indicate an old settlement; and here is a little inn which recalls our idea of the primitive English alehouse. It has a little Dutch porch, a sunny garden, the liquor is served from the square bottles of Holland, the back-parlor is retired and neat, and the landlady sits all day in the window at her sewing, and, when a little acquainted, will tell you all about the love-affairs of the village; the cheese and sour-krout at dinner suggest a Flemish origin.

The old sign that hangs at the road-side was brought

to this country by an English publican, when the fine arts were supposed to be at so low a stage as to furnish no Dick Tinto equal to such an achievement. It represents the arms of Great Britain, and doubtless beguiled many a trooper of his Majesty when Long Island was occupied by the English; no sooner, however, had they retreated, than the republican villagers forced the landlord to have an American eagle painted above the king's escutcheon. Indeed, it is characteristic of inns that they perpetuate local associations: put your head into an Italian boarding-house in New York, and the garlic, maccaroni, and red wine lead you to think yourself at Naples; the snuff, dominos, and gazettes mark a French *café* all the world over; in Montreal you wake up in a room like that you occupied at Marseilles; and at Halifax the malt liquor is as English as the currency.

"The sports of the inn-yards" are noted often in the memoirs of Elizabeth's reign. In a late biography of Lord Bacon, his brother Anthony is spoken of as "having taken a house in Bishopsgate Street, near the famous Ball Inn, where plays are performed before cits and gentlemen, very much to the delight of Essex and his jovial crew." And in allusion to the Earl's conspiracy the lower class of inns then and there are thus described: "From kens like the Hart's Horn and the Shipwreck Tavern, haunts of the vilest refuse of a great city, the spawn of hells and stews, the vomit of Italian cloisters and Belgian camps, Blount, long familiar with the agents of disorder, unkennels in the Earl's name a pack of needy ruffians eager for any device that seems to promise pay to their greed or license to their lust." It has been justly remarked by Letitia

Landon that "after all the English hostel owes much of its charm to Chaucer; our associations are of his haunting pictures, — his delicate prioress, his comely young squire, with their pleasant interchange of tale and legend:" still less remote and more personal associations endear and identify these landmarks of travel and sojourn in Great Britain. Scarcely a pleasant record of life or manners, during the last century, is destitute of one of these memorable resorts. Addison frequented the White Horn at the end of Holland House Lane. When Sir Walter visited Wordsworth, he daily strolled to the Swan beyond Grasmere, to atone for the plain fare of the bard's cottage. "We four," naïvely writes the Rev. Archibald Carlyle, speaking of his literary comrades, "frequently resorted to a small tavern in the corner of Cockspur Street, at the Golden Ball, where we had a frugal supper and a little punch, as the finances of none of the company were in very good order; but we had rich enough conversation on literary subjects, enlivened by Smollett's agreeable stories, which he told with peculiar grace." And his more than clerical zest for such a rendezvous is apparent in his notice of another favorite inn: "It was during this assembly that the inn at the lower end of the West Bow got into some credit, and was called the Diversorium. Thomas Nicholson was the man's name, and his wife's Nelly Douglass. Nelly was handsome, Thomas a rattling fellow." Here often met Robertson the historian, Horne the dramatist, Hume, Jardine, and other notable men of the Scotch metropolis. To facilitate their intercourse when in London, they also "established a club at a coffee-house in Saville Row; and dined together daily at three with Wedderburn and Jack Dalrymple." By the same candid autobiographer we are informed that at a tavern "in Fleet Street, a physicians' club met, had original papers laid before them, and always waited supper for Dr. Armstrong to order." These casual allusions indicate the essential convenience and social importance of the inn, before clubs had superseded them in Britain, and *cafés* on the Continent. A writer whose "Itinerary" is dated 1617 thus describes entertainment at the English inns of his day: "As soone as a passenger comes to an inne, the servants run to him, and one takes his horse and walkes him about till he is cool, then rubs him down and gives him feed; another servant gives the passenger his private chamber, and kindles his fire; the third pulls off his bootes and makes them cleane; then the host and hostess visit him, and if he will eate with the hoste, or at a common table with the others, his meale will cost him sixpence, or, in some places, fourpence; but if he will eat in his own chamber, he commands what meat he will, according to his appetite; yea, the kitchen is open to him to order the meat to be dressed as he likes beste. After having eaten what he pleases, he may with credit set by a part for next day's breakfast. His bill will then be written for him, and should he object to any charge, the host is ready to alter it." An Italian nobleman of our own day,* his appreciation of free discussion quickened by political exile, was much impressed with the influence and agency of the English inn in public affairs. "Taverns," he writes, "are the forum of the English; it was here that arose the triumph of Burdett when he left the Tower, and the curses of Castlereagh when he descended into the tomb; it is

* Count Pecchio.

here that begins the censure or the approval of a new law."

Charles Lamb delighted to smoke his pipe at the old Queen's Head, and to quaff ale from the tankard presented by one Master Cranch (a choice spirit) to a former host, and in the old oak-parlor where tradition says "the gallant Raleigh received full souse in his face the contents of a jolly black-jack from an affrighted clown, who, seeing clouds of tobacco-smoke curling from the knight's mouth and nose, thought he was all on fire."

"A relic of old London is fast disappearing," says a journal of that city, — "the Blue Boar Inn, or the George and Blue Boar, as it came to be called later, in Holborn. For more than two hundred years this was one of the famous coaching-houses, where stalls arrived from the Northern and Midland counties. It is more famous still as being the place — if Lord Orrery's chaplain, Morrice, may be credited — where Cromwell and Ireton, disguised as troopers, cut from the saddle-flap of a messenger a letter which they knew to be there, from Charles the First to Henrietta Maria."

The Peacock, at Matlock on the Derwent, was long the chosen resort of artists, botanists, geologists, lawyers, and anglers; and perhaps at no rural English inn of modern times has there been more varied and gifted society than occasionally convened in this romantic district, under its roof.

The Hotel Gibbon, at Lausanne, suggests to one familiar with English literature the life of that historian, so naïvely described by himself, and keeps alive the associations of his elaborate work in the scene of its production; and nightly colloquies, that are embalmed and embodied in genial literature, immortalize the "sky-blue parlor" at Ambrose's Edinburgh tavern.

Few historical novelists have more completely mastered the details of costume, architecture, and social habits in the old times of England than James; and his description of the inns of Queen Anne's day is as elaborate as it is complete: "Landlords in England at that time — I mean, of course, in country towns — were very different in many respects, and of a different class, from what they are at present. In the first place, they were not fine gentlemen; in the next place, they were not discharged *valets-de-chambre* or butlers, who, having cheated their masters handsomely, and perhaps laid them under contribution in many ways, retire to enjoy the fat things at their ease in their native town. Then, again, they were on terms of familiar inter course with two or three classes, completely separate and distinct from each other, — a sort of connecting link between them. At their door, the justice of the peace, the knight of the shire, the great man of the neighborhood, dismounted from his horse, and had his chat with mine host. There came the village lawyer, when he gained a cause or won a large fee or had been paid a long bill, to indulge in his pint of sherry, and gossiped as he drank it of all the affairs of his clients. There sneaked in the doctor to get his glass of *eau-de-vie*, or plague-water, or *aqua mirabilis*, or strong spirits, in short, of any other denomination, and tell little dirty anecdotes of his cases and his patients. There the alderman, the wealthy shopkeeper, and the small proprietor, or the large farmer, came to take his cheerful cup on Saturdays, or on market-day. But, besides these, the inn was the resort — though approached by another door — of a lower and a poorer class, with whom the landlord was still upon as good terms as with the others. The wagoner, the carter, the lawyer's and the banker's clerk, the shopman, the porter, even, all came there; the landlord was civil and familiar and chatty with them all."

Geoffrey Crayon's "Shakspearian Research" culminated at the Boar's Head, Eastcheap; his story of the "Spectre Bridegroom" was appropriately related in the kitchen of the Pomme d'Or, in the Netherlands; and he makes Rip's congenial retreat from his virago spouse, the "coin of vantage" in front of the village inn. Irving's own appreciation of these vagabond shrines and accidental homes is emphatic; he commends the "honest bursts of laughter in which a man indulges in that temple of true liberty, an inn," and quotes zestfully the maxim that "a tavern is the rendezvous, the exchange, the staple of good-fellows." His personal testimony is characteristic: "To a homeless man there is a momentary feeling of independence, as he stretches himself before an inn-fire: the arm-chair is his throne, the poker is his sceptre, and the little parlor his undisputed empire." How little did the modest author imagine, when he thus wrote, that the poker with which he stirred the fire in the parlor-grate of the Red Lion would become a sacred literary relic wherewith his partial countrymen are beguiled of extra fees, while the bard of Avon and the gentleman of Sunnyside mingle in the reverie of fond reminiscence.

"I went by an indirect route to Litchfield," writes Hawthorne, in his English sketches, "and put up at the Black Swan. Had I known where to find it, I would rather have established myself at the inn kept by

Mr. Boniface, and so famous for its ale in Farquhar's time." Gossip and gayety, the poor man's arena and the "breathing-time of day" of genius, thus give to the inn a kind of humane scope. Beethoven, wearied of his palace-home and courtly patronage and the "stately houses open to him in town and country, often forsook all for solitude in obscure inns, escaping from all conventionalities to be alone with himself." "*Nous voyons*," says Brillat-Savarin, "*que les villageois font toutes les affaires au cabaret;*" Rousseau delighted in the frugal liberty thereof; and the last days of Elia are associated with the inn which was the goal of his daily promenade. "After Isola married," writes one of his friends, "and Mary was infirm, he took his lonely walk along the London road, as far as the 'Bell of Edmonton;' and one day tripped over a stone and slightly wounded his forehead; erysipelas set in, and he died." Somewhat of the attractiveness of the inn to the philosopher is that its temporary and casual shelter and solace accords with the counsel of Sydney Smith, "to take short views," and Goethe's, to "cast ourselves into the sea of accidents;" and a less amiable reason for the partiality has been suggested in "the wide capability of finding fault which an inn affords." A genial picture of one is thus drawn by a modern poet: —

'This cosy hostelrie a visit craves;
Here will I sit awhile,
And watch the heavenly sunshine smile
Upon the village graves.
Strange is this little room in which I wait,
With its old table, rough with rustic names.
'T is summer now; instead of blinking flames,
Sweet-smelling ferns are hanging o'er the grate.
With curious eyes I pore
Upon the mantel-piece, with precious wares,

Glazed Scripture prints in black, lugubrious frames,
Filled with old Bible lore:
The whale is casting Jonah on the shore;
Pharoah is drowning in the curly wave;
And to Elijah, sitting at his cave,
The hospitable ravens fly in pairs,
Celestial food within their horny beaks;
On a slim David, with great pinky cheeks,
A towered Goliath stares.
Here will I sit at peace,
While, piercing through the window's ivy veil,
A slip of sunshine smites the amber ale;
And as the wreaths of fragrant smoke increase,
I 'll read the letter which came down to-day." *

As a contrast to this, take Longfellow's "Wayside Inn," at Sudbury, Massachusetts: —

"As ancient is this hostelry
As any in the land may be,
Built in the old colonial day,
When men lived in a grander way,
With ampler hospitality;
A kind of old Hobgoblin hall,
Now somewhat fallen to decay,
With weather-stains upon the wall,
And stair-ways worn, and crazy doors,
And creaking and uneven floors,
And chimneys huge and tiled and tall.
A region of repose it seems,
A place of slumber and of dreams,
Remote among the wooded hills!"

The facilities of modern travel and its vast increase, while they have modified the characteristic features of the inn, have given it new economical importance; and not long since, the American hotel-system was earnestly discussed in the English and French journals as a substitute for the European: the method by which all the wants of the traveller are supplied at an established

* Alexander Smith.

price per diem, instead of the details of expense and the grades of accommodation in vogue abroad. In Paris, London, some of the West India Islands, and elsewhere, the American hotel has, in a measure, succeeded. But it is in its historical and social aspect that we find the interest of the subject; as regards convenience, economy, and comfort, the question can perhaps only be met in an eclectic spirit, each country having its own merits and demerits as regards the provision for public entertainment of man and beast. The inns of Switzerland will bear the test of reminiscence better than those of any other part of the Continent: the solitary system of the English inn is objectionable; discomfort is proverbial in Havana hotels; the garden-tables and music in the German hostels are pleasant social features; and, with all their frugal resources, the farm-stations in Norway boast the charm of a candid and *naïve* hospitality which sweetens the humble porridge of the weary traveller. "It is scarcely credible," says an "unprotected female," in her record of travel there, "that such Preadamite simplicity of heart still exists on earth." In pictures and diaries, the German landlord is always light-haired, and holds a beer tankard; and the hotels in the British West Indies, according to a recent traveller, are always kept by "fat, middle-aged, colored ladies, who have no husbands." Rose, writing to Hallam from Italy, hints the union of romantic and classical associations which some of the inns conserve and inspire; that of Civita Castellana, he remarks, "is on the classic route from Rome to Florence, and is a type of the large Italian inns such as one finds in romances: balconies, terraces, flowers of the south, large courts open for post-chaises, — nothing is wanting." When

Heine revisited Germany, he tells us how the conservative habits of his father-land newly impressed him in the familiar and old-fashioned dishes, "sour-krout, stuffed chestnuts in green cabbages, stockfish swimming in butter, eggs and bloaters, sausages, fieldfares, roasted angels with apple-sauce, and goose."

In mediæval times, in that part of Europe, from the isolation of inns they were emphatically the places to find an epitome of the age: soldiers, monks, noblemen, and peasants surrounded the same stove, shared the contents of the same pot, and often the straw which formed their common bed; the proverb was, "inns are not built for one;" the salutations, benisons, and curses, the motley guests, the lack of privacy, the *trinkgeld* and stirrup-cup, the murders and amours, the converse and precautions, the orgies and charities thereof, were each and all characteristic of the unsettled state of society, the diversities of rank, the common necessities, and the priestly, military, and boorish elements of life and manners. But the rarity of any public house, as we understand the term, is more characteristic of those times than the incongruous elements therein occasionally exhibited. "There seem," says an eminent historian, "to have been no inns or houses of entertainment for the reception of travellers during the Middle Ages. This is a proof of the little intercourse which took place between different nations. The duty of hospitality was so necessary in that state of society that it was enforced by statutes; it abounded, and secured the stranger a kind reception under any roof where he chose to take shelter." *

On first entering an inn at Havre de Grace, I found the landlady taking leave of the captain of an Ameri-

* Prescott's Robertson's *Charles Fifth*, vol. 1, p. 355.

can packet-ship; he had paid his bill, not without some remonstrance, and his smiling hostess, with true French tact, was now in the act of bidding so pleasing a farewell as would lure him to take up his quarters there on the return voyage. She had purchased at the market a handsome bouquet and tied it up jauntily with ribbons. The ruddy sea-dog face of the captain was half turned aside with a look of impatience at the idea of being inveigled into good-nature after her extortion; but she, not a whit discouraged, held her flowers up to him, and smiling, with her fair hand on his rough dreadnaught overcoat, turned full to his eye a sprig of yellow blossom, and with irresistible *naïveté* whispered,— "*Mon cher Capitaine, c'est immortel comme mon attachment pour vous.*" It was a little scene worthy of Sterne, and brought the agreeableness and the imposition of the innkeepers of the Continent at once before me. One evening in Florence I was sent for by a countryman who lodged at the most famous hotel in the city, and found him perambulating his apartment under strong excitement of mind. He told me, with much emotion, than the last time he had visited Florence was twenty years before with his young and beautiful wife. The belle of the season that winter was the Marchesa ——. She gave a magnificent ball, and in the midst of the festivities took the young American couple into her boudoir and sung to them with her harp; her vocal talent was celebrated, but it was a rare favor to hear her, and this attention was prized accordingly. "You know," added my friend, "that I came abroad to recover the health which grief at my wife's death so seriously impaired; and you know how unavailing has proved the experiment. On my arrival here, I inquired for the best inn, and was directed hither; upon entering this chamber which was assigned me, something in the frescoes and tiles struck me as familiar; they awoke the most vivid associations, and at last I remembered that this is the very room to which the beautiful Marchesa brought us to hear her sing on that memorable evening; the family are dispersed, and her palace is rented for a hotel; hence this coincidence."

Among the minor local associations to be enjoyed at Rome, not the least common and suggestive are those which belong to the old Bear Inn where Montaigne lodged. Not only the vicissitudes but the present fortunes of European towns are indicated by the inns. I arrived at ancient Syracuse at sunset on a spring afternoon, and dismounted at an inn that looked like an episcopal residence or government house, so lofty and broad were the dimensions of the edifice; but not a person was visible in the spacious court, and as I wandered up the staircases and along the corridors, no sound but the echo of my steps was audible. At length a meagre attendant emerged from an obscure chamber and explained that this grand pile was erected in anticipation of the American squadron in the Mediterranean making their winter quarters in the harbor of Syracuse: a project abandoned at the earnest request of the King of Naples, who dreaded the example of a republican marine in his realm; and then so rarely did a visitor appear, that the poor lonely waiter was thrown into a fit of surprise, from which he did not recover during my stay.

To the stranger no more characteristic evidence of our material prosperity and gregarious habits can be imagined than that afforded by the large, showy, and thronged hotels of our principal cities. They are epitomes of the whole country; at a glance they reveal the era of upholstery, the love of ostentation, the tendency to live in herds, and the absence of a subdued and harmonious tone of life and manners. The large mirrors and bright carpets which decorate these resorts are entirely incongruous — the brilliancy of the sunshine and the stimulating nature of the climate demands within doors, a predominance of neutral tints to relieve and freshen the eye and nerves. It is characteristic of that devotion to the immediate which De Tocqueville ascribes to republican institutions, that these extravagant and gregarious establishments in our country are so often named for living celebrities in the mercantile, literary, and political world. This custom gives those who enjoy this distinction while living "the freedom of the house." It greatly amused the friends of our modest Geoffrey Crayon, when, encouraged by his affectionate kinswoman and his friend Kennedy to "travel on his capital," under the pressure of necessity, he once thus desperately claimed the privileges of his honored name, wherefrom his sensitive nature habitually shrunk. "I arrived in town safe," he writes from New York to his niece, "and proceeded to the Irving House, where I asked for a room. What party had I with me? None. Had I not a lady with me? No; I was alone. I saw my chance was a bad one, and I feared to be put in a dungeon as I was on a former occasion. I bethought myself of your advice; and so, when the book was presented to me, wrote my name at full length — 'from Sunnyside.' I was ushered into an apartment on the first floor, furnished with rosewood, yellow damask, and pier-glasses, with a bed large enough for an alderman and his wife, a bath-room adjoining. In a word, I was accommodated completely *en prince.* The negro waiters all call me by name, and vie with each other in waiting on me. The chambermaid has been at uncommon pains to put my room in first-rate order; and, if she had been pretty, I absolutely should have kissed her; but as she was not, I shall reward her in sordid coin. Henceforth I abjure all modesty with hotel-keepers, and will get as much for my name as it will fetch. Kennedy calls it travelling on one's capital."

The extravagant scale upon which these establishments are conducted is another national feature, at once indicating the comparative ease with which money is acquired in the New World, and the passion that exists here for keeping up appearances. It would be useful to investigate the influence of hotel-life in this country upon manners: whatever may be the result as to the coarser sex, its effect upon women and children is lamentable, lowering the tone, compromising the taste, and yielding incessant and promiscuous excitement to the love of admiration; the change in the very nature of young girls, thus exposed to an indiscriminate crowd, is rapid and complete; modesty and refinement are soon lost in over-consciousness and moral hardihood. But perhaps the most singular trait in the American hotel, is the deference paid to the landlord: instead of being the servant of the public, he is apparently the master; and a traveller who makes the now rapid transition from a New York to a Liverpool hotel, might think himself among a different race; the courteous devotion, almost subserviency in the one case, being in total contrast with the nonchalance and even despotism of the other. The prosperous security of the host with us, and the dependence of his guest for any choice of accommodation, is doubtless the most obvious reason for this anomaly; but it is also, in a degree at least, to be referred to the familiarity with which even gentlemen treat the innkeepers; to use a vulgar phrase, they descend to curry favor and minister to the self-esteem of a class of men in whom it is already pampered beyond endurable bounds; no formula of republican equality justifies this behavior; and it usually reacts unfavorably for the self-respect of the individual. Some foreigner remarked, with as much truth as irony, that our aristocracy consisted of hotel-keepers and steamboat-captains; and appearances certainly warrant the sarcasm. It was not always thus. When Washington lodged at the old Walton Mansion-House, which had been converted to an inn, the old negro who kept it was the ideal of a host; an air of dignity as well as comfort pervaded the house; through the open upper half of the broad door played the sunshine upon the sanded threshold; at the head of the long easy staircase ticked the old-fashioned clock; full-length portraits, by Copley, graced the parlor-wall; the old Dutch stoop looked the emblem of hospitality; no angular figures were ranged to squirt tobacco-juice; no pert clerks lorded it from behind a mahogany barricade; but the glow of the windows at night, the alacrity of the sedate waiter, the few but respectable guests, and the prolonged meals, of which but two or three partook, gave to the inn the character of a home. Lafayette wrote to his wife in 1777, while descanting with enthusiasm upon the simplicity of manners in this country: "The very inns are different from those in Europe; the host and hostess sit at table with you and do the honors of a comfortable meal; and on going away, you pay your fare without higgling." An English traveller, who visited this country soon after the Revolutionary War, speaks of the "uncomplying temper of the landlords of the country inns in America." "They will not," says another, "bear the treatment we too often give ours at home. They feel themselves in some degree independent of travellers, as all of them have other occupations to follow; nor will they put themselves into a bustle on your account; but, with good language, they are very civil, and will accommodate you as well as they can. The general custom of having two or three beds in a room to be sure is very disagreeable; it arises from the great increase of travelling within the last few years, and the smallness of their houses, which were not built for houses of entertainment."

It is a most significant indication of our devotion to the external, that ovations at which the legislators of the land discourse, and eulogies that fill the columns of the best journals, celebrate the opening of a new tavern, or the retirement of a publican. The confined and altitudinous cells into which so many of the complacent victims of these potentates are stowed, and their habits of subserviency to the rules of the house which are perked up on their chamber-walls, induced a Sicilian friend of mine to complain that sojourners at inns in this land of liberty were treated like friars. The gorgeous luxury of the metropolitan inns is reversed in the small towns, where, without the picturesque situation, we often find the discomfort of the Continent.

Under date of March 4, 1634, John Winthrop, first

governor of Massachusetts, records in his journal, "Samuel Cole set up the first house of common entertainment" in Boston. According to the famous literary ruse of Irving and Wirt, Knickerbocker's facetious history and the "Letters of a British Spy" were found in the inn-chamber of a departed traveller. Of old, the American inn, or tavern as it was called, subserved a great variety of purposes. One of New England's local historians says: —

"The taverns of olden time were the places of resort for gentlemen; and one consequence was, good suppers and deep drinking. They also performed the office of newspapers. The names posted on the several tavern-doors were a sufficient notice for jurors. Saturday afternoon was the time when men came from all quarters of the town to see and hear all they could at the tavern, where politics and theology, trade, barter, and taxes, were all mixed up together over hot flip and strong toddy.

"The taverns served also as places for marketing. During most of the winter they were filled every night with farmers who had brought their pork, butter, grain, seeds, and poultry to market. Most families supplied themselves through these opportunities, and purchased the best articles at moderate prices.

"Landlords could not grow rich very fast on country custom. The travelling farmer brought all his food for himself in a box, and that for his horse in a bag. He therefore paid only twelve cents for his bed, and as much for horse-keeping. It was not uncommon to have six days' expenses amount only to two dollars. Auctions, theatricals, legerdemain, caucuses, military drills, balls, and dancing-schools, all came in place at the tavern. Especially, sleigh-riding parties found them convenient." *

"You will not go into one," wrote Brissot in 1788, "without meeting with neatness, decency, and dignity. The table is served by a maiden well-dressed and pretty, by a pleasant mother whose age has not effaced the agreeableness of her features, and by men who have that air of respectability which is inspired by the idea of equality, and are not ignoble and base, like the greater part of our own tavern-keepers." In 1792, Wansey, the commercial traveller already cited, tells us he lodged at the Bunch of Grapes, in Boston, and paid five shillings a day, including a pint of Madeira He had an interview with Citizen Genet and Dr. Priestley at the Tontine near the Battery in New York; and saw Frenchmen with tricolor cockades at the Indian Queen on the Boston road; — trivial data for his journal then, and yet now suggestive of the political and economical condition of the land, whereof even tavern bills and company are no inadequate test. A sagacious reminiscent informs us that "the taverns of Boston were the original business Exchanges: they combined the Counting-house, the Exchange-office, the Reading-room, and the Bank; each represented a locality. To the Lamb Tavern, called by the sailors 'sheep's baby,' people went to 'see a man from Dedham' — it was the resort of Norfolk County; the old Eastern Stage-House in Ann Street, was frequented by 'down-easters,' captains of vessels, formerly from the Penobscot and Kennebec; there were to be seen groups of sturdy men seated round an enormous fireplace, chalking down the price of bark and lumber, and skippers bringing in

* Brooks's *History of Medford.*

a vagrant tarpaulin to 'sign the articles.' To the Exchange Coffee-House resorted the nabobs of Essex County; here those aristocratic eastern towns, Newburyport and Portsmouth, were represented by ship-owners and ship-builders, merchants of the first class. Dealers in butter and cheese went to the City Tavern in Brattle Street — a favorite sojourn of 'members of the General Court,' — its court-yard crowded with teams loaded with the best pork from Vermont and Western Massachusetts, and the 'wooden notions' of Yankee rustics. The last of the old Boston taverns was the once famous Elm-Street House, a rendezvous of stage-coaches, teams, and transient boarders, which was kept up in the old style until fairly drawn from the field by 'modern improvements.'" Indeed, this slight mention of the functions and fortunes of inns in the New England metropolis, hints, more than a volume of statistics, the process of her growth and the cause of her social transitions; locomotion has completely done away with the local affinities of the past, and emigration modified the individuality of class and character which of old gave such special interest to the inn; we are too gregarious, luxurious, and hurried to indulge in these primitive expedients.

At the old Raleigh tavern in Virginia, — not long since destroyed by fire, — Patrick Henry lodged when he made his memorable *début*, as a patriotic orator, in the House of Burgesses; and it was in a chamber of this inn that he prepared his speeches, and that the great leading men of the Revolution, in that State, assembled to consult. Some of the inns in Canada are named for the Indian chiefs mentioned in the earliest record of exploration by Cartier. At the Frauncis tavern in New

York, Washington took leave of his officers, and the "Social Club" — still famous in the annals of the city — met. Military men appreciate good inns; Washington wrote to Frauncis, and Lafayette praised him. One of the latest of memorable associations connected with the inns of New York is that which identifies the City Hotel with the naval victories of the last war with England. No one who listened to the musical voice of the late Ogden Hoffman, as he related to the St. Nicholas Society, at their annual banquet, his personal memories of that favorite hotel, will fail to realize the possible dramatic and romantic interest which may attach to such a resort, even in our unromantic times and in the heart of a commercial city. Visions of naval heroes, of belles in the dance, witty coteries, and distinguished strangers, — political crises and social triumphs flitted vividly before the mind as the genial reminiscent called up the men, women, fêtes, and follies there known. A recent English traveller in the United States, in alluding to the resemblance he discovered to what was familiar at home, speaks of one relic which has caught the eye of few as suggestive of the old country. "There is," he observes, "in Baltimore an old inn, with an old sign, standing at the corner of Eutaw and Franklin streets, just such as may still be seen in the towns of Somersetshire; and before it are to be seen old wagons, covered and soiled and battered, about to return from the city to the country, just as the wagons do in our own agricultural counties." *

How near to us the record of "baiting at an inn" brings the renowned! "After dinner," writes Washington in the diary of his second visit to New England,

* A. Trollope.

"through frequent showers, we proceeded to the tavern of a Mrs. Haviland, at Rye, who keeps a very neat and decent inn." Mendelssohn, ideal as was his tone of mind, wrote zestfully to his sister: — "A neat, civil Frenchwoman keeps the inn on the summit of the Simplon; and it would not be easy to describe the sensation of satisfaction caused by its thrifty cleanliness, which is nowhere to be found in Italy." Lockhart, when an assiduous Oxford scholar, found his choicest recreation in "a quiet row on the river, and a fish-dinner at Godstow;" and there is not one of his surviving associates, says his biographer, "who fails to look back at this moment, with melancholy pleasure on the brilliant wit, the merry song, and the grave discussion which gave to the sanded parlor of the village ale-house the air of the Palæstra at Tusculum, or the Amaltheum of Cumæ."

It is impossible to conceive any house of entertainment more dreary than some of the stage-houses, as they were called in New England: the bar-room with an odor of stale rum, the parlor with its everlasting sampler over the fireplace, weeping willow, tombstone, and inscription; the peacock's feathers or asparagus boughs in the chimney as if in cheerful mockery, the looking-glass that reflects every feature awry, the cross-lights of the windows, inquisitive loungers, pie-crust like leather, and cheese of mollified oak, — all defied both the senses and digestion, and made the crack of the coachman's whip a joyful alarum.

The inns near famous localities identify themselves to the memory with the most attractive objects of travel; thus the inn, so rural and neat, at Edensor, with the marvels of Chatsworth; the Red Horse at Stratford, with Shakspeare's tomb; and the Nag's Head, at Uxoter, with Johnson's penance. It was while "waiting for the train," at an inn of Coventry, that Tennyson so gracefully paraphrased the legend of Godiva; and the sign of the "Flitch" is associated with the famous bequest of the traditional patron of conjugal harmony. "A wayside inn at which we tarried, in Derbyshire, I fancied must have sheltered Moreland or Gainsborough, when caught in the rain, while sketching in that region. The landlady had grenadier proportions and red cheeks; a few peasants were drinking ale beneath a roof whence depended flitches of bacon, and with the frocks, the yellow hair, and the full, ruddy features we see in their pictures; the windows of the best room had little diamond-shaped panes, in which sprigs of holly were stuck. There were several ancient engravings in quaint-looking frames on the wall; the chairs and desk were of dark-veined wood that shone with the polish of many a year's friction; a great fire blazed in the chimney, and the liquor was served in vessels only seen on this other side of the water, in venerable prints. It was a hostel where you would not be surprised to hear the crack of Tony Lumpkin's whip, or to see the Vicar of Wakefield rush in, in search of Olivia, — an ale-house, that you knew at once, had often given "an hour's importance to the poor man's heart," and where Parson Adams or 'Squire Western would have felt themselves entirely at home." *

Goldsmith has genially celebrated the humble, rustic inn in the "Deserted Village," and his own habits confirmed the early predilection. "His favorite festivity," says one of his biographers, "his holiday of holidays, was to have three or four intimate friends to breakfast

* *A Month in England.*

with him at ten, to start at eleven for a walk through the fields to Highbury Barn, where they dined at an ordinary frequented by authors, templars, and retired citizens, for ten pence a head; to return at six to White's, Conduit Street, and to end the evening with a supper at the Grecian or Temple Exchange Coffee-House; the whole expense of the day's *fête* never exceeded a crown, for which the party obtained "good air, good living, and good conversation;' "he, Goldsmith, however," adds Forster, "would leave a tavern if his jokes were not rewarded with a roar." One of Ben Jonson's best comedies is the "New Inn," and Southey's most popular ballad is "Mary of the Inn." Chaucer makes his Canterbury pilgrims set out from an inn at Southwark. We all remember the inns described by Scott. Elliston's "larks" at the White Hart and Red Cow were comical episodes, that read like a vaudeville. "She Stoops to Conquer," "L'Auberge Pleine," and "The Double-Bedded Room," are a few of the countless standard plays of which an inn is the scene. "What befell them at the Inn," is the heading of Don Quixote's best chapters, for the knight always mistook inns for castles. Grammont's adventures frequently boast the same scene, and it was "in the worst room of the worst inn" that the accomplished and dissolute Villiers died. Foote frequented the Bedford in Covent Garden, and old Macklin doffed the buskin for the apron and carver. Philosophers, from Horace, at the inn of Brundusium, to Montaigne, noting the furniture, dishes, and prices at the inns where he rested on his "Journey into Italy," have found this a most suggestive and characteristic theme.

In German university towns, the professors frequent

the Hereditary Prince, or some other inn at evening, to drink beer, smoke pipes, and discuss metaphysics. The jocose reproof which Lamb administers to the sentimental donor of "Cœlebs" was —

"If ever I marry a wife,
I'll marry a landlord's daughter,
And sit in the bar all day,
And drink cold brandy and water."

Quaintly pious is the allusion of John Winthrop in a letter — more than two centuries old — to his father, the first governor of Massachusetts, when the project of emigration was about to be realized: "For the business of New England, I can say no other thing but that I believe confidently that the whole disposition thereof is from the Lord; and for myself, I have seen so much of the vanity of the world that I esteem no more of the diversities of countries, than as so many inns, whereof the traveller that hath lodged in the best or in the worst findeth no difference when he cometh to his journey's end." *

It has been said of Socrates that he "looked upon himself as a traveller who halts at the public inn of the Earth." "Was I in a condition to stipulate with death," writes Sterne, "I should certainly declare against submitting to it before my friends, and therefore I never seriously think upon the mode and the manner of this great catastrophe, but I constantly draw the curtain across it with this wish, that the Disposer of all things may so order it, that it happen not to me in my own house, but rather in some decent inn." Aaron Burr realized in a forlorn manner Yorick's desire when,

* *Life and Letters of John Winthrop*, by Robert C. Winthrop, p. 306.

after years of social ostracism, he expired at a tavern on Staten Island.

The beautiful significance of the first incident in the life of Christ is seldom realized, offering, as it does, so wonderful and affecting a contrast between the humblest mortal vicissitude in the outward circumstances of birth and the highest glory of a spiritual advent: they "laid him in a manger because there was no room for them in the inn." It was to an inn that the Good Samaritan carried the traveller who had "fallen among thieves." Joseph's brethren rested at an inn on their way to Egypt; and it was at the Three Taverns, in the suburbs of Rome, that Paul was met by the brethren. Venerable as are these allusions in sacred history, the visible token of the antiquity of inns that strikes our imagination most vividly are the wine-stains on the marble counter in Pompeii.

Falstaff absolutely requires the frame of an inn to make his portrait intelligible, with the buxom figure of Mrs. Quickly in the background; and it may safely be asserted that no public house of entertainment has afforded such world-wide mirth as the Boar's Head, Eastcheap. The freaks of Tony Lumpkin have their natural scope at an ale-house; and Goldoni's *Locandiera* is a fine colloquial piece of real life; even the most eloquent of England's historians cites the superior inns that existed in the range of travel there, during the early part of the seventeenth century, as a reliable evidence of the prosperity and civil advancement of the nation. These inns are, in fact, the original retreats for "freedom and comfort," whence our pleasant ideas on the subject are derived; they still exist in some of the rural districts of the kingdom; and the cleanliness, good fare, and retirement of the old-fashioned English inn, as well as the freshness and urbanity of the host, wholly justify their renown. The exigencies of the climate, and the domestic habits of the people, explain this superiority; where so much enjoyment is sought within doors, and the national character is reserved and individual, better provision is naturally made both for the physical well-being and the privacy of the wayfarer than is required under less inclement skies, and among a more vivacious and social race.

A most characteristic note of Boswell's is that which records his idol's hearty encomiums on a tavern, while dining at one in London; both the man and the place then combined to realize the perfection of the idea, for that dim and multitudinous city invites to secluded conviviality; and that irritable, dogmatic, yet epicurean sage required the liberty of speech, an absolute deference, and the solid physical comforts so easily obtained at a London tavern. There he could make "inarticulate, animal noises over his food" without restraint; there he could bring only such companions as would bear to be contradicted, and there he could refresh body and mind without fear of intrusion from a printer's devil or needy author. Bores and duns away, a good listener by, surrounded with pleasant viands and a cheerful blaze, a man so organized and situated might, without extravagance, call a tavern-chair the throne of human felicity, and quote Shenstone's praise of inns with rapture. Beneath this jovial appreciation, however, there lurks a sad inference; it argues a homeless lot, for lonely or ungenial must be the residence, contrast with which renders an inn so attractive; and we must bear in mind that the winsome aspect they wear in English literature is based on their casual and temporary enjoyment; it is as recreative, not abiding places that they are usually introduced; and, in an imaginative point of view, our sense of the appropriate is gratified by these landmarks of our precarious destiny, for we are but "pilgrims and sojourners on the earth." Jeremy Taylor compared human life to an inn, and Archbishop Leighton used to say he would prefer to die in one.

AUTHORS.

"High is our calling, friend! Creative Art,
  Whether the instrument of words she use,
  Or pencil pregnant with ethereal hues,
Demands the service of a mind and heart,
Though sensitive, yet in their weakest part
  Heroically fashioned — to infuse
  Faith in the whispers of the lonely muse,
While the whole world seems adverse to desert."

WORDSWORTH.

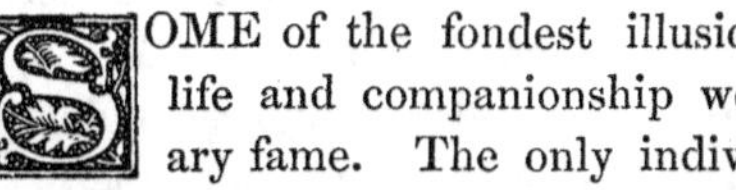

SOME of the fondest illusions of our student-life and companionship were based on literary fame. The only individuals, of the male gender, who then seemed to us (indiscriminate and mutual lovers of literature) worthy of admiration and sympathy, were authors. Our ideal of felicity was the consciousness of distributing ideas of vital significance, and causing multitudes to share a sentiment born in a lonely heart. The most real and permanent sway of which man is capable we imagined that of ruling and cheering the minds of others through the medium of literature. Our herbals were made up of flowers from the graves of authors; their signatures were our only autographs. The visions that haunted us were little else than a boundless panorama that displayed scenes in their lives. We used continually to see, in fancy, Petrarch beside a fountain, under a laurel, with the sweet *penseroso* look visible in his portraits; Dante in the corridor of a monastery, his palm laid on a friar's breast, and his stern features softened as he craved the only blessing life retained for him —*peace ;* rustic Burns, with his dark eye proudly meeting the curious stare of an Edinburgh coterie ; Camœns breasting the waves with the Lusiad between his teeth ; Johnson appalling Boswell with his emphatic "*Sir ;*" Milton — his head like that of a saint encircled with rays — seated at the organ ; Shakspeare walking serenely, and with a benign and majestic countenance, beside the Avon ; Steele jocosely presiding at table with liveried bailiffs to pass the dishes ; the bright face of Pope looming up from his deformed body in the cool twilight of a grotto ; Voltaire's sneer withering an auditor through a cloud of snuff; Molière reading his new comedy to the old woman ; Landor standing in the ilex path of a Tuscan villa ; Savage asleep on a bulk at midnight in one of the London parks ; Dryden seated in oracular dignity in his coffee-house arm-chair ; Metastasio comparing notes with a handsome *prima donna* at Vienna ; Alfieri with a magnificent steed in the midst of the Alps ; Swift stealing an interview with Miss Johnson, or chuckling over a chapter of Gulliver ; the funeral pyre of Shelley lighting up a solitary crag on the shores of the Mediterranean ; and Byron, with marble brow and rolling eye, guiding the helm of a storm-tossed boat on the Lake of Geneva ! Such were a few only of the *tableaux* that haunted our imaginations. We echoed heartily Akenside's protest against the sermon on Glory :

"Come, then, tell me, sage divine,
  Is it an offence to own
That our bosoms e'er incline
  Towards immortal glory's throne ?
For with me nor pomp nor pleasure,
Bourbon's might, Braganza's treasure,

So can fancy's dream rejoice,
So conciliate reason's choice,
As one approving word of her impartial voice.

"If to spurn at noble praise
Be the passport to thy heaven;
Follow thou those gloomy ways;
No such law to me was given;
Nor, I trust, shall I deplore me,
Faring like my friends before me;
Nor a holier place desire
Than Timoleon's arms acquire,
And Tully's curule chair, and Milton's golden lyre."

In our passion for native authors we revered the memory of Brockden Brown, and detected in his romantic studies the germs of the supernatural school of fiction; we nearly suffocated ourselves in the crowded gallery of the old church at Cambridge, listening to Sprague's Phi Beta Kappa poem; and often watched the spiritual figure of the "Idle Man," and gazed on the white locks of our venerable painter, with his "Monaldi" and "Paint King" vividly remembered. We wearied an old friend of Brainard's by making him repeat anecdotes of the poet; and have spent hours in the French coffee-house which Halleck once frequented, eliciting from him criticisms, anecdotes, or recitations of Campbell. New Haven people that came in our way were obliged to tell all they could remember of the vagaries of Percival, and the elegant hospitality of Hillhouse. We have followed Judge Hopkinson through the rectangular streets of his native metropolis, with the tune of "Hail Columbia" humming in our ears; and kept a curious eye on Howard Payne through a whole evening party, fondly cognizant of "Sweet Home." Beaumont and Fletcher were our Damon and Pythias. The memorable occurrence of our childhood was the advent of a new Waverley novel, and of our youth a fresh Edinburgh Review. We loved plum color because poor Goldy was vain of his coat of that hue; and champagne, partly because Schiller used to drink it when writing; we saved orange-peel because the author of the "Rambler" liked it; and put ourselves on a course of tar-water, in imitation of Berkeley. Roast-pig had a double relish for us after we had read Elia's dissertation thereon. We associated gold-fish and china jars with Gray, skulls with Dr. Young, the leap of a sturgeon in the Hudson with Drake's "Culprit Fay," pine-trees with Ossian, stained-glass windows with Keats (who set one in an immortal verse), fortifications with Uncle Toby, literary breakfasts with Rogers, water-fowl with Bryant, foundlings with Rousseau, letter-writing with Madame de Sévigné, bread and butter with the author of Werther, daisies with Burns, and primroses with Wordsworth. Mrs. Thrale's acceptance of Piozzi was a serious trouble to our minds; and whether "little Burney" would be happy after her marriage with the noble *emigré* was a problem that made us really anxious until the second part of her Diary was procurable and relieved our solicitude. An unpatriotic antipathy to the Pilgrim Fathers was quelled by the melodious pæan of Mrs. Hemans; and we kept vigils before a portrait of Mrs. Norton, at an artist's studio, with a chivalric desire to avenge her wrongs.

This enthusiasm for authors was not altogether the result of a literary idiosyncrasy or local influences; it grew out of a consciousness of personal obligation. Mrs. Radcliffe, Miss Porter, and Maturin were the clandestine intimates of childhood; the English poets became the confidants of youthful sentiment, which met but a cool reception from those by whom we were surrounded; and when judgment was enough matured to discriminate the charms of style, a new world opened under the guidance of Mackenzie and Sterne, Lady Montagu and Sir Thomas Browne. Books are endeared, like people, by the force of circumstances; ideal tendencies, a spirit of inquiry, a thirst for sympathy, will often drive minds whose environment is uncongenial, to seek therein what is elsewhere denied; and when, in early life, this resource becomes habitual, it is not surprising that a deep personal feeling should be gradually engendered; and that we should come to regard favorite authors as the most reliable and dearest of our companions; and this without an inkling of pedantry, or a title to scholarship, but from a thoroughly human impulse intellectually vindicating itself. To such a pitch did the feeling once possess us that we resented any imputation cast upon our chosen authors as if they were actual friends. We honored the critic that defended Bacon from the charge of meanness, and longed to applaud his prowess; we disliked to admit the evidence that Johnson was dogmatic, and ascribed his arrogance to a kind of excusable horse-play; we contended that Thomson was not lazy, but encouraged ease to escape ambition; we grew very warm if any one really believed Shelley an atheist, and argued that his faith transcended that of the majority of so-called Christians; we never would admit that Sterne was heartless, or Moore a toady. We could have embraced Dr. Madden after reading his "Infirmities of Genius," and thought the most brave of Sidney's deeds his "Defence of Poesy." How we longed to go a-fishing with Walton, to walk in Cowley's garden, to see Roscoe's library, to hear Coleridge talk, to feel the grasp of Burns's hand, to drink whiskey with John Wilson, to pat Scott's dogs, to go to the theatre with Lamb, to listen to D'Israeli the elder's anecdotes, to look on the lakes of Westmoreland at the side of Wordsworth, and to ride through "our village" in Miss Mitford's pony chaise!

The first time we saw an author was an epoch. It was in a church. Some one whispered, just as the sermon began, that a lady in the next pew was the writer of a moral tale then rated high in our little circle. We did nothing the rest of the service but watch and speculate upon this, to us, wonderful personage. We were disappointed at her every-day look and attire; there was no fine frenzy in eye or gesture; there she sat, for all the world like any other lady — mild, quiet, and attentive. We were somewhat consoled by noting the extreme paleness of her complexion, and a kind of abstraction in her gaze. Her habiliments were dark and faded; in fact, as we afterward discovered, she was poor, and her book had been printed by subscription. Thenceforth, for a long time, we imagined all female authors were dressed in black, looked pensive, and had no color. This illusion, however, was banished, some years later, when we were taken to a literary *soirée* where all the female authors were fat, dressed in a variety of colors, and, instead of being melancholy, had an overwhelming vivacity that made us realize how the type had changed. By degrees we became enlightened, and our authormania cooled. In the first place, we were shocked by seeing a pathetic writer, whose universal tribute was tears, in a flashy vest; then we encountered a psychologist, whose forte was sublimity, enacting the part of a mendicant; it was our misfortune to conduct a bard, whose highly imaginative strain had often roused our aspirations, home from a party in a state of inebriety; one author we were prepared to love turned out a disagreeable egotist; another wearied us by the exactions of his vanity; a third repelled by intense affectation, and a fourth by the bitterness of his comments; one, who had written only the most refined sentiment, proved, upon acquaintance, an acute Yankee; one who had sung the beauty of Nature we found to be an inveterate dandy; and another, whose expressed ideas betokened excess of delicacy, grossly violated the ordinary instincts of gentle blood.

On one of our earliest visits to ——— the illusive charm attached to the idea of a female author became, indeed, changed to a horror from which we have never wholly recovered. We were requested to escort a lady to what we understood was an ordinary social gathering. After entering a rather small and somewhat obscure drawing-room, saluting the hostess and taking the proffered seat, we were struck with the formal arrangement of the company. They formed an unbroken row along the walls of the room, except at one end, at which stood a table surmounted by an astral lamp; and in an arm-chair beside it, in a studied attitude, like one *posèd* for a daguerreotype, sat a woman of masculine proportions, coarse features, and hair between yellow and red, which fell in unkempt masses down each side of her broad face. She was clad in white muslin of an antiquated fashion. We noticed that the guests cast looks, partly of curiosity, partly of uneasiness, upon this Herculean female, who rolled her eyes occasionally, and smiled on us all with a kind of complacent pity. We ventured, amidst the silence, to ask our neighbor the name of the gigantic unknown. She appeared extremely surprised at the very natural question. "Why, don't you know? We 're invited here to meet her, and, I assure you, it is a rare privilege. That is Mrs. Jones, the celebrated author of the 'Affianced One!'" At this moment, a brisk little woman in the corner, with accents slightly tremulous, and a manner intended to be very *nonchalant*, broke the uncomfortable hush of the room. "My dear Mrs. Jones," said she, "as one of your earliest and most fervent admirers, allow me to inquire if your health does not suffer from the intense state of feeling in which you evidently write?" The Amazonian novelist sighed, — it was funny to see that operation on so large a scale, — and then, in a voice so like the rougher sex that we began to think she was a man in disguise, replied: "When I reach the catastrophe of my stories, it is not uncommon for me to faint dead away; and, as I always write in a room by myself, it has happened more than once that I have been found stretched, miserable and cold, on the floor, with a pen grasped in my fingers, and the carpet littered with manuscript blotted with tears!" The Siddonian pathos of this announcement sent a thrill round the circle; glances of admiration and pity were thrown upon the self-immolated victim at the shrine of letters, and other inquiries were adventured, which elicited equally impressive replies, until the psychological throes of authorship — particularly in the female gender — assumed the aspect of an experience combined of epilepsy and nightmare. The tragic egotism of these revelations at length overcame our patience; and, leaving our fair companion to another's escort, we slipped out of the room. A thunder-storm had arisen; the rain was pouring down in torrents; upon the door-steps we encountered a very pale, thin, little man, with an umbrella under his arm and a pair of overshoes in his hands. As we passed, he addressed us in a very meek and frightened voice: "Please, sirs, is there a party here?" "Yes." "Please, sirs, is the celebrated Mrs. Jones here?" "Yes." "Please, sirs, do you think I could step into the entry? I'm Mr. Jones!"

Hastening to our lodgings in another metropolis at twilight, we passed a dwarf standing on a threshold, who leaped down and caught us by the arm, eagerly pronouncing our name, and requesting a moment's interview. He led the way to a little room lighted by a single candle, closed the door, and, with a quivering impatience of gesture, introduced himself. We remembered his name at once. He was the author of a feeble imitation of Pope. We never beheld such an ogre. His little green eyes, ape-like limbs, and expression indicative of sensitiveness and conceit, in that lone and dusky cabinet, were appalling. From a cupboard he took down what we supposed to be a ledger, and, placing it on the table, gave an emphatic slap to the worn brown cover. "There," said he, "is garnered the labor of years. I have heard of your enthusiasm for authors, and I will read you specimens of a poem destined to see the light a twelve-month hence. Listen!" It was an epic in blank verse, — dreary, monotonous, and verbose. His recitation was like the refrain of a bull-frog; it grated on the ear and made the nerves shrink. The candle burned thick; the air seemed mephitic, and, in a little while, we were oppressed and fevered as by a glamour cast over our brain; we looked toward the door and moved uneasily; the green eye was cast fiercely up from the page, and the tone of the deformed became malicious. We had heard of his vindictive spirit, and felt as if in the cave of an imp, spellbound and helpless. The complacent hardihood with which he read on made us inwardly frantic. We thought of the fair being who waited for us at a neighboring fireside, of the free air we had quitted, and we writhed under the infliction. Hours passed; a numb, half-unconscious sense of misery stole over us, and still the little demon glared and spouted. "Words, words, words," — how detestable seemed they then! At last, in a fit of desperation, we clapped our hand to our forehead, and murmuring something about a congestive tendency, sprang up, ran through the hall and out the door, and looking back, after hurrying on a few yards, beheld the dwarf, with his enormous book clasped to his heart, gazing after us with the implacable look of a disappointed savage.

Literature is no more regulated by accident than nature; lucky hits and the tricks of pencraft are as temporary as all other artificial expedients. The authors truly remembered and loved are *men* in the best sense of the term; the human, the individual informs and stamps their books with an image or an effluence not born of will or mere ingenuity, but emanating from the soul; and this is the quality that endears and perpetuates their fame. Hence Goldsmith is beloved, Milton reverenced, and the grave of Burns a "Mecca of the mind." At the commencement of the last century there appeared in the London Gazette the offer of a reward of fifty pounds for the discovery of a certain person thus described: "A middle-sized, spare man, about forty years of age, of a brown complexion and dark brown hair, though he wears a wig, having a hooked nose, a sharp chin, gray eyes, and a large mole near his mouth." This was Daniel De Foe, the victim of partisan injustice, for whose rights every schoolboy would fight now, out of sheer gratitude to the author of "Robinson Crusoe." Let the writers who debase authorship into a perversion of history, a sickly medium for egotistical rhetoric, a gross theft of antecedent labors, a base vehicle for spite, or a mechanical knack of book-making, realize that they are foredoomed to contempt, and that character is as little disguised by types as by costume. The genuine author is recognized at once; his integrity is self-evident.

It was sunset on the Arno; far down the river, over mountain ranges where snow yet lingered, a warm tint, half rose and half amethyst, glowed along the horizon; beside the low parapet that bordered the street, people were loitering back from their afternoon promenade at the Cascine: here a priest, there a soldier, now an Englishman on horseback, and then a bearded artist; sometimes an oval-faced *contadina*, the broad brim of whose finely-woven straw hat flapped over eyes of mellow jet; and again a trig nurse with Saxon ringlets, dragging a petulant urchin along; and over all these groups and figures was shed the beautiful smile of parting day, and by them, under graceful bridges, flowed the turbid stream, its volume doubled by the spring freshets. I surveyed the panorama from an overhanging balcony, where I stood awaiting the appearance of a friend upon whom I had called. Hearing a movement behind, I stepped back into the *salon*, and found a middle-aged gentleman seated on a divan near the window. We exchanged salutations, and began to converse. He alluded, in unexceptionable English, to the beauty of the hour. "I come here from Geneva," he said. "There I work; in Italy I recreate; and it is wonderful how this country ministers to intellectual repose, even by the very associations it excites. We feel a dream-like relation with the past, and enter readily, for a time, into the *dolce far niente* spirit of the people; and then return to task-work invigorated and with new zest." There was a bland, self-possessed, and paternal look about this chance acquaintance that insensibly won my confidence and respect. He was the image of a wise and serene maturity. His ample brow, his strong physique, his affable manner and kindly eye, suggested experience, intelligence, and benignity. I was certain that he was a philosopher of some kind, and fancied him an optimist; but the utter absence of pretension and the simple candor of his address gave no hint of a man of renown. Accordingly, I soon found myself engaged in a most pleasant, and to me, instructive colloquy. Following up the hint he had thrown out, I spoke of the difficulty of combining mental toil with health, — reverting in my own mind to our American race of scholars, a majority of whom are confirmed invalids. "Ah!" said he, "there is vast error on this subject. Be assured that we were intended for intellectual labor, and that there is a way of making it subservient to health. I will tell you a few rules founded on experience: Vary the kind of work, — let it be research one hour, meditation another; collation to-day, and revision to-morrow; do this on system; give the first part of the day to the hardest study, the afternoon to exercise, and the evening to social intercourse; let the mind be tasked when the brain is most vigorous, that is, after sleep; and woo the latter blessing not in the feverish hour of thought and emotion, but after the gentle exercise of the mind which comes from pastime and friendliness." I looked at the hale, contented face of the speaker, about whom no sign of nervous irritability or exhaustion was discoverable, and asked myself what experience of mental toil could have led him to such inferences. He looked like a temperate country gentleman, or unambitious and well-to-do citizen. He then spoke of the changes he observed upon each successive visit to Italy, of the climate of Switzerland, and the society of Geneva; then he referred to America, divining at once that it was my country, and exhibiting entire familiarity with all that had been accomplished there in literature. He betrayed a keen sense of enjoyment, recognized a genial influence in the scene before us, and gradually infected me with that agreeable feeling only to be derived from what poor Cowper used to call "comfortable people." I led him to speak of his own method of life, which was one of the most philosophical order. He considered occasional travel and prudent habits the best hygiene for a man of sedentary pursuits; and the great secret both of health and successful industry, the absolute yielding up of one's consciousness to the business and the diversion of the hour, — never permitting the one to infringe, in the least degree, upon the other. I felt an instinctive respect toward him, but, at the same time, entirely at home in his company; the gentleman and the scholar appeared to me admirably fused in, without overlaying, the man. Presently the friend we mutually expected came in, and introduced me to Sismondi. I was fresh from his "Italian Republics" and "Literature of the South of Europe," and he realized my ideal of a humane and earnest historian.

Quite in contrast with this tranquil and robust votary of letters was the appearance and manner of Silvio Pellico. No one who has ever read the chronicle of his imprisonments can forget the gentle and aspiring nature, just blooming into poetic development, which, by the relentless fiat of Austrian tyranny, was cut off in a moment, from home, intelligent companionship, and graceful activity, and subjected to the loneliness, privation, and torments of long and solitary confinement; nor is the spirit in which he met the bitter reverse less memorable than its tragic detail, recorded with so much simplicity, and borne with such loving faith. When I arrived in Turin, he was still an object of espionage, and it was needful to seek him with caution. Agreeably to instructions previously received, I went to a *café* near the Strada Alfieri, just at nightfall, and watched for the arrival of an *abbé* remarkable for his manly beauty. I handed him the card of a mutual friend, and made known my wishes. The next day he conducted me through several arcades, and by many a group of noble-looking Piedmontese soldiers, to a gateway, thence up a long flight of steps to a door, at which he gave a significant knock. In a few moments it was quietly opened; he whispered to the old *serva*, and we tarried in an antechamber until a diminutive figure in black appeared, who received me with a pensive kindliness that, to one acquainted with *Le Mie Prigioni*, was fraught with pathos. I beheld in the pallor of that mild face and expanded brow, and the purblind eyes, the blight of a dungeon. His manner was subdued and nervous, and his very tones melancholy. I was unprepared to find, after years of liberty, the effects of his experience so visible, and felt almost guilty of profane curiosity in having thus intruded upon his cherished seclusion. I had known other victims of the same infernal tyranny, but they were men of sterner mould, who had resisted their cruel fate by the force of will rather than the patience of resignation. Pellico's very delicacy of organization barbed the arrows of persecution; and when at length he was released, loneliness, hope deferred, and mental torture had crushed the energy of his nature. The sweetness of his autobiography was but the fragrance of the trampled flower, — too unelastic ever again to rise up in its early beauty. A smile lighted up his brooding expression when I told him of the deep sympathy his book had excited in America, and he grasped my hand with momentary ardor; but the man too plainly reflected the martyr. The stifling air he breathed under the leads of Venice, and the damps of his Spielberg cell, seemed yet to weigh upon his soul; no glimmer of the patriotic fire which beams from Francesca da Rimini, no ray of the vivacious observation that beguiled his solitude and quickened his pen, redeemed the hopeless air of the captive poet; the shadow of the power he had braved yet lay on his form and face; and only the solace of filial love and the consolations of religion gave hope to his existence.

That is but a vulgar idea of authorship which estimates its worth by the caprices of fashion or the prestige of immediate success. Like art, its value is intrinsic. There are books, as there are pictures, which do not catch the thoughtless eye, and yet are the gems of the virtuoso, the oracles of the philosopher, and the consolations of the poet. We love authors, as we love individuals, according to our latent affinities; and the extent of the popular appreciation is no more a standard to us than the world's estimate of our friend, whose nature we have tested by faithful companionship and sympathetic intercourse. He who has not the mental independence to be loyal to his own intellectual benefactors, is as much a heathen as one who repudiates his natural kin. Indeed, an honest soul clings more tenaciously to neglected merit in authors as in men; there is a chivalry of taste as of manners. Doubtless Lamb's zest for the old English dramatists, Addison's admiration of Milton's poetry, and Carlyle's devotion to German favorites were all the more earnest and keen because they were ignored by their neighbors. In the library, an original mind is conscious of special and comparatively obscure friends, as the lover of Nature has his pet flower and the lover of Art his favorite old master. It is well to obey these decided idiosyncrasies. They point, like the divining-rod, to hidden streams peculiarly adapted to our refreshment. I knew an old merchant that read no book except "Boswell's Johnson," and a black and humpbacked cook whose only imaginative feast was the "Arabian Nights."

No one really can, indeed, love authors as a class, without a catholic taste. If thus equipped, how inexhaustible the field! He is independent of the world. Is he retrospective in mood? Plutarch will array before him a procession of heroes and sages. Does he yearn for conviviality? Fielding will take him to a jolly tavern. Is he eager for intellectual communion? Landor is at hand with a choice of "imaginary conversations." Would he exercise causality? Bishop Butler will put to the test his power of reasoning. Is he in need of a little gossip by way of recreation? Horace Walpole will amuse by the hour. Is the society of a sensible woman wanted? Call in Maria Edgeworth or Jane Austin. Is the bitterness of a jilted lover in his heart? "Locksley Hall" will relieve it. Would he stroll in the forest? Evelyn or Bryant will take him there in a moment. By the sea-shore? Crabbe and Byron are sympathetic guides. Are his thoughts comprehensive and inclined for the generalities of literature? Open De Staël or Hallam.

The relation of authorship to society varies with political influences and average culture; the class of degraded penwrights so often alluded to by Fielding, the ferocious quarrels recorded of and by Pope and Johnson with critics and publishers, are phases of literary life, which, if not extinct, have become essentially modified with the progress of civilization. Yet a quite recent quarterly reviewer speaks of this class of men as "a kind of ticket-of-leave lunatics"; and modern experiences, if less dark than old annals of Grub Street, include some quite as remarkable instances of reckless extravagance in prosperity and barbarous neglect in adversity. The Bohemian class is confined to no epoch or country. Yet charming is the group of authors that illustrate and signalize every period of British history,—an intellectual alleviation to the monotony of fashionable, and the rancor of political life. Every era of French government also has its brilliant *salon* of philosophers and poets. Mrs. Carter and Mrs. Montague assembled, in their day, as exclusive a coterie as used to cluster about Dryden's chair, dine with Sir Joshua Reynolds, keep Burns's birthday at Edinburgh with Scott at the head of the table, rally at Jeffrey's call, dispute with Hume, chat over Rogers's breakfasts, fraternize with the lakers at Keswick and Grasmere, or pass an evening with Lamb. From the days of Shakspeare to those of Evelyn and Sydney Smith, from La Fontaine to Lamartine, from Klopstock to Goethe, and from Mather to Channing, every cultivated city abroad and at home, has boasted its author circle, to which kindred tastes ever revert with zest, and whose traditions as well as "works" prolong a spell more refined and memorable than any other social prestige. Weimar, Bordeaux, Florence, Edinburgh, and Boston, as well as London and Paris, are thus consecrated by reminiscences of Goethe, Schiller, Montaigne, Alfieri, Wilson, Mackenzie, some Concord Sage, or Spanish Historian, some Autocrat, Wizard of the North, or Ettrick Shepherd of the pen. To have seen Niccolini on the Lung 'Arno; Elizabeth Browning at a Casa Guidi window; Rossini, the historical novelist, at a bookstore in Pisa; Hillhouse under the New Haven elms; Hawthorne at the Athenæum; Elia at his India-house desk; poor Heine on his "mattress grave," or Freiligrath at his bank-counter, requires but the perspective of time to be as impressive or winsome an experience as the first survivors of Pope, Chatterton, Milton, or Burke realized in rehearsing their personal cognizance of these famous authors. Such is the instinctive attraction of congenial or eminent authorship. If this subject were nomenclated and analyzed in the naturalistic way, there is scarcely a sphere of humanity or a form of character which might not be identified with or illustrated by authorship; the mad, the mendicant, the charlatan, — combative, contemplative, heroic, and sybarite,— are but a few of the varieties which literary biography reveals. Their amours, diseases, profits, calamities, triumphs, quarrels, personal tastes and habits, domestic life, and most individual traits and fortunes, have been minutely recorded, so as to form, on the whole, the best and most accessible psychological cabinet for the student of human nature. Of no other class of men and women with whom we never had personal acquaintance, do we know so many details; Chatterton's despair, Young's skull-light, Milton's organ, Berkeley's tar-water, Coleridge's opium, Swift's lady-loves, Cowper's hymns and hares, Rogers's table-talk, Scott's dogs, Steele's debts, Lamb's folios, are as familiar to us as if they appertained to some neighbor or kinsman. The prisons of Cervantes, Raleigh, Pellico, Hunt, and Montgomery, have a pathetic charm which no other record of captivity boasts. Even the self-delusions of authors awaken a considerate interest; the mistaken judgment of Petrarch and Milton, in regard to the comparative merit of their writings; and the exaggerated estimate of their own verses by such able statesmen as Frederic and Richelieu, tend to enhance the mysteries of the craft and sanction its illusions. But it must be confessed that the romance of authorship is fast disappearing in its reality; so numerous have become the votaries of a once rare pursuit, so common the renown, so universal the practice, that the individual and characteristic, the curious and interesting elements thereof, are more and more merged in the commonplace and familiar.

A distinction has often been insisted on between the critical and the creative in literature; but modern criticism, in its best development, is essentially reproductive; so intimate, deep, and affluent is its dealing with authors, that they often are restored in all their vital worth; and the process has endeared such writers as Lamb, Hazlitt, Carlyle, Arnold, and St. Beuve, as true intellectual benefactors. Such philosophical and æsthetic interpreters of authorship have engendered an eclectic appreciation and enjoyment of authors, and made us what Allston calls "wide likers." Hence the prevalence and promise of what may be called a cosmopolitan, in distinction to a provincial taste, whereby we learn to value the greatest diversities of style, subject, and character in literature. Fastidious and severely disciplined minds, indeed, coldly ignore certain authors and warmly espouse others; but to a spirit at once generous and cultivated, sympathetic and intelligent, though a special charm will invest favorite authors, — all of the fraternity who are genuine, have a recognized claim to grateful recognition; and even the unequal and incongruous development of modern English literature incident to the absence of what Matthew Arnold calls "any centre of intelligent and urbane spirit," like the French Academy. Desirable as such a discipline and standard is in quelling eccentricity and incorrectness, the free and energetic development, the honest, though sometimes rude, exercise of authorship in our vernacular, is no small compensation. We confess a partiality for the richly diversified phases of mental life thus induced, — an eclectic relish for the varieties of national and personal characteristics. The artistic French, the meditative German, the practical English writers, have each their attraction and use; the desultory style of Richter, the quaint individuality of Lamb, the verbose dignity of Johnson, the mosaic finish of Gray, the grotesque eloquence of Carlyle, the flowing rhetoric of Macaulay, Wordsworth's pastoral isolation, Scott's feudal enthusiasm, Byron's intense consciousness, Shelley's disinterested idealism, the homely images of Crabbe, and the sensuous luxury of Keats, are all, in their way and at times, accordant with our mental wants, congenial to our receptive moods. Why should not we tolerate and enjoy the various elements of literature as fully and fondly as those of nature and society? Does it not argue a narrowness of mind inconsistent with genuine, intellectual, and moral health, to perversely confine our appreciation of authorship to certain schools, forms, and individuals? Are not the philosophical, the piquant, the earnest, the playful, the solemn, gay, impressive, winsome, acute, wise, and humorous traits and triumphs of written thought, as legitimate, in their infinite variety, as means of human culture, discipline, and pleasure, as the myriad tints and tones of Nature, and the diversities of character and manners? A true lover of authors will not only find something to enjoy and appropriate in the most diverse forms of expression and qualities of genius, both in the literature of power and in that of knowledge as finely discriminated by De Quincey; but will separate the inspired and the journeyman work of each author, and do justice to what is genuine while repudiating the conventional. If what Goethe maintained is literally true, and genuine authorship is the reflex of consciousness upon outward life, — then all its spontaneous products must have a vital element of human life, love, and truth more or less congenial to all readers of candid, clear, and humane instincts: for we agree with a liberal and acute critic when he says that the gift of literary genius "lies in the faculty of being happily inspired by a certain intellectual and spiritual atmosphere, — by a certain order of ideas; of dealing divinely with these ideas, presenting them in the most effective and attractive combinations, making beautiful works of them."

It is a new and glorious era in our experience of books, when the vital significance of authorship is heartily realized ; dilletantism, excusable in the novice, gives place to the worship of truth; to write for the mere sake of writing, to amuse with the pen, becomes in our estimation what it is, — a thing of less interest than the most simple and familiar phenomena of Nature; as life reveals itself, and character matures, we long above all, for reality; we perceive that growth is our welfare, and that earnestness, faith, and new truth the only joy of a manly intellect. Then we read to nerve our moral energies, to extend the scope of perception, and to deepen the experience of the soul: the butterflies of literature allure no longer; the imitators we pass by; but the deep thinkers, the original, the brave, lead us on to explore, analyze, and conquer. "Literature," says Schlegel, "according to the spirit in which it is pursued, is an infamy, a pastime, a dry labor, a handicraft, an art, a science, a virtue;" and this diversity is true, not only of authors in general, but sometimes of the same individual. Many a poet whose early utterance was inspired, has degenerated into a hack, a truckster, and a mercenary penman; and many a youthful dabbler in letters by some deep experience has been matured into the bold advocate or heroic pioneer in the world of thought.

We soon learn heartily to sympathize with one of the unfortunate originals of Goethe's Werther, and declare with him, — "I have resolved in future to take good care how I write anything to an author, save what all the world may see;" only extending the prudential resolve to conversation, — for whatever advance has been made in refinement in the use of language, in the abuse of confidence modern writers are so destitute of scruples, that the sanctities of life and social intercourse have no greater or more profane intruder than the author.

Nor is the "heart of courtesy" the only high quality risked by the vocation; it almost seems, in vain and unchivalric natures, to sap manhood itself; some one has said, — "The man who has learned to read has lost one portion of his courage; if he writes verses, he has lost a double portion." There is a fatal fluency, an arrogant expressiveness, whereby the robust and honest material of character is, as it were, evaporated in words; for nothing characterizes the genuine author more than a reticent tone, an integrity of utterance, which makes it apparent that his authorship, instead of a graft, is a growth of his best humanity. So proverbial is the social barrenness of the craft, in its average conventional scope, that a facetious Florentine barber, in one of the best of modern historical novels (Romola), is quite appropriately made to say, — "I am sorely afraid that the good wine of my understanding is going to run off at the spigot of authorship, and I shall be left an empty cask, with an odor of dregs, like many other incomparable geniuses of my acquaintance." All meanness is disenchanting; but selfish economy of intellectual treasures, and egotistical insensibility to the merit of others, not only robs the author of all sympathetic charm, but almost invariably signalizes his essential mediocrity or unfounded pretensions.

Under the two diverse aspects of an inspiration and a career, authorship thus offers the extremes of attraction and antagonism to candid and earnest souls; if the spontaneous gift and charm of the former are justly endeared to all lovers of humanity, the artificial conditions, worldly motives, and forced relations of the latter, often dispel the illusions of fame in the realities of vulgar notoriety and mercenary zeal. We can well understand how a reverent, delicate, and true nature, like Maurice de Guèrin, shrinks from professional authorship, when the original beauty and truth of his utterances led his friends to urge that vocation upon him: "The literary career," he writes, "seems to me unreal, both in its own essence and in the rewards one seeks from it; and, therefore, fatally marred by a secret absurdity."

At this moment our vernacular is the only tongue in which men can express themselves fearlessly; it appropriately enshrines the literature of freedom. We seldom realize this noble distinction of the English language. I was half-asleep one afternoon, in the cabin of a steamer in the Bay of Naples, when suddenly the violent pitching of the vessel ceased, and I hastened on deck to learn the reason of the change, and found, to my surprise, that we were returning into the harbor, the captain having decided that it was too great a risk to venture to sea in such a gale. Pleasant as was the transition from tossing waves to smooth water, every traveller in that region who has gone through the business of a departure, — the passport signatures, the tussle with porters, drivers, and boatmen, the leave-takings, packings-up, directions at post-office and banker's, an embarkation in the midst of cries, rushings to and fro, disputes for gratuities, beggars, missing baggage, attempts to secure a berth, wringing of hands, waving of handkerchiefs, and, it may be, embraces at parting, — every traveller cognizant of this experience, will understand how vexatious it was, within an hour after this tantalizing process, to find one's self, in travelling costume, once more in the city, for the afternoon, with no lodging, no appointment, and no sight-seeing to do. I was not long in resolving to visit once more my old dining-place, the *Corona di Ferro.* At the opposite table to that at which I was seated, appeared a handsome young man, with a dark, intelligent eye, and a bearing indicative of spirit and courtesy. Seeing me hesitate over the *carte,* he suggested a dish which had proved *molto buono* that day, and having followed the kindly counsel, we engaged in a desultory chat about the weather, the Opera, the last news from France, etc., and by the time dessert came on, had established quite a pleasant understanding; at length he made an inquiry based upon the idea that he was addressing an Englishman. I corrected the error, and his politeness at once warmed into enthusiasm at the discovery that he was talking with an American. After dinner he invited me to his apartments. I found the sitting-room adorned with pictures and littered with books. Having ordered coffee, we were soon engaged in a serious discussion of literary subjects, in which my new friend proved a tasteful votary. He wished for a definite statement as to the extent of the liberty of the press in the United States. I explained it; and he became highly excited, paced the room, quoted Alfieri, sighed, pressed his brow, and at length flung himself into a chair, declaring that, if it were not for kindred who had claims upon him, he would emigrate at once to America. To account for his feelings, he showed me a pile of MSS. the publication of which had been prohibited by the government censors on account of their liberal sentiment. He then exhibited several beautiful poems founded on scientific truths, yet mystically involving great and humane principles, — a *ruse* he had been compelled to resort to in order to express publicly his opinions. As I recognized the evidences of genius, watched his chafed mood, and noted his manly spirit, I felt deeply the crushing influence of despotism upon authorship, and realized the natural antagonism between poets and kings.

There is no greater fallacy than that involved in the notion of an essential diversity between an author and his books: professed opinions do not reveal the truth of character, but unconscious phases of style, habits of thought, and tones of expression, like what is called natural language, make us thoroughly acquainted with the man. Is not Jeremy Taylor's religious sentiment manifest in the very method of his utterance? Can we not see at a glance the improvidence and the fascination of Sheridan in the tenor of his plays? Who would not avouch the honesty of John L. Stephens after reading his travels? What reverent heart is not magnetized by the genuineness of devotion in Watts, however crudely expressed? Is not prudence signified in the very style of Franklin? Are we not braced with the self-confident frankness of Cooper in the spirit as well as the characters of his nautical and forest tales? Critics betray their arrogant temper under the most courteous phrases; a gentleman is still a gentleman, and a puppy a puppy, on paper as in life; the sham and the true are equally discernible in print and in society. Montaigne exhibits his worldly wisdom as plainly in his essays as he ever did in his acts. It is not, therefore, the insidious but the obvious perils of authorship that threaten the novice. Lamentable is it to see mediocre men take up as a vocation either literature or art, for in both a certain amount of *character* alone insures respectability; and this is less requisite in pursuits that do not so openly challenge observation.

One day I was told a gentleman had called and waited for me in the drawing-room. As I entered, he was gazing from the window in the shadow of a damask curtain, which threw a warm tint upon as strongly moulded a face as I remembered to have seen in one so young. His forehead was compactly rounded, his hair curly and raven, and his eye dark and luminous. As I approached, he handed me a note of introduction from a friend, refused the proffered seat, and wore so earnest and grave an expression that I almost thought he was the bearer of a challenge. "Sir," he began, "I have come to you for sympathy in a great undertaking. I wish to be cheered in a mission, encouraged in a career, advised in an experiment!" There was a certain wildness in the manner of this sententious address which breathed of an excited fancy. I expressed a willingness to aid him to the extent of my humble ability. He drew a thick packet from his coat, and proceeded: "I am a native of a little village in a neighboring State. My father is an agriculturist, and has endeavored to render me content with that lot; but there is something *here*" — and he laid a large red hand on his capacious breast — "that rebels against the decree. I aspire to the honors of literature. I long to utter myself to the world. Here is a tragedy and some lyrics; and I have come to town to test my fortune as an author." I saw that he was an enthusiast, and calmly pointed out the obstacles to success. He became impatient. I enlarged on the healthfulness and wisdom of a country life, on the precarious subsistence incident to pencraft. His eye flashed with anger. I urged him to consider well the risk he incurred, the danger of failure, the advantages of a reliable vocation, the comfort of an independent though secluded existence. He advanced toward me with an indignant stride. "Sir," he exclaimed, "I have been misinformed; you are not the man I took you for; farewell, forever!" and he rushed from the house. Six months had elapsed, and I was sitting over a book in my quiet room one day, when a terrific knock at the door aroused me, and an instant after the stranger entered and impetuously grasped my hand. "Sir, — my dear friend, I mean," — he said, "I have done you injustice, and I have come to apologize. For a month after my former interview, I passed a feverish novitiate, hawking my manuscripts around, deceived by plausible members of the trade, snubbed by managers, frozen out of the sanctums of editors, yawned at by casual audiences, baffled at every turn, until worn out, mortified, and despairing, I went home. The feel of the turf, the breath of the wind, the lowing of the kine, the very scent of hay was refreshing. I thought over your counsel and found it true. I now farm the paternal acres on shares, write verses during the long winter evenings, lead the choir on Sundays, am to marry the pride of the village next week, and am here to beg your pardon, and invite you to my wedding."

The delectable quality of authorship is its impersonality. Consider a moment the privilege and the immunity. If we address a multitude or an individual, the impression may be pleasing or wearisome, but courtesy requires that it be endured with equanimity. A book is unobtrusive, silent, objective. It can be taken up or let alone. In it, if genuine, there is a thought that craves hospitality to be caught in a favorable mood, as the fallow hillock receives the seed borne on the vagrant wind. It may take root, and the originator thereof has unconsciously given birth to an undying impulse or yielded spiritual refreshment. The whole process is like that of Nature, — unostentatious, benign, and of inestimable benefit; and yet how latent, beyond observation, secreted in consciousness! All power of expression — whether by means of pen, color, or chisel, — all artistic development, — is but a new vocabulary that reveals character. The author and the artist differ from their less gifted fellows simply in this, — that they have more language; the endowment does not change their natures; if coarse, artificial, vain, — if brave, truthful, or shallow, — they thus appear in books and marble or on canvas; and hence it is that character is the true gauge of authorship, and wins or repels confidence, respect, and love, in the same proportion as do living men. "By their fruit shall ye know them." Therefore authors themselves most effectually disenchant readers. They are disloyal to their high mission; they compromise their own ideal, write gossip instead of truth, describe themselves instead of Nature, dip their pens in the venom of malevolence, corrupt their style with vulgarity, keep no faith with aspiration, truckle to power and interest, and so bring their vocation itself into merited disdain.

How charming, on the other hand, is the spontaneous bard, who sings from an overflowing and musical nature! There is a court in one of the most populous quarters of London which rejoices in the name of Spring Gardens; doubtless the spot, at one time, was a rural domain; at present, a few trees peering over a wall, and a retired and quaint look about some of the brick domiciles that line the street, alone justify the pleasant name it bears. In one of these houses is the office of the Commissioners of Lunacy; and there, one winter morning, I had the satisfaction of a brief *tête-à-tête* with Procter. His plainly cut frock-coat, long and black, his white hair and quiet bearing, made him appear a curate such as Goldsmith portrayed. It is a curious vocation for a poet, — that of testing the wits of people suspected of being out of their mind, — and a painful one for a sensitive nature to inspect the asylums devoted to their use. But I remembered that Procter's early taste drew him into intimate love and recognition of the old English dramatists, whose natural element was the terrible in human passion and woe; I considered the profound tenderness of his muse, and I felt that even the tragic scenes it was his duty to witness and to study, were not without a certain sad affinity with genius. Kean visited mad-houses to perfect his conception of Lear; and he who sings of human weal and sorrow is taught to deepen and hallow his strain by the misery as well as the amenities of his life. The heart of courtesy, the mood of aspiration, have not been quelled in Procter by the stern professional business which is his daily task. They loomed up even in that dusky office, and kept faith with my previous ideal; but it was especially in the poet's eye that I read the spirit of his muse; ineffably mild and tender is its expression, deepening under the influence of emotion like the tremulous cadence of music that is born of sentiment. I saw there the soul that dictated "How many summers, love, hast thou been mine?" "Send down thy pitying angel, God!" and so many other lays of affection endeared to all who can appreciate the genuine lyrics of the heart identified with the name of Barry Cornwall.

With all its occasional disenchantment, my love of authors imparted a singular charm to the experience of travel; the lapse of time and new localities united then to revive the dreams of youth. What a new grace the first view of the hills of Spain derived from the memory of Cervantes, and the gleanings in that romantic field of Lockhart and Irving; how rife with associations was the dreary night-ride beyond Terracina, near the scene of Cicero's murder; and what an intense life awoke in desolate Ravenna, at the sight of Dante's tomb! The rustling of dry reeds in the gardens of Sallust had an eloquent significance; the figures on Alfieri's monument, in Santa Croce, seemed to breathe in the twilight; the rosemary plucked in Rousseau's old garden at Montmorency had a scent of fragrant memory; in the *cafés* at Venice, Goldoni's characters appeared to be talking, and Byron's image floated on her waters like a sculptor's dream; in the Florentine villa Boccacio's spirit lingered; in the Cenci palace Shelley's deep eyes glistened; in the shade of the pyramid of Cestus the muse of Keats scattered flowers; on the shores of Como hovered the creations of Manzoni, and a cliff in Brittany rose like a cenotaph to Chateaubriand; while the cadence of Virgil's line chimed with the lapsing wave on the beach at Naples. I thought, at Lausanne, of Gibbon's last touch to the "Rise and Fall," and his revery that night; sought the tablet that covers Parnell's dust at Chester, craved Montgomery's blessing at Sheffield, looked for Sterne's monk at

Calais, and beheld the crown on Tasso's cold temples beneath the cypresses of St. Onofrio. De Foe lighted up gloomy Cripplegate, Addison walked in the groves of Oxford, Johnson threaded the crowd in Fleet Street, and Milton's touch seemed to wake the organ-keys of St. Giles. But it is not requisite to wander from home for such experiences.

It was a delicious morning in June. I had passed the previous night at a village on the Hudson; a violent thunder-storm just before dawn had laid the dust, freshened the leaves, and purified as well as cooled the sultry air. Attracted by the sweet breath and vivid tints of the landscape, I determined to walk to a steamboat-landing four miles off, and on my way make a long-meditated visit to Sunnyside. Taking an umbrageous path that wound through a shady lane, I sauntered along, sometimes in view of the crystal expanse of Tappan Zee, sometimes catching a glimpse of the hoary and tufted Palisades, and again pausing under a majestic elm on whose pendent spray a yellow-bird chirped and swung, or from whose dense green canopy a locust trilled its drowsy note. The breeze was scented with clover and woodbine; sleek cattle grazed in the meadows; amber clouds flecked a heaven of azure; fields of grain waved like a shoreless lake of plumes; the maize stood thick and tasselled; the lofty chestnuts shook their feathery bloom; now and then a solitary crow hovered above, or a brown robin hopped cheerily by the wayside. It was one of those clear, serene, luxurious days of early summer which, in our capricious climate, occasionally unite the gorgeous hues of the Orient with the balm and the softness of Italy; pearly outlines stretched along the hills, the broad river gleamed in sunshine, and every shade of emerald flashed or deepened over the wide groves and teeming farms. As I drew near to Irving's cottage, the bees were contentedly humming round the locusts, and the ivy-leaves, that clustered thickly about the old gables, were dripping with the tears of night; every bugle of the honeysuckle was a delicate censer, and the turf and hedge wore their brightest colors; even the old weathercock, trophy of an ancient colonial Stadt-house, dazzled the eye as it caught the lateral rays of the sun; the fowls strutted about with unwonted complacency, and the house-dog bounded through the beaded grass as if exhilarated by the scene. On the veranda that overlooks the river, from which it is divided by a little grove, sat our favorite author, with a book on his knee, the embodiment of thoughtful content. His home looked the symbol of his genius, and his expression the reflex of his life. They harmonized with a rare completeness, and fulfilled to the heart the picture which imagination had drawn. Here was no castle in the air, but a realized day-dream. Sleepy Hollow was at hand: an English cottage, like that to which poor Leslie brought his angel wife; a Dutch roof such as covered Van Tassell's memorable feast; the stream up which floated the incorrigible Dolph; the mountain range whose echoes resounded with the mysterious bowls, and where Rip took his long nap, — all identified with the author's virgin fame, — gave the vital interest of charming association to the silent grace of Nature; and, above all, the originator of the spell was there, as genial, humorous, and imaginative, as if he had never wandered from the primal haunts of his childhood and his fame. That he had done so, and to good purpose, however, was evident in his conversation. News had just arrived of a new French *émeute*, and that led us to speak of the first Revolution; and Irving gave some impressive reminiscences of his visits to the localities of Paris which are identified with those scenes of violence and blood. He recurred to them with keen sensibility and in graphic details. It was delightful thus to commune with a man whose name was associated with my first conscious relish of native authorship, and detect the same moral zest and picturesque insight in his talk which so long ago had endeared his writings. I felt anew the conservative power of a love of Nature and an artistic organization; they had kept thus fresh the sympathies and thus enjoyable the mind. Retirement was as grateful now as when he sought it as a juvenile dreamer; the noble river won as fond a glance as when first explored as a truant urchin; and the kindly spirit beamed as truly in his smile as when he mused in the Alhambra, or walked to Melrose with Scott for a *cicerone*. My authormania revived in all its original fervor; here were the mellow hues on the picture that beguiled my boyhood; and the man, the scene and the author blended in a graceful unity of effect, without a single incongruity.

PICTURES.

"Look on this picture and on this."
HAMLET.

IT is not surprising that pictures, with all their attraction for eye and mind, are, to many honest and intelligent people, too much of a riddle to be altogether pleasant. What with the oracular dicta of self-constituted arbiters of taste, the discrepancies of popular writers on Art, the jargon of connoisseurship, the vagaries of fashion, the endless theories about color, style, chiaroscuro composition, design, imitation, nature, schools, etc., painting has become rather a subject for the gratification of vanity and the exercise of pedantic dogmatism, than a genuine source of enjoyment and culture, of sympathy and satisfaction, — like music, literature, scenery, and other recognized intellectual recreations. In these latter spheres it is not thought presumptuous to assert and enjoy individual taste; the least independent talkers will bravely advocate their favorite composer, describe the landscape which has charmed or the book which has interested them; but when a picture is the subject of discussion, few have the moral courage to say what they think; there is a self-distrust of one's own impressions, and even convictions, in regard to what is represented on canvas, that never intervenes between thought and expression, where ideas or sentiments are embodied in writing or in melody. Nor is this to be ascribed wholly to the technicalities of pictorial art, in which so few are deeply versed, but, in a great measure, to the incongruous and irrelevant associations which have gradually overlaid and mystified a subject in itself as open to the perception of a candid mind and healthy senses as any other department of human knowledge. Half the want of appreciation of pictures arises from ignorance, not of the principles of Art, but of the elements of Nature. Good observers are rare. The peasant's criticism upon Moreland's "Farm-yard"—that three pigs never eat together without one foot at least in the trough—was a strict inference from personal knowledge of the habits of the animal; so the surgeon found a head of the Baptist untrue, because the skin was not withdrawn somewhat from the line of decollation. These and similar instances show that some knowledge of or interest in the thing represented, is essential to the appreciation of pictures. Sailors and their wives crowded around Wilkie's "Chelsea Pensioners,"* when first exhibited; French soldiers enjoy the minutiæ of Vernet's battle-pieces; a lover can judge of his betrothed's miniature; and the most unrefined sportsman will point out the niceties of breed in one of Landseer's dogs. To the want of correspondence so frequent between the subject of a picture and the observer's experience, may, therefore, be attributed no small degree of the prevalent want of sympathy and confident judgment. "Gang into an Exhibition," says the Ettrick Shepherd, "and only

* "I would not" observes Washington Irving in one of his letters, "give an hour's conversation with Wilkie about paintings, in his earnest but precise and original enthusiasm, for all the enthusiasm and declamation of the common run of amateurs and artists."

look at a crowd o' cockneys, some with specs, and some wi' quizzing-glasses, and faces without ae grain o' meaning in them o' ony kind whatsomever, a' glowering, perhaps, at a picture o' one o' Nature's maist fearfu' or magnificent warks! What, I ask, could a Prince's-Street maister or missy ken o' sic a wark mair than a red deer wad ken o' the inside o' George's-Street Assembly-Rooms?"

The incidental associations of pictures link them to history, tradition, and human character, in a manner which indefinitely enhances their suggestiveness. Horace Walpole wove a standard collection of anecdotes from the lives and works of painters. The frescos of St. Mark's, at Florence, have a peculiar significance to the spectator familiar with Fra Angelico's life. One of the most pathetic and beautiful tragedies in modern literature is that which a Danish poet elaborated from Correggio's artist career. Lamb's great treasure was a print from Da Vinci, which he called "My Beauty," and its exhibition to a literal Scotchman gave rise to one of the richest jokes in Elia's record. The pen-drawing Andre made of himself the night before his execution, — the curtain painted in the space where Faliero's portrait should have been, in the ducal palace at Venice, — and the head of Dante, discovered by Mr. Kirkup, on the wall of the Bargello, at Florence, — convey impressions far beyond the mere lines and hues they exhibit; each is a drama, a destiny. And the hard but true lineaments of Holbein, the aërial grace of Malbone's "Hours," Albert Durer's mediæval sanctities, Overbeck's conservative self-devotion, a market-place by Ostade, Reynolds's "Strawberry Girl," one of Copley's colonial grandees in a New England farmer's parlor, a cabinet gem by Greuze, a dog or sheep of Landseer's, the misty depths of Turner's "Carthage," Domenichino's "Sibyl," Claude's "Sunset," or Allston's "Rosalie," — how much of eras in Art, events in history, national tastes, and varieties of genius do they each foreshadow and embalm! Even when no special beauty or skill is manifest, the character of features transmitted by pictorial art, their antiquity or historical significance, often lends a mystery and meaning to the effigies of humanity. In the carved faces of old German church choirs and altars, the existent facial peculiarities of race are curiously evident; a Grecian life breathes from many a profile in the Elgin marbles, and a sacred marvel invests the exhumed giants of Nineveh; in the cartoons of Raphael, and the old Gobelin tapestries, are hints of what is essential in the progress and the triumphs of painting. Considered as a language, how definitely is the style of painters associated with special forms of character and spheres of life! "There certainly never was a painter," — says a traveller in Spain of Murillo, — "who, without much imagination, and telling no story, could yet vision his eyes with such pure love, and make lips so parting with prayer as Murillo; himself a father, he loved to paint the child-Saviour in conjunction with thin-faced saints." It is this variety of human experience, typified and illustrated on canvas, that forms our chief obligations to the artist; through him our perception of and acquaintance with our race, its individuality and career, its phases and aspects, is indefinitely enlarged. "The greatest benefit," says a late writer, "we owe to the artist, whether painter, poet, or novelist, is the *extension of our sympathies*. Art is the nearest thing to life; it is a mode of amplifying our experience and extending our contact with our fellow-creatures beyond the bounds of our personal lot."

"A room with pictures in it, and a room without pictures," says an æsthetic essayist, "differ by nearly as much as a room with windows and a room without windows. Nothing, we think, is more melancholy, particularly to a person who has to pass much time in his room, than blank walls with nothing on them; for pictures are loopholes of escape to the soul, leading it to other spheres. It is such an inexpressible relief to the person engaged in writing, or even reading, on looking up, not to have his line of vision chopped square off by an odious white wall, but to find his soul escaping, as it were, through the frame of an exquisite picture, to other beautiful, and perhaps idyllic scenes, where the fancy for a moment may revel, refreshed and delighted. Is it winter in your world? Perhaps it is summer in the picture; what a charming momentary change and contrast! And thus pictures are consolers of loneliness; they are a sweet flattery to the soul; they are a relief to the jaded mind; they are windows to the imprisoned thought; they are books; they are histories and sermons — which we can read without the trouble of turning over the leaves."

The effect of a picture is increased by isolation and surprise. I never realized the physiognomical traits of Madame de Maintenon, until her portrait was encountered in a solitary country-house, of whose drawing-room it was the sole ornament; and the romance of a miniature by Malbone first came home to me, when an ancient dame, in the costume of the last century, with trembling fingers drew one of her husband from an antique cabinet, and descanted on the manly beauty of the deceased original, and the graceful genius of the young and lamented artist. Hazlitt wrote an ingenious essay on "A Portrait by Vandyck," which gives us an adequate idea of what such a masterpiece is to the eye and mind of genuine artistic perception and sympathy. Few sensations, or rather sentiments, are more inextricably made up of pleasure and sadness than that with which we contemplate (as is not infrequent in some old gallery of Europe) a portrait which deeply interests or powerfully attracts us, and whose history is irrevocably lost. A better homily on the evanescence of human love and fame can scarcely be imagined: a face alive with moral personality and human charms, such as win and warm our stranger eyes, — yet the name, subject, artist, owner, all lost in oblivion! To pause before an interesting but "unknown portrait" is to read an elegy as pathetic as Gray's.

The mechanical processes by which Nature is so closely imitated, and the increase of which during the last few years is one of the most remarkable facts in science, may, at the first glance, appear to have lessened the marvellous in Art, by making available to all the exact representation of still-life. But, when duly considered, the effect is precisely the reverse; for exactly in proportion as we become familiar with the mechanical production of the similitudes of natural and artificial objects, do we instinctively demand higher powers of conception, greater spiritual expression in the artist. The discovery of Daguerre and its numerous improvements, and the unrivalled precision attained by photography, render exact imitation no longer a miracle of crayon or palette; these must now create as well as reflect, invent and harmonize as well as copy, bring out the soul of the individual and of the landscape, or their achievements will be neglected in favor of the fac-similes obtainable through sunshine and chemistry. The best photographs of architecture, statuary, ruins, and, in some cases, of celebrated pictures, are satisfactory to a degree which has banished mediocre sketches, and even minutely finished but literal pictures. Specimens of what is called "Nature-printing," which gives an impression directly from the veined stone, the branching fern, or the sea-moss, are so true to the details as to answer a scientific purpose; natural objects are thus lithographed without the intervention of pencil or ink. And these several discoveries have placed the results of mere imitative art within reach of the mass; in other words, her prose language, that which mechanical science can utter, is so universal, that her poetry, that which must be conceived and expressed through individual genius, the emanation of the soul, is more distinctly recognized and absolutely demanded from the artist, in order to vindicate his claim to that title, than ever before.

Perhaps, indeed, the scope which Painting offers to experimental, individual, and prescriptive taste, the loyalty it invokes from the conservative, the "infinite possibilities" it offers to the imaginative, the intimacy it promotes with Nature and character, are the cause of so much originality and attractiveness in its votaries. The Lives of Painters abound in the characteristic, the adventurous, and the romantic. Open Vasari, Walpole, or Cunningham, at random, and one is sure to light upon something odd, genial, or exciting. One of the most popular novelists of our day assured me, that, in his opinion, the richest unworked vein for his craft, available in these days of civilized uniformity, is artist-life at Rome, to one thoroughly cognizant of its humors and aspirations, its interiors and vagrancies, its self-denials and its resources. I have sometimes imagined what a story the old white dog who so long frequented the Lepri and the Caffè Greco, and attached himself so capriciously to the brother artists of his deceased master, could have told, if blest with memory and language. He had tasted the freedom and the zest of artist-life in Rome, and scorned to follow trader or king. He preferred the odor of canvas and oil to that of conservatories, and had more frolic and dainty morsels at an *al fresco* of the painters, in the Campagna, than the kitchen of an Italian prince could furnish. His very name betokened good cheer, and was pronounced after the manner of the pert waiters who complacently enunciate a few words of English. *Bif-steck* was a privileged dog; and though occasionally made the subject of a practical joke, taught absurd tricks, sent on fools' errands, and his white coat painted like a zebra, these were but casual troubles; he was a sensible dog to despise them, when he could enjoy such quaint companionship, behold such experiments in color and drawing, serve as a model himself, and go on delicious sketching excursions to Albano and Tivoli, besides inhaling tobacco-smoke and hearing stale jests and love soliloquies *ad infinitum*. I am of *Bif-steck's* opinion. There is no such true, earnest, humorous, and individual life, in these days of high civilization, as that of your genuine painter; impoverished as it often is, baffled in its aspirations, unregarded by the material and the worldly, it often rears and keeps pure bright, genial natures whose contact brings back the dreams of youth. It is pleasant, too, to realize, in a great commercial city, that man "does not live by bread alone," that fun is better than furniture, and a private resource of nature more prolific of enjoyment than financial investments. It is rare comfort, here, in the land of bustle and sunshine, to sit in a tempered light and hear a man sing or improvise stories over his work; to behold once more vagaries of costume; to let the eye rest upon pictorial fragments of Italy, — the "old familiar faces" of Roman models, the endeared outlines of Apennine hills, the *contadina* bodice and the brigand hat, until these objects revive to the heart all the romance of travel.

Vernet's sympathies were excited by the misfortunes of a worthy tradesman of Marseilles, and he attended the sheriff's auction at the bankrupt's house, where, among the crowd, he recognized a would-be *connoisseur* in art, of ample wealth; the painter fixed his eyes upon a dim and mediocre picture on the wall, and bid fifteen francs; immediately the rich amateur scented a prize; a long contest ensued, and at length the picture was knocked off to Vernet's antagonist for so large a sum that the honest bankrupt was enabled to pay his creditors in full, and recommence business with a handsome capital. With the progress of civilization pictures have grown in permanent market value: a Quaker who incurred the reproach of his brethren for securing a Wouverman for a large sum, was excused for this "vanity" by his shrewd friends, when he demonstrated to them that he had made an excellent investment. Literature affords many illustrations of the romance of the pictorial art, of which, among our own authors, Allston and Hawthorne have given memorable examples in "Monaldi," and "Twice-Told Tales." Unknown portraits have inspired the most attractive conjectures, and about the best known and most fascinating hover an atmosphere of intensely personal interest or historical association. Vasari, Mrs. Jameson, Hazlitt, and other art-writers have elaborated the most delectable facts and fancies from this vast individual sphere of the picturesque.

The technicalities of Art, its refinements of style, its absolute significance, are, indeed, as dependent for appreciation on a special endowment as are mathematics; but the general and incidental associations, in which is involved a world of poetry, may be enjoyed to the full extent by those whose perception of form, sense of color, and knowledge of the principles of sculpture, painting, music, and architecture are notably deficient. It is a law of life and nature, that truth and beauty, adequately represented, create and diffuse a limitless element of wisdom and pleasure. Such memorials are talismanic, and their influence is felt in all the higher and more permanent spheres of thought and emotion; they are the gracious landmarks that guide humanity above the commonplace and the material, along the "line of infinite desires." Art, in its broad and permanent meaning, is a language, — the language of sentiment, of character, of national impulse, of individual genius; and for this reason it bears a lesson, a charm, or a sanction to all, — even those least versed in its rules and least alive to its special triumphs. Sir Walter Scott was no amateur, yet, through his reverence for ancestry and his local attachments, portraiture and architecture had for him a romantic interest. Sydney Smith was impatient of galleries when he could talk with men and women, and made a practical joke of buying pictures; yet Newton and Leslie elicited his best humor. Talfourd cared little and knew less of the treasures of the Louvre, but lingered there because it had been his friend Hazlitt's Elysium. Indeed, there are constantly blended associations in the history of English authors and artists; Reynolds is identified with Johnson and Goldsmith, Smibert with Berkeley, Barry with Burke, Constable and Wilkie with Sir George Beaumont, Haydon with Wordsworth, and Leslie with Irving; the painters depict their friends of the pen, the latter celebrate in verse or prose the artist's triumphs, and both intermingle thought and sympathy; and from this contact of select intelligences of diverse vocation has resulted the choicest wit and the most genial companionship. If from special we turn to general associations, from biography to history, the same prolific affinities are evident, whereby the artist becomes an interpreter of life, and casts the halo of romance over the stern features of reality. Hampton Court is the almost breathing society of Charles the Second's reign; the Bodleian Gallery is vivid with Britain's past intellectual life; the history of France is pictured on the walls of Versailles; the luxury of color bred by the sunsets of the Euganean hills, the waters of the Adriatic, the marbles of San Marco, and the skies and atmosphere of Venice, are radiant on the canvas of Titian, Tintoretto, and Paul Veronese; Michel Angelo has embodied the soul of his era and the loftiest spirit of his country; Salvator typified the half-savage picturesqueness, Claude the atmospheric enchantments, Carlo Dolce the effeminate grace, Titian the voluptuous energy, Guido the placid self-possession, and Raphael and Correggio the religious sentiment of Italy; Watteau put on canvas the *fête champêtre;* the peasant-life of Spain is pictured by Murillo, her asceticism by the old religious limners; what English rustics were before steam and railroads, Gainsborough and Moreland reveal; Wilkie has permanently symbolized Scotch shrewdness and domesticity, and Lawrence framed and fixed the elegant shapes of a London drawing-room; and each of these is a normal type and suggestive exemplar to the imagination, a chapter of romance, a sequestration and initial token of the characteristic and the historical, either of what has become traditional or what is forever true.

The indirect service good artists have rendered by educating observation has yet to be acknowledged. The Venetian painters cannot be even superficially regarded, without developing the sense of color; nor the Roman, without enlarging our cognizance of expression; nor the English, without refining our perception of the evanescent effects in scenery. Raphael has made infantile grace obvious to unmaternal eyes; Turner opened to many a preoccupied vision the wonders of atmosphere; Constable guided our perception of the casual phenomena of wind; Landseer, that of the natural language of the brute creation; Lely, of the coiffure; Michel Angelo, of physical grandeur; Rolfe, of fish; Gerard Dow, of water; Cuyp, of meadows; Cooper, of cattle; Stanfield, of the sea; and so on through every department of pictorial art. Insensibly these quiet but persuasive teachers have made every phase and object of the material world interesting, environed them with more or less of romance, by such revelations of their latent beauty and meaning; so that, thus instructed, the sunset and the pastoral landscape, the moss-grown arch and the craggy seaside, the twilight grove and the swaying cornfield, an old mill, a peasant, light and shade, form and feature, perspective and anatomy, a smile, a gesture, a cloud, a waterfall, weather-stains, leaves, deer, — every object in Nature, and every impress of the elements, speaks more distinctly to the eye and more effectively to the imagination.

The vicissitudes which sometimes attend a picture or statue furnish no inadequate materials for narrative interest. Amateur collectors can unfold a tale in reference to their best acquisitions which outvies fiction. Beckford's table-talk abounded in such reminiscences. An American artist, who had resided long in Italy, and made a study of old pictures, caught sight at a shop-window in New Orleans of an "Ecce Homo" so pathetic in expression as to arrest his steps and engross his attention. Upon inquiry, he learned that it had been purchased of a soldier fresh from Mexico, after the late war between that country and the United States; he bought it for a trifle, carried it to Europe, and soon authenticated it as an original Guercino, painted for the royal chapel in Madrid, and sent thence by the government to a church in Mexico, whence, after centuries, it had found its way, through the accidents of war, to a pawnbroker's shop in Louisiana. A lady in one of our eastern cities, wishing to possess, as a memorial, some article which had belonged to a deceased neighbor, and not having the means, at the public sale of her effects, to bid for an expensive piece of furniture, contented herself with buying for a few shillings a familiar chimney-screen. One day she discovered a glistening surface under the flowered paper which covered it, and when this was torn away, there stood revealed a picture of Jacob and Rebecca at the Well, by Paul Veronese; doubtless thus concealed with a view to its secret removal during the first French Revolution. The missing Charles First of Velasquez was lately exhibited in this country, and the account its possessor gives of the mode of its discovery and the obstacles which attended the establishment of its legal ownership in England is a remarkable illustration both of the tact of the connoisseur and the mysteries of jurisprudence.*

Political vicissitudes not only cause pictures to emigrate like their owners, but to change their costume — if we may so call a frame — with equal celerity: that which now encloses Peale's Washington, at Princeton, once held the portrait of George the Third; and there is an elaborate old frame which holds the likeness of a New England poet's grandfather whence was hurriedly taken the portrait of Governor Hutchinson, in anticipation of a domiciliatory visit from the "Sons of Liberty."

There is scarcely, indeed, an artist or a patron of art, of any eminence, who has not his own "story of a picture." Like all things of beauty and of fame, the very desire of possession which a painting excites, and the interest it awakens, give rise to some costly sacrifice, or incidental circumstance, which associates the prize with human fortune and sentiment.

A friend of mine, in exploring the more humble class

* One of the recently discovered gems of pictorial art in Florence is the "coach-house picture"; so called from being a fresco on a stable-wall; and under the head of "Romance of a Portrait," the "London Athenæum" publishes a statement which seems to show conclusively that the famous portrait of Addison at Holland House, which has been copied and engraved time and again, and has been mentioned as authentic by Macaulay, is in fact not a portrait of Addison, but a portrait of Sir Andrew Fountaine, of Narford Hall, in Norfolk, vice-chamberlain to Queen Caroline, and the successor of Sir Isaac Newton in the wardenship of the Mint.

of boarding-houses in one of our large commercial towns, in search of an unfortunate relation, found himself, while expecting the landlady, absorbed in a portrait on the walls of a dingy back-parlor. The furniture was of the most common description. A few smutched and faded annuals, half-covered with dust, lay on the centre-table, beside an old-fashioned astral lamp, a cracked porcelain vase of wax-flowers, a yellow satin pincushion embroidered with tarnished gold-lace, and an album of venerable hue filled with hyperbolic apostrophies to the charms of some ancient beauty; which, with the dilapidated window-curtains, the obsolete sideboard, the wooden effigy of a red-faced man with a spyglass under his arm, and the cracked alabaster clock-case on the mantel, all bespoke an impoverished establishment, so devoid of taste that the beautiful and artistic portrait seemed to have found its way there by a miracle. It represented a young and *spirituelle* woman, in the costume, so elegant in material and formal in mode, which Copley has immortalized; in this instance, however, there was a French look about the coiffure and robe. The eyes were bright with intelligence chastened by sentiment, the features at once delicate and spirited, and altogether the picture was one of those visions of blended youth, grace, sweetness, and intellect, from which the fancy instinctively infers a tale of love, genius, or sorrow, according to the mood of the spectator. Subdued by his melancholy errand, and discouraged by a long and vain search, my friend, whose imagination was quite as excitable as his taste was correct, soon wove a romance around the picture. It was evidently not the work of a novice; it was as much out of place in this obscure and inelegant domicile, as a diamond set in filigree, or a rose among pig-weed. How came it there? who was the original? what her history and her fate? Her parentage and her nurture must have been refined; she must have inspired love in the chivalric; perchance this was the last relic of an illustrious exile, the last memorial of a princely house.

This reverie of conjecture was interrupted by the entrance of the landlady. My friend had almost forgotten the object of his visit; and when his anxious inquiries proved vain, he drew the loquacious hostess into general conversation, in order to elicit the mystery of the beautiful portrait. She was a robust, gray-haired woman, with whose constitutional good-nature care had waged a long and partially successful war. That indescribable air which speaks of better days was visible at a glance; the remnants of bygone gentility were obvious in her dress; she had the peculiar manner of one who had enjoyed social consideration; and her language indicated familiarity with cultivated society; yet the anxious expression habitual to her countenance, and the bustling air of her vocation which quickly succeeded conversational repose, hinted but too plainly straitened circumstances and daily toil. But what struck her present curious visitor more than these casual traits were the remains of great beauty in the still lovely contour of the face, the refined lines of her mouth, and the depth and varied play of the eyes. He was both sympathetic and ingenious, and ere long gained the confidence of his auditor. The unfeigned interest and the true perception he manifested in speaking of the portrait rendered him, in its owner's estimation, worthy to know the story his own intuition had so nearly divined. The original was Theodosia, the daughter of Aaron Burr. His affection for her was the redeeming fact of his career and character. Both were anomalous in our history. In an era remarkable for patriotic self-sacrifice, he became infamous for treasonable ambition; among a phalanx of statesmen illustrious for directness and integrity, he pursued the tortuous path of perfidious intrigue; in a community where the sanctities of domestic life were unusually revered, he bore the stigma of unscrupulous libertinism. With the blood of his gallant adversary and his country's idol on his hands, the penalties of debt and treason hanging over him, the fertility of an acute intellect wasted on vain expedients, — an outlaw, an adventurer, a plausible reasoner with one sex and fascinating betrayer of the other, poor, bereaved, contemned, — one holy, loyal sentiment lingered in his perverted soul, — love for the fair, gifted, gentle being who called him father. The only disinterested sympathy his letters breathe is for her; and the feeling and sense of duty they manifest offer a remarkable contrast to the parallel record of a life of unprincipled schemes, misused talents, and heartless amours. As if to complete the tragic antithesis of destiny, the beloved and gifted woman who thus shed an angelic ray upon that dark career was, soon after her father's return from Europe, lost in a storm at sea, while on her way to visit him, thus meeting a fate which, even at this distance of time, is remembered with pity. Her wretched father bore with him, in all his wanderings and through all his remorseful exile, her picture, — emblem of filial love, of all that is beautiful in the ministry of woman, and all that is terrible in human fate. At length he lay dangerously ill in a garret. He had parted with one after another of his articles of raiment, books, and trinkets, to defray the expenses of a long illness; Theodosia's picture alone remained; it hung beside him, — the one talisman of irreproachable memory, of spotless love, and of undying sorrow; he resolved to die with this sweet relic of the loved and lost in his possession; there his sacrifices ended. Life seemed slowly ebbing; the unpaid physician lagged in his visits; the importunate landlord threatened to send this once dreaded partisan, favored guest, and successful lover to the almshouse; when, as if the spell of woman's affection were spiritually magnetic, one of the deserted old man's early victims — no other than she who spoke — accidentally heard of his extremity, and, forgetting her wrongs, urged by compassion and her remembrance of the past, sought her betrayer, provided for his wants, and rescued him from impending dissolution. In grateful recognition of her Christian kindness, he gave her all he had to bestow, — Theodosia's portrait.

The indiscriminate disparagement of the old masters which has so long been the parodox of Ruskin's beautiful rhetoric, Haydon's suicidal devotion to the "grand style," Mrs. Jameson's gracious exposition of religious art, and the extravagant encomiums which the fashionable painter of the hour elicits from accredited critical journals, indicate the antagonistic theories and tastes that prevail; and yet these are all authentic and recognized oracles of artistic knowledge — all more or less true; and yet, in a comparative view, offering such violent contrasts as to baffle and discourage a novice in search of the legitimate picturesque.

So thoroughly identified with the possibility and probability of deception is the very name of a Picture-dealer, that to the multitude an "Old Master" is a bugbear; — the tricks of this trade form a staple of Paris correspondents and travelled *raconteurs.* The details of manufacture in perhaps this most lucrative branch of spurious traffic are patent; and, although the legitimate products of world-renowned painters are authenticated and on record, scarcely a month passes without some extensive fraud. The amateur in literature, sculpture, and music, is comparatively free from this perpetual danger; the sense of mystery does not baffle his enthusiasm; and while the pictorial votary or victim is disputing about an "Andrea del Sarto," or a "Teniers," or bewildered by the conflicting theories of rival artists in regard to color, tone, composition, foreshortening *chiaro-oscuro,* etc., he enjoys, without misgiving, the *noi ci darem* of Mozart, revels over the faded leaves of his first edition of a classic, or discourses fluently about the line of beauty in his copy of a Greek statue. "God Almighty's daylight," wrote Constable, "is enjoyed by all mankind, excepting only the lovers of old dirty canvas, perished pictures at a thousand guineas each, cart-grease, tar, and snuff of candle." The practical lesson derivable from these anomalous results of "Pictures," is that we should rely upon our individual impressions, enjoy what appeals gratefully to our consciousness, and repudiate hackneyed and conventional terms, judgments, and affectations, and boldly declare with the poet, before the picture which enchants us —

> I leave to learned fingers and wise hands
> The artist and his ape, to teach and tell
> How well his connoisseurship understands
> The graceful bend and the voluptuous swell:
> Let these describe the undescribable;

I would not their vile breath should crisp the stream
Wherein that image shall forever dwell;
The unruffled mirror of the loveliest dream
That ever left the sky on the deep soul to beam.

There are heads of men and women delineated hundreds of years ago, so knit into the mystic web of memory and imagination, so familiar through engravings, cameos, and other reproductive forms of art, and so identified with tragic experience, ideal aspiration or heroic deeds, that the first view of the originals is an epoch in life; we seem to behold them down a limitless vista of time, and they appeal to our consciousness like the faces of the long-loved, long-lost, and suddenly restored. It is as if we had entered a spiritual realm, and were greeted by the vanished idols of the heart, or the "beings of the mind and not of clay," once arbiters of destiny and oracles of genius. Beatrice Cenci, through soulful eyes infinitely deepened by a life of tears dried up by the fever of intense anguish, looks the incarnation of beauty and woe, — beauty we have adored in dreams, woe we have realized through sympathy. With the first sight of that alabaster skin, those lips quivering with pain, those golden locks, the theme of poets, that corpse-like head-band; the fragility, the fervor, the sensibility, and the chaste, ineffable grace; above all, the soulful world of terror, pity, and meekness in the lustrous and melancholy orbs, how familiar, yet how new, how pathetic, yet sublime! The hoary wretch who called her child, seems lurking somewhere in that hushed and sombre palace; the brother whose fair brow was lacerated by parental violence; the resigned mother, the infernal banquet, the prison, the tribunal, the bloody axe, flit with fearful distinctness between our entranced vision and the picture; for tradition, local association, Shelley's muse, the secret pen of the annalist, and the pencil of Guido, combine to make absolutely real an unparalleled story of loveliness and persecution, maidenhood and martyrdom. It is but recently that the true history of this picture has been authenticated. According to Guerazzi, who has minutely explored contemporary archives, the "study" from which it was painted, Ubaldo Ubaldini made from memory, to console his sister for the loss of Beatrice. He was one of the many artists who loved the beautiful victim with the passion of youth, and the fancy of a painter; one of the courageous but inadequate band who conspired to rescue her at the scaffold;* and it

* Another current tradition is the following: "So great was the excitement of the Roman populace against the condemnation of Beatrice, that on her way to the scaffold, three attempts were made by concerted bands of young men to rescue her from the officers' hands. On the eve of the fatal day she sat meditating her doom so intently, that for some time she did not notice a young man who had bribed the jailer to admit him into the cell for the purpose of making a sketch of her. Her appearance is thus described: 'Beatrice had risen from her miserable pallet, but, unlike the wretched inmate of a dungeon, resembled a being from a brighter sphere. Her large brown eyes were of liquid softness, her forehead broad and clear, her countenance of angelic purity, mysteriously beautiful. Around her head a fold of white muslin had been carelessly wrapped, from whence in rich luxuriance fell her fair and waving hair. Profound sorrow and recent bodily anguish imparted an air of touching sensibility to her lovely features. Suddenly turning, she discovered a stranger seated with pencil and paper in hand looking earnestly at her — it was Guido Reni. She demanded who he was, and what he did there; the frank young artist told his name and object, when, after a moment's hesitation, Beatrice replied, "Signor Guido, your great name and my sad story may make my portrait interesting, and the picture will awaken compassion if you write on one of its angles the word *innocent*."' Thus was birth given an inspired picture, which, to contemplate, is itself worth a visit to Rome; which once seen, haunts the memory as a supernatural mystery — as the beautiful apparition of sublimated suffering."

was long believed that he died of indignant grief after the catastrophe. Imagine him with the shadow of that mighty sorrow upon his soul, his hand inspired by tender recollection, secluded with her image stamped on his broken heart, and patiently reproducing those delicate features and that anguished expression — his last offering to her he so quickly followed into the valley of death! His "study" fell into the hands of Maffei Barberini, and furnished Guido Reni the materials for this, his most effective and endeared creation. Its marvellous, almost magnetic expression, doubtless gave rise to the belief, so long current, that he sketched Beatrice on her way to execution; but the later explanation is more accordant with probability and more satisfactory to the mind, for such a work requires for the conditions of success, both the inspiration of love and the aptitude of skill. Ubaldini furnished one and Guido the other.

Many travellers, especially women, have expressed great disappointment with the "Fornarina." They cannot associate a figure so much the reverse of ethereal, and charms so robust, with the refined taste and delicate person of Raffaelo. But such objections are founded on an imaginative not philosophic theory of love. There never was a genuine artist who, in matters of feeling, was not a child of Nature; and we have but to recognize the idiosyncrasies of poet and painter to find a key to their human affinities. What a peculiar interest we feel in the objects of love whose affection cheered, and whose sympathy inspired those products of pen and pencil, which have become part of our mental being! I have seen a crowd of half-bashful and wholly intent English girls watch the carriage which contained the obese, yet still fair-haired Countess, whose youthful charms so long made Byron a methodical hermit at Ravenna; and the respectable matron, who as a child was deemed by sentimentalists in Germany and her own exaggerated fancy, the object of Goethe's senile passion, was long courted, on that account, at tea-drinkings, by foreign visitors enamored of Faust and Wilhelm Meister. Still more natural is the sentiment which lures us to earnest acquaintance with the countenance on which he who gave an angelic semblance to maternity and caught the most gracious aspect of childhood, used to gaze with rapture; the eye that responded to his glance, the smile that penetrated his heart, and were fixed on his canvas. The impression which the "Fornarina" of the Tribune instantly gives, is that of genuine womanhood: there is generosity, a repose, a world of latent emotion, an exuberance of sympathetic power, in the full impassioned eye, the broad symmetrical bosom, the rich olive tint; it is precisely the woman to harmonize by her simple presence, and to soothe or exalt by her spontaneous love, the mood of a man of nervous organization and ardent temper. There is a tranquil self-possession in the face and figure which the sensitive and excitable artist especially finds refreshing, — a candid nature such as alone can inspire such a man's confidence, a majestic simplicity, peculiar to the best type of Roman women, more delightful to the over-tasked brain and sensibilities than the highest culture of an artificial kind; and there is the fresh, unperverted, richly developed, harmoniously united heart and physique, which, notwithstanding the modern standard of female charms, is the normal and the essential basis of honest, natural affinity. I could never turn, in the Florence Gallery, from the pale, delicately rounded, ideal brow, the almost pleading eye, and the cherubic lips of Raffaello, instinct with the needs as well as the immortal longings of genius, to the mellow, calm, self-sustained and healthful "Fomarina," without fancying the support, the rest, the inexhaustible comfort — in Othello's sense of that expressive word — which the sensitive artist could find in the cheerful baker's daughter, the irritable seeker in the serene and satisfied woman, the delicate in the strong, the gentle in the hearty, the ideal in the real, the poetic in the practical, the spiritual in the human; and I contemplated her noble contour, her contented smile, her beaming cheek, and eye undeepened by the experience that withers as it teaches, — yet soulful with latent emotion, with an ever-increasing sense of her native claims to Raphael's love.

Musical organizations are especially sensitive to the pictorial spell; the letters of Mendelssohn indicate how it influenced his development. Writing from Venice of church services he attended, he says: — "Nothing impressed me with more solemn awe than, when on the very spot for which they were originally created, the "Presentation of Mary as a child in the Temple," "the Assumption of the Virgin," "The Entombment of Christ," and "The Martyrdom of St. Peter," in all their grandeur, gradually steal forth out of the darkness in which the long lapse of time has veiled them. Often I feel a musical inspiration, and since I came here have been busily engaged in composition." And from Florence he writes: — "There is a small picture here which I discovered for myself. It is by Fra Bartolomeo, who must have been a man of most devout, tender, and earnest spirit. The figures are finished in the most exquisite and consummate manner. You can see in the picture itself that the pious master has taken delight in painting it and in finishing the most minute details, probably with a view of giving it away to gratify some friend; we feel as if the painter belonged to it, and still ought to be sitting before his work or had this moment left." This personal magnetism about pictures is an authentic evidence of their vital relation to character, and it is felt often in an incredible way by the imaginative and susceptible. The same gifted and generous composer who thus wrote of Titian and Fra Bartolomeo, speaks of the impression he received from Raphael's portrait by himself: "Youthful, pale, delicate, and with such inward aspirations, such longing and wistfulness in the mouth and eyes, that it is as if you could see into his very soul; that he cannot succeed in expressing all that he sees and feels, and is thus impelled to go forward, and that he must die an early death; — all this is written on his mournful, suffering, yet fervid countenance."

Vandyke's portraits of Charles the First, impress the spectator with regal fanaticism, and a tragic destiny more than some of the written histories of his reign. The exquisite hands of Leonardo's "Gioconde," are as eloquent of feminine grace and sensibility as the most elaborate description. Correggio's "Magdalen" in the remorseful *abandon* and beautiful sadness of its expression, reveals her who "loved much," repented, and was forgiven. Giovanni di Medici, in the Uffizzi Gallery, fulfils to the imagination the ideal of mediæval Italian soldiership. Stuart's "Washington" embodies the serene conscience, the self-control, the humane dignity and birthright of command which consecrate our peerless chief; and Delaroche's "Napoleon Crossing the Alps," perpetuates the intense purpose and insatiable ambition that won so many battles and died of anxiety on an ocean-rock. Such instances, which might easily be multiplied, prove how a single department of Art, and that the least estimated, is allied to history, patriotism, and sentiment, and capable of touching their secret springs and unveiling their limitless perspective at a glance. Guercino's "Hagar" is a biblical poem. Hamlet's filial reproaches borrow their keenest sting from two "counterfeit presentments," and Trumbull's faithful and assiduous pencil has transmitted the individualities of our Revolutionary drama. And thus the art of portraiture, even in its general relations, may become, through illustrious subjects and rare fidelity, the romance which association of ideas breeds from reality.

I was never more impressed with the absolute line of demarcation between the imitative and the inventive, even in the lighter processes of Art, than when examining the graphic series of illustrations of "The Wandering Jew." Nature is represented under all forms, — the woods, the desert, the ocean, caves, meadows, and skies, and these fixed elemental features might be well reflected by mechanical aids — photographed or reproduced through chemical and optical means; but the true meaning of each picture consisted in the ever-present shadow pursuing the Wanderer — the form of the Holy One bowed under his cross: it glimmered in the water, was stamped on the rock, outlined in the gnarled forest branches, pencilled in the floating vapor, reflected in the ice-mirrored lake, with a latent and inevitable yet unobtrusive and apparently accidental omnipresence, as if wrought into the texture of Nature through the creative anguish of conscience — which emphatically announced an intelligence far beyond all mechanical art, and interfused the material with the abstract, the imaginative, and the human as only genius can. The same thing is evinced by comparing the best photographs of architecture, figures, or landscape with the sketch-book of a genuine artist; in certain points, there will be found a special intelligence and feeling which transcends the most remarkable imitative truth. How much of this is suggested, for instance, by the mere catalogue of an album on the table at a Parisian *soirée:* fleurs de Redonté, chevaux de Carl Vernet, Bedouins d'Horace, aquarelles de Ciceri, petit paysages de Géniole, caricatures de Grandville et de Monnier, beaux brigands de Schnetz — "tous chéfs d'œuvre au petit pied."

A portrait of little Fritz, drumming, in the Berlin Gallery, Carlyle hails in his "Life of Frederick the Great" as "one tiny islet of reality amid the shoreless sea of fantasms; Flaying of Bartholomews, Rape of Europas, etc." Napoleon was delighted to remember that his mother reclined on tapestry representing the heroes of the Iliad, when she brought him into the world.

For how long and with what vividness are certain pictures associated with localities. Gainsborough's "Blue Boy," and Reynolds's "Strawberry Girl," are among the salient retrospective images of the English school at the Manchester Exhibition. We think of Correggio with Parma, Perugino with Perugia, Fra Angelico with Florence, Da Vinci's Last Supper and Guercino's Hagar with Milan, Murillo with Seville, Vandyke with Madrid, Rubens with Antwerp, Watteau with Paris, and Paul Potter's Bull with the Hague.

The Dutch School, in a philosophical estimate, is but

the compensation afforded by the romance of Art for its deficiency in Nature; the element of the picturesque not found in mountains, forests, and cataracts, the low-land painters wrought from flowers and firesides; the radiant tulips and exquisite interiors, the humble but characteristic in life and manners. To seize upon individuality is the conservative tact of both painter and poet; whoever does this effectively contributes to the world's gallery of historical portraits, and keeps before the living, the faces, costume, and action of bygone races and heroes. Catlin's aboriginal portraits introduced the American native tribes to Europe; a naturalist abroad has but to turn over Audubon's portfolio to become intimately acquainted with every bird whose plumage or song makes beautiful our woodlands and sea-shore; the traveller who rests an hour at Perugia, may trace on the walls of a church the original, crude, yet pious expression which Raphael developed into angelic beauty. Vernet has, by the very multiplicity of his battle-pieces, signalized on canvas the military genius of the French nation; the faith which so distinguishes the fifteenth from the speculation of the eighteenth century, is manifest to us most eloquently in the master-pieces of religious art, which yet remain in peerless beauty to attest the holy convictions that inspired them; and all that is peculiar in Grecian culture has found no exponent like the statues of her divinities. Hogarth preceded Crabbe and Dickens in making palpable the shadows of want, crime, and luxury. The Italian satirist who endowed animals with speech and made them represent the absurdities of humanity, hinted their possible significance less than Landseer who, by individualizing their most salient traits, or Kaulbach who revealed the brute creation in the highest intuitive expression. There is a piquant rustic beauty by Greuze, which embodies and embalms, in its exquisite suggestiveness, the special claim of naive brightness and grace that belongs almost exclusively to French lovable women ; and there is a portrait of an American matronly belle of the days of Washington, by Stuart, which represents the type of mingled self-reliance and womanly loveliness that has made the ladies of our Republican court so memorably attractive.

DOCTORS.

Throw physic to the dogs.
MACBETH.

Friend of my life, which did not you prolong,
The world had wanted many an idle song.
POPE.

IN the moving panoramas of cities are to be seen certain vehicles of all degrees of locomotive beauty and convenience, from the glossy and silver-knobbed carriage with its prancing grays, to the bacheloric-looking sulky with its one gaunt horse, in which are seated gentlemen of a learned and professional aspect, usually wearing spectacles, and always an air of intense respectability, or of contemplation and seriousness. They recognize numerous acquaintances as they pass with a peculiar smile and nod, and are usually accompanied by "a little man-boy to hold the horse," as the French cook in the play defines a *tigre*. These mysterious personages rejoice in the title of Doctor, — once a very distinctive appellation, but now as common as authorship and travelling. A moralist, watching them gliding by amid fashionable equipages, crowded omnibuses, hasty pedestrians, and all the phenomena of life in a metropolis, would find a striking contrast between the rushing tide around, and the hushed rooms they enter. To how many their visit is the one daily event that breaks in upon the monotony of illness and confinement; how many eyes watch them with eager suspense, and listen to their opinion as the fiat of destiny; how many feverishly expect their coming, shrink from their polished steel, rejoice in their cheering ministrations, or dread their long bills! "The Doctor!" — a word that stirs the extremest moods — despair and jollity!

There is no profession which depends so much for its efficiency on personal traits as that of medicine; for the utility of technical knowledge here is derived from individual judgment, tact, and sympathy. In other words, the physician has to deal with an unknown element. Between the specific ailment and the remedy there are peculiarities of constitution, the influence of circumstances, and the laws of Nature to be considered; so that although the medical adviser may be thoroughly versed in physiology, the materia medica, and the symptoms of disease, if he possess not the discrimination, the observant skill, and the reflective power to apply his learning wisely, it is comparatively unavailing. The aim of the divine and the attorney, however impeded by obstacles, is reached by a more direct course; logic, eloquence, and zeal, united to professional attainment, will insure success in law and divinity; but in physic, certain other qualities in the man are requisite to give scope to the professor. Hence we associate a certain originality with the idea of a doctor; are apt to regard the vocation at the two extremes of superiority and pretension, and justly estimate the individuals of the class according to their capacity of insight and their principles of action, rather than by their mere acquisitions or rank as teachers. The uncertainty of medicine, as a practical art, thus induces a stronger reliance on individual endowments than is the case in any other liberal pursuit.

A philosophical history of the art of healing would be not less curious than suggestive. The absurd theories which checked its progress for centuries, the secrets hoarded by Egyptian priests, the union of medical knowledge with ancient systems of philosophy, the epoch of Galen, the Arabian and Salerno schools, the reformation of Paracelsus, the brilliant discoveries which, at long intervals, illumined the track of the science, and the enlightened principles now realized, — if fully discussed, would form an extraordinary chapter in the biography of man. Herein, as with other vocations, modern division of labor has concentrated professional aptitudes. " L' affluence des postulants," says Balzac, " a forcé la médecine a se diviser en catégories ; il y a le médecin qui professe, le médecin politique et le médecin militant et la cinquieme divisions, celle des docteurs qui vendent des remédes."

St. Luke and the Good Samaritan are yet the favorite signs of apothecaries, confirming the original charity of the art; and in the south of Europe may still be seen over the barbers' shops, the effigy of a human arm spouting blood from an open vein, an indication of the once universal custom of periodical depletion. It is now acknowledged that diverse climates require modified treatment of the same disease; that nervous susceptibility is far greater in one latitude than another, and that habits of life essentially individualize the constitution. Indeed, the widest difference exists in the relation of persons to the doctor; some never see him, and others must have a consultation upon the most trifling ailment, — so great is the dependence which can be had upon nature, and so extreme both the faith and the scepticism which exists in regard to curative science.

Popular literature is full of hits at the profession: "La barber fait plus de la moitié d'un médecin," says Molière, who, in "La Malade Imaginaire," has so acutely given the current philosophy of the subject, by satirizing the pedantry and charlatanism of the doctors of his day: "Nous voyons que, dans la maladie tout le monde a recours aux médecins; — ce'st une marque de la faiblesse humaine et non pas de la vérité de leur art;" and of all ailments the hardest to cure is "la maladie des médecins." Imagination has been called by a German philosopher "the mediatrix, the nurse, the mover of all the several parts of our spiritual organism." "I have the worst luck of any physician under the cope of heaven," complains Sancho Panza; "other doctors kill their patients and are paid for it too, and yet they are at no further trouble than scrawling two or three cramp words for some physical slip-slop, which the apothecaries are at all the pains to make up."

It would seem, indeed, as if the advance of science improved medical practice negatively, that is, by inducing what in politics has been called a masterly inactivity; and there is no doubt that no small degree of the success attending Hahnemann's theory is to be attributed to the comparative abstinence it inculcates in the use of remedial agents. The fact is a significant one, as indicative of the want of positive science in the healing art; and the consequent wisdom of leaving to nature, as far as possible, the restorative process. Indeed, to assist nature is acknowledged, by just observers, to be the only wise course; and this brings us to the inference that a good physician is necessarily a philosopher;

it is incumbent on him, of all men, to exercise the inductive faculty; he must possess good causality, not only to reason justly on individual cases, but to apply the progress of science to the exigencies of disease. It is related of Bixio that such was his zeal for science, having long wished to ascertain whether a man instinctively turns when wounded in a vital part, asked his adversary in a duel to aim at one, and, although fatally hurt, exclaimed with ardor, as he involuntarily spun round — "It is true, they do turn!"

The comparatively slow accumulation of scientific truth in regard to the treatment of disease, is illustrated by the fact that not until the lapse of two thousand years after medicine had assumed the rank of a science, under the auspices of Hippocrates, was the circulation of the blood discovered, — an era in its history. The fiery discussion of the efficacy of inoculation and its gradual introduction, is another significant evidence of the same general truth. But, in our own day, the rapid and valuable developments of chemistry have, in a measure, reversed the picture. Numerous alleviating and curative agents have been discovered; the gas of poisonous acids is found to eradicate, in many cases, the most fatal diseases of the eye; heat, more penetrating than can be created by other means, is eliminated from carbon in an aeriform state, passes through the cuticle, without leaving a mark on its surface, and restores aching nerves or exhausted vitality. Vegetable and mineral substances are refined, analyzed, and combined with a skill never before imagined; opium yields morphine, and Peruvian bark quinine, and all the known salubrious elements are thus rendered infinitely subservient to the healing art. Chloroform is one of the most beneficent of these new agents; and has exorcised the demon of physical pain by a magical charm, without violating, in judicious hands, the integrity of Nature.

There is a secret of curative art in which consists the genius of healing; it is that union of sympathy with intelligence, and of moral energy with magnetic gifts, whereby the tides of life are swayed, and one "can minister to a mind diseased." Fortunate is the patient who is attended by one thus endowed — but such are usually found out of the professional circle — they are referees ordained by Nature to settle the difficulties of inferior spirits; the arbiters recognized by instinct who soothe anger, reconcile doubt, amuse, elevate, and console by a kind of moral alchemy; and potent coadjutors are they to the material aids of merely technical physicians. "Who dare say," asks Rénan, in allusion to the calming and purifying influence of Jesus, "that in many cases, and apart from injuries of a dreaded character, the contact of an exquisite person is not worth all the resources of pharmacy?" "It was agony to me," wrote Hahnemann, "to walk in darkness, with no other light than could be derived from books." One of his opponents from this confession infers the fallacy of his system; "the conviction," he observes, "is irresistibly forced upon us that he was not a *born physician.*" If our ancestors were less enlightened in regard to hygiene, and if their physicians were less scrupulous in tampering with the functions of nature, they had one signal advantage over us in escaping the inhuman comments, made after every fatal issue, on the practice and the treatment adopted — no matter with how much conscientious intelligence; we not only suffer the pangs of bereavement, but the reproaches of devotees of each school of medicine, and of rival doctors — of having by an unwise choice sacrificed the life for which we would have cheerfully resigned our own! Somewhat of this occult healing force might have been read in the serene countenance of Dr. Physic of Philadelphia; it predominated in the benevolent founder of the Insane Asylum of Palermo, who learned from an attack of mental disorder how to feel for, and minister to, those thus afflicted. The late Preissnitz, of Graefenberg, seems to have enjoyed the gift which is as truly Nature's indication of an aptitude for the art, as a sense of beauty in the poet. But this principle is "caviare to the general."

Medicine has lost much of its inherent dignity by the same element, in modern times, that has degraded art, letters, and society, — the spirit of trade. This agency encourages motives, justifies means, and leads to ends wholly at variance with high tone and with truth. The gentleman, the philosopher, the man of honor, and with them that keystone in the arch of character — self-respect, are wholly compromised in the process of sinking a liberal art into a common trade. In the economy of modern society, however, the physician has acquired a new influence; he has gained upon the monopoly of the priest, for while the spirit of inquiry, by trenching on the mysterious prerogatives which superstition once accorded, has retrenched the latter's functions, the same agency, by extending the domain of science and rendering its claims popular, has enlarged the sphere of the other profession. To an extent, therefore, never before known, the doctor fills the office of confessor; his visits yield agreeable excitement to women with whom he gossips and sympathizes; admitted by the very exigency of the case to entire confidence, often revered as a counsellor and friend, as well as relied on as a healer, not infrequently he becomes the oracle of a household. Privileges like these, when used with benevolence and integrity, are doubtless honorable to both parties, and become occasions for the exercise of the noblest service and the highest sentiments of our nature; while, on the other hand, they are liable to the grossest abuse, where elevation of character and gentlemanly instincts are wanting. Accordingly there has sprung into existence, in our day, a personage best designated as the medical Jesuit; whose real vocation, as well as the process by which he acquires supremacy, fully justifies the appellation. Like his religious prototype, he operates through the female branches, who, in their turn, control the heads of families; and the extent to which the domestic arrangements, the social relations, and even the opinions of individuals are thus regulated, is truly surprising. "Women," says Mrs. Jameson, "are inclined to fall in love with priests and physicians, because of the help and comfort they derive from both in perilous moral and physical maladies. They believe in the presence of real pity, real sympathy, where the look and tone of each have become merely habitual and conventional, I may say professional." Yet a popular novelist, in his ideal portrait of the physician, justly claims superiority to impulse and casual sympathy, as an essential requisite to success. "He must enter the room a calm intelligencer. He is disabled for his mission if he suffer aught to obscure the keen glance of his science." *

The natural history of the doctor has not yet been

* Bulwer's *Strange Story.*

written, but the classes are easily nomenclated; we have all known the humorous, the urbane, the oracular, the facetious, the brusque, the elegant, the shrewd, the exquisite, the burly, the bold, and the fastidious; and the character of people may be inferred by their choice of each species. Those in whom taste predominates over intellect, will select a physician for his agreeable personal qualities; while such as value essential traits, will compromise with the roughest exterior and the least flattering address for the sake of genuine skill and a vigorous and honest mind. As a general rule, in large cities, vanity seems to rule the selection; and it is a lamentable view of human nature to see the blind preference given to plausible but shallow men, whose smooth tongues or gallant air win them suffrages denied to good sense and candid intercourse. The most detestable genus is that we have described under the name of medical Jesuits; next in annoyance are the precisians; the most harmless of the weaker order are the gossips; and there is often little to choose in point of risk to "the house of life" between the very timid and the dare-devils; in a great exigency the former, and in an ordinary case the latter are equally to be shunned. In the "Horæ Subsecivæ" of Dr. John Brown, we find some apt and needed counsel to the aspirants for medical success: — "The young doctor must have for his main faculty, *sense;* but all will not do if Genius is not there; such a special therapeutic gift had Hippocrates, Sydenham, Pott, Purcell, John Hunter, Delpech, Dupuytren, Kellie, Cheyne, Baillie, and Abercrombie. Moreover, let me tell you, my young doctor friends, that a cheerful face and step and neckcloth and button-hole, and an occasional hearty and kindly joke, and the power of executing and setting a-going a good laugh, are stock in our trade not to be despised." Brillat Savarin declares, doctors easily become gourmands because so well received.

In Paris, Edinburgh, and Philadelphia all the world over, the medical student is an exceptional character; their pranks are patent; the rough ones like to kick up rows, and the more quiet are unique at practical jokes. Bob Sawyer is a typical hero. If, like the portrait-painter, doctors are often the playthings of fortune in cities, where the arbitrary whims of fashion decree success; in the country, their true worth is more apt to find appreciation; and the individualities of character, having free scope, quite original children of Apollo are the result. The name of Hopkins is still memorable in the region where he practised, as one of the literary clique of which Humphries, Dwight, and Barlow were members. Dr. Osborn, of Sandwich, Mass., wrote the popular whaling-song yet in vogue among Nantucketers. Dr. Holyoke of Salem, is renowned as a beautiful instance of longevity; and the wit of Dr. Spring was proverbial in Boston. The best example of a medical philosopher, in our annals, is that of Dr. Rush of Philadelphia; he reformed the system of practice; first treated yellow fever successfully, made climate a special study, and, like Burke, laid every one he encountered under contribution for facts. His life of seventy years was passed in ardent investigation. It is remarkable that the first martyr to American liberty was a physician; and before he fell, Warren eloquently avowed his principles, like Körner in Germany, rousing the spirit of his countrymen, and then consecrating his sentiments with his blood. Boylston, the ancestral portraits of whose family are among the best of Copley's American works, nearly fell a victim to public indignation for his zealous and intelligent advocacy of inoculation, and natural science owes a debt to Barton, Morton, and De Kay, which is acknowledged both at home and abroad. A French doctor has noted the historical importance of his *confréres,* and tells us Hamond was Racine's master, Lestocq helped elevate Catharine to the Russian throne, Haller was a poet and romancer, Cuvier was the greatest naturalist of his age, and Murat was a doctor. French *médecins* have figured in the Chamber and on the Boulevards.

If, by virtue of the philosophic instinct and liberal tastes, the doctor is thus allied to belles-lettres, he is allured into the domain of science by a still more direct sympathy. To how many has the study of the materia medica and the culling of simples, proved the occasion of botanical research; and hence, by an easy transition, of exploring the entire field of natural science. Thus Davy was beguiled into chemical investigation; and Abercrombie, by the vestibule of physiological knowledge, sought the clue to mental philosophy; while Spurzheim and Combe ministered to a great charity by clearly explaining to the masses the natural laws of human well-being. It is an evidence of the sagacity of the Russian Peter, that he sought an interview with Boerhaäve; for by these varied links of general utility, the medical office enters into every branch of social economy; and is only narrowed and shorn of dignity by the limited views or inadequate endowments of its votaries. The Jewish physician preserved and transmitted much of the learning of the world after the fall of the Alexandrian school.* Life-insurance and quarantines, have become such grave interests, that through them the responsibility of the physician to society is manifest to all; that to individuals is only partially recognized. How Cowper and Byron suffered for wise medical advice, and what ameliorations in states of mind and moral conditions, have been induced by the now widely-extended knowledge of hygienic laws! Charles Lamb reasons wisely as well as quaintly in this wise: — "You are too apprehensive of your complaint. The best way in these cases is to keep yourself as ignorant as the world was before Galen, of the entire construction of the animal man; not to be conscious of a midriff; to hold kidneys to be an agreeable fiction; to account the circulation of the blood an idle whim of Harvey's; to acknowledge no mechanism not visible. For once, fix the seat of your disorder, and your fancies flux into it like bad humors. Above all, take exercise, and avoid tampering with the hard terms of Art. Desks are not deadly. It is the mind, and not the limbs, that taints by long sitting. Think of the patience of the tailors; think how long the Lord Chancellor sits; think of the brooding hen."

In literature the doctor figures with a genial dignity;

* "Mohammedanism had been the patron of physical science; paganizing Christianity not only repudiated it, but exhibited towards it sentiments of contemptuous disdain and hatred; hence physicians were viewed by the Church with dislike and regarded as atheists by the people, who had been taught that cures must be wrought by relics of martyrs and bones of saints: for each disease there was a saint. Already it was apparent that the Saracenic movement would aid in developing the intelligence of barbarian Western Europe, through Hebrew physicians, in spite of the opposition encountered from theological ideas imported from Constantinople and Rome." — *Draper's Intellectual Development of Europe*, p. 414.

he has affinities with genius and a life-estate in the kingdom of letters: witness Garth's poem of "The Dispensary;" Akenside's "Pleasures of the Imagination;" Armstrong's "Art of Health;" Cowley's verses, Sprat's Life of him, and Currie's of Burns; Beattie's "Minstrel;" Darwin's "Botanic Garden;" Moore's "Travels in Italy;" Zimmerman's "Solitude;" Goldsmith's "Vicar and Village;" Aikin's "Criticisms;" Joanna Baillie's gifted brother, and Lady Morgan's learned husband. Burke found health at the house of the benign Dr. Nugent of Bath, at the outset of his career, and married the daughter of his medical friend. "Les médecins sont souvent tout a la fois conseillors, arbitres et magistrats au sein des familles." The best occasional verses of Dr. Johnson are those that commend the humble virtues of Levett, the apothecary.* Dr. Lettson wrote the life of Carver, the American traveller, and his account of that adventurous unfortunate led to the establishment of the Literary Fund Society. Among the graves near Archibald Carlyle's old church at Inveresk, where that handsome clerical and convivial gossip is buried, is that of the sweet versifier, beloved as the "Delta" of Blackwood, Dr. Moir, who so genially

* When fainting Nature called for aid,
And hovering Death prepared the blow,
His vigorous remedy displayed
The power of Art without the show.
In Misery's darkest caverns known,
His useful help was ever nigh,
Where hopeless Anguish poured his groan,
Or lonely Want retired to die.
No summons mocked by chill delay,
No petty gains disdained by pride,
The modest wants of every day,
The toil of every day supplied.

united the domestic lyrist and the good doctor, a Delta framed in bay adorns the pedestal of his monument. Rousseau, an invalid of morbid sensibility, recognizes the professional superiority of the physician as a social agent: "Par tous le pays ce sont les hommes les plus veritablement utiles et savants." The "Médecin de Campagne" of Balzac, and the "Dr. Antonio" of Ruffini, are elaborate and charming illustrations of this testimony of the author of "Emile." What a curious chapter would be added to the "Diary of a Physician," had Cabanis kept a record of his interviews with those two illustrious patients — Mirabeau and Condorcet. The social affinities of the doctor prove indirectly what we before suggested, that it is in the character more than in the learning, in the mind rather than the technical knowledge, that medical success lies. One of the shrewdest of the profession, Abernethy, declared thereof — "I have observed, in my profession, that the greatest men were not mere readers, but the men who reflected, who observed, who fairly thought out an idea." Almost intuitive is the venerable traditional ideal of the physician; among the aborigines of this continent, the "medicine man" was revered as nearest to the "Great Spirit." "I hold physicians," said Dr. Parr, "to be the most enlightened professional persons in the whole circle of human arts and sciences." In our own day, Lever's Irish novels, and in our own country the writings of Drake, Mitchell, Holmes, Bigelow, Francis, and others, indicate the literary claims of the profession. Think of Arbuthnot beside Pope's sick-bed, and the latter's apostrophe —

"Friend of my life, which did not you prolong,
The world had wanted many an idle song;"

of Garth ministering to Johnson, and Rush philosophizing with Dr. Franklin, and the friendship of Pope and Cheselden. Bell's comments on Art, Colden's "Letters to Linnæus," and Thatcher's "Military Journal," are attractive proofs of that liberal tendency which leads the physician beyond the limits of his profession into the field of philosophical research. The bequest of Sir Hans Sloane was the nucleus of the British Museum. We all have a kind of affection for Dr. Slop, who, drawn from Dr. Burton of York, — a cruel, instrumental obstretician, — is the type of an almost obsolete class, as the doctor in "Macbeth" is of the sapient pretender of all time. As to ideal doctors, how real to our minds is that Wordsworthean myth, Dr. Fell, the physician of Sancho Panza, and the Purgon of Molière, while Dulcamara is a permanent type of the clever quack, Dr. Bartolo of the solemn professor, and Sangrado of the merciless phlebotomist. To think it "more honorable to fail according to rule than to succeed by innovation," is a satire of no local significance, but the constant creed of the medical pedant. Satirized years ago by the French comic dramatist, the profession was caricatured the other day by a young disciple of Esculapius, who in a clever drawing represented the votary of homœopathy with a little globule between thumb and finger, engaged in a kind of airy swallowing; the allopathic patient in an easy-chair is making wry faces over a large spoonful of physic; the believer in hydropathy sits forlorn and shivering in a sitz-bath, with a large goblet of water raised to his lips; while the Thomsonian victim is writhing and nauseating in anguish; and in the midst a skeleton, with a syringe for a baton, is dancing in a transport of infernal joy. Southey took a wise advantage of the popular idea of a doctor, in the genial and speculative phase of the character, when he gave the title to his last rambling, erudite, quaint, and charming production. Men of letters accordingly are wont to fraternize with the best of the profession; and there has always been a reciprocal interchange between them both of affection and wit. Thus Halleck tells us in "Fanny" —

> In Physic, we have Francis and M'Neven,
> Famed for long heads, short lectures, and long bills;
> And Quackenboss and others, who from heaven
> Were rained upon us in a shower of pills:
> They 'd beat the deathless Esculapius hollow,
> And make a starveling druggist of Apollo.

The record of our surgeons in the war for the Union is alike honorable to their patriotism, humanity, and skill.

Popular writers have indicated the claims and character of the profession, not only in a dramatic or anecdotal way, but by personal testimony and observation; and those who have had the best opportunities and are endowed with liberal sympathies, warmly recognize the possible usefulness and probable benevolence of a class of men more often satirized than sung. The privations and toil incident to country practice half a century ago, are scarcely imagined now. Sir Walter Scott tells us: "I have heard the celebrated traveller Mungo Park, who had experienced both courses of life, rather give the preference to travelling as a discoverer in Africa, than to wandering by night and day the wilds of his native land in the capacity of a country practitioner." Dr. Johnson, a livelong invalid, and not apt to overlook professional foibles, gives a high average character to the doctor. "Whether," he observes, "what Sir William

Temple says be true, that the physicians have more learning than the other faculties, I will not stay to inquire ; but I believe every man has found in physicians great liberality and dignity of sentiment, very prompt effusion of beneficence and willingness to exert a lucrative art where there is no hope of lucre."

It is a nervous process to undergo the examination of a Parisian medical professor of the first class. Auscultation was first introduced by one of them; Laennec, and diagnosis is their chief art. In their hands the stethoscope is a divining rod. So reliable is their insight, that they seem to read the internal organism as through a glass ; and one feels under Louis's inspection as if awaiting sentence. The laws of disease have been thoroughly studied in the hospitals of Paris, and the philosophy of symptoms is there understood by the medical *savans* with the certainty of a natural science, but the knowledge and application of remedies is by no means advanced in equal proportion. Accordingly, the perfection of modern skill in the art seems to result from an education in the French schools, combined with experience in English practice ; thorough acquaintance with physiology, and habits of acute observation and accurate deduction, are thus united to executive tact and ability. And similar eclectic traits of character are desirable in the physician, especially the union of solidity of mind with agreeableness of manner; for in no vocation is there so often demanded the blending of the *fortiter in re* with the *suaviter in modo.*

The absence of faith in positive remedies that obtains in Europe, is very striking to an American visitor, because it offers so absolute a contrast to the system pursued at home. I attended the funeral of a countryman, a few days after reaching Paris, and, on our way to Père la Chaise, his case and treatment were fully discussed; his disease was typhus fever. Previous to delirium he had designated a physician, a celebrated professor, who only prescribed *gomme syrop.* For a week I travelled with a Dominican friar who had so high a fever, that in America he would have been confined to his bed; he took no nourishment all the time but a plate of thin soup once a day; and when we reached our destination, he was convalescent. Abstinence and repose are appreciated on the continent as remedial agencies; but they are contrary to the genius of our people, who regard active enterprise as no less desirable in a doctor than a steamboat captain.

Veteran practitioners have demonstrated that certain diseases are self-limited, that the art of treating diseases is still "a conjectural study," and avowed the conviction that "the amount of death and disaster in the world would be less, if all disease were left to itself, than it now is under the multiform, reckless, and contradictory modes of practice." A conscientious student, of high personal character, entered upon the profession with enthusiastic faith; experience in the use of remedies made him sceptical, and he resorted to evasion by giving water only under various pretexts and names; his success was so much greater than that of his brethren, that he felt bound to reveal the ruse, but continued thenceforth to assert that, all things being equal, more patients would survive, if properly guarded and nourished, without medicine than with.

The influence of the mind upon the body is, in some instances, so great, that it accounts for that identity of superstition and medicine which is one of the most remarkable traits in the history of the science. Sir Walter Raleigh's cordial was as famous in its day as Mrs. Trulbery's water praised by Sir Roger de Coverley. In Egypt, old practitioners cure with amulets and charms; among the Tartars they swallow the name of the remedy with perfect faith; and from the Puritan horse-shoe, to keep off witchcraft, to Perkins' tractors to annihilate rheumatism, the history of medical delusions is rife with imaginary triumphs. As late as the seventeenth century, when Arabian precepts and the Jewish leech of chivalric times had disappeared, when the square cap and falling beards had given place to the wig and cane, in some places the mystic emblems of skull, stuffed lizards, pickled fœtus, and alembic gave a necromantic air to the doctor's sanctum.

The unknown is the source of the marvellous, and the relation between a disease and its cure is less obvious to the common understanding, than that between the evidence and the verdict in a law case, or religious faith and its public ministration in the office of priest. The imagination has room to act, and the sense of wonder is naturally excited, when, by the agency of some drug, mechanical apparatus, or mystic rite, it is attempted to relieve human suffering and dispel infirmity. Hence the most enlightened minds are apt to yield to credulity in this sphere, much to the annoyance of the "regular faculty," — who complain with reason that quackery, whether in the form of popular specifics or the person of a charlatan, derives its main support from men of civic and professional reputation. Think of Dr. Johnson, in his infancy, being touched for King's Evil by Queen Anne, in accordance with a belief in its sovereign efficiency, unquestioned for centuries. Sir Kenelm Digby was as much celebrated in his day for his recipe for a sympathetic powder, which he obtained from an Italian friar, as for his beautiful wife or his naval victory; and the good Bishop Berkeley gave as much zeal to the "Treatise on the Virtues of Tar-Water," as to that on the "Immateriality of the Universe."

Shakspeare has drawn a quack doctor to the life in Caius, the French physician, in the "Merry Wives of Windsor," and uttered an impressive protest against the tribe in "All 's Well that Ends Well": —

"*King.* —— But may not be so credulous of cure, —
When our most learned doctors leave us; and
The congregated college have concluded
That laboring art can never ransom nature
From her inaidable estate: I say we must not
So stain our judgment, or corrupt our hope,
To prostitute our past-cure malady
To empirics; or to dissever so
Our great self and our credit, to esteem
A senseless help, when help past sense we deem."

An American member of the medical profession* has traced in the great bard of Nature a minute knowledge of the healing art, — citing his various allusions to diseases and their remedies: thus we have in Coriolanus the "post-prandial temper of a robust man," and the physiology of madness in Hamlet and Lear. The wasting effects of love, melancholy, the processes of digestion, respiration, circulation of the blood, infusion of humors, effects of passions on the body, of slow and swift poisons, insomnia, dropsy, and other phenomena described with accuracy. Cæsar's fever in Spain, Gratiano's warning, "creep into a jaundice by being

* *Shakspeare's Medical Knowledge*, by Charles W. Stearns, M. D. New York: D. Appleton & Co.

peevish;" the physical effects of sensualism in Antony and Cleopatra, the external signs of sudden death from natural causes in Henry VI., and summary of diseases in Troilus and Cressida, are described with professional truth. How memorable his Apothecary's portrait! while the medical critic assures us that, in a passage in "Midsummer-Night's Dream," the "accessories of a sickly season are poetically described," and that Falstaff admirably satirizes the "ambiguities of professional opinion," while, in Mrs. Quickly's description of his death, and the dying scene of Cardinal Beaufort, as well as the senility of Lear, the mellow virility of old Adam, the "thick coming fancies" of remorse, and Ophelia's aberration — every minute touch in the memorable picture of "a mind diseased" — indicate a profound insight, and suggest, as no other poet can, how intimately and universally the "ills that flesh is heir to" and the vocation of those who minister to health, are woven into the web of human destiny and the scenes of human life. Who has so sweetly celebrated "Nature's sweet restorer" and the "healing touch"? or more emphatically declared, "when the mind 's free, the body 's delicate," and —

> "We are not ourselves
> When nature, being oppressed, commands
> The mind to suffer with the body."

The memoirs of celebrated men abound with physiological interest; their eminence brings out facts which serve to vindicate impressively the phases of medical experience, and the relation of the soul to its tabernacle. Madden's "Infirmities of Genius" is a book which suggests an infinite charity, as well as exposes the fatal effects of neglecting natural laws. Lord Byron used to declare that a dose of salts exhilarated him more than wine. Shelley was a devoted vegetarian. Cowper spoke from experience when he sang the praises of the cups "that cheer but not inebriate." Johnson had faith in the sanative quality of dried orange peel. When Dr. Spurzheim was first visited by the physicians in his last illness, he told them to allow for the habitual irregularity of his pulse, which had intermitted ever since the death of his wife. George Combe used to tell a capital story, in his lectures, of the manner in which a pious Scotch lady made her grandson pass Sunday, whereby, while outwardly keeping the Sabbath, he violated all the rules of health. Two of the most characteristic books in British literature are Greene's poem of the "Spleen," and Dr. Cheyne's "English Malady;" and another is the history of the "Gold-Headed Cane," or rather of the five doctors that successively owned it. The cane, indeed, was ever an indispensable symbol of medical authority; the story of Dr. Radcliffe's illustrates its modern significance, but the association of the walking-staff and the doctor comes down to us from mediæval times. "He smelt his cane," in the old ballads, is a phrase suggestive of a then common expedient; the head of the physician's cane was filled with disinfectant herbs, the odor of which the owner inhaled when exposed to miasma. Even at this day, in some of the provincial towns in Italy, we encounter the doctor in the pharmacist's shop, awaiting patients, — his dress and manner such as are reproduced in the comic drama, while the quack of the Piazza is recognized on the Operatic stage.

How unprofessional medicine is becoming, may be seen in current literature, when De Quincey's metaphysical account of the effects of opium, and Bulwer's fascinating plea for the Water-Cure, are ranked as light reading. To the lover of the old English prose-writers, there is no more endeared name than Sir Thomas Browne, and his "Religio Medici" and quaint tracts are among the choicest gifts for which philosophy is indebted to the profession; while the classical student owes to Dr. Middleton a "Life of Cicero." The vivacious Lady Montagu is most gratefully remembered for her philanthropic efforts in behalf of inoculation for small-pox; and our Brockden Brown has described the phenomena of an epidemic, in one of his novels, with more insight though less horror than De Foe.

It is in pestilence and after battle that the doctor sometimes rises to the moral sublime, in his disinterested and unwearied devotion to others. It must, however, be confessed that, notwithstanding these incidental laurels, the authority of the profession has so declined, the *malades imaginaires* so increased with civilization, and the privileges of the faculty been so encroached upon by what is called "progress," that a doctor of the old school would scorn to tolerate the fallen dignity of a title that once rendered his intercourse with society oracular, and authorized him with impunity, to whip a king, as in the case of Dr. Willis and George the Third.

"The philosophy of medicine, I imagine," observed Dr. Arnold, "is zero; our practice is empirical, and seems hardly more than a course of guessing, more or less happy." None have been more sceptical than physicians themselves in regard to their own science: Broussais calls it illusory, like astrology; and Bichat declares, "it is, in respect to its principles, taken from most of our *materia medicas*, impracticable for a sensible man;

an incoherent assemblage of incoherent opinions, it is, perhaps, of all the physiological sciences, the one which shows plainest the contradictions and wanderings of the human mind." Montaigne used to beseech his friends that, if he fell ill, they would let him get a little stronger before sending for the doctor. Louis XIV., who was a slave to his physicians, asked Molière what he did for his doctor. "Oh sire," said he, "when I am ill, I send for him. He comes, we have a chat, and enjoy ourselves. He prescribes; I don't take it, — and I am cured."

"There is a certain analogy," says an agreeable writer, "between naval and medical men. Neither like to acknowledge the presence of danger." On the other hand, each patient's character as well as constitution makes a separate demand upon his sympathy; for in cases where fortitude and intelligence exist, perfect frankness is due, and in instances of extreme sensibility it may prove fatal; so that the most delicate consideration is often required to decide on the expediency of enlightening the invalid. If it is folly to theorize in medicine, it is often sinful to flatter the imagination for the purpose of securing temporary ease. A physician's course, like that of men in all pursuits, is sometimes regulated by his consciousness, and he is apt to prescribe according to his own rather than his patient's nature; thus a fleshy doctor is inclined to bleed, and recommend generous diet; a nervous one affects mild anodynes; a vain one talks science; and a thin, cold-blooded, speculative one, makes safe experiments in practice, and is habitually non-committal in speech. Almost invariably short-necked plethoric doctors enjoy freeing the vessels of others by copious depletion, and those more delicately organized advocate fresh air and tonics; the one instinctively reasoning from the surplus, and the other from the inadequate vitality of which they are respectively conscious. I knew a doctor who scarcely ever failed to prescribe an emetic, and his expression of countenance indicated chronic nausea.

Medicine enjoys no immunity from the spirit of the age. Who does not recognize in the popularity of Hahnemann's system the influence of the transcendental philosophy, a kind of intuitive practice analogous to the vague terms of its disciples in literature; those little globules with the theoretical accompaniment catch the fancy; castor-oil and the lancet are matter-of-fact in comparison. And so with hydropathy. There is in our day what may be called a return-to-nature school. Wordsworth is its expositor in poetry; Fourier in social life, the Pre-Raphaelites in painting. The newly appreciated efficacy of water accords with this principle. It is an elemental medicament, limpid as the style of Peter Bell, free from admixture as the individual labor in a model community, and as directly caught from Nature as the aerial perspective of England's late scenic limner. Even what has been considered the inevitable resort to dissection in order to acquire anatomical knowledge, it is now pretended, has a substitute in clairvoyance. Somewhat of truth in this spiritualizing tendency of science, there doubtless is, but Fact is the basis of positive knowledge, and the most unwarrantable of all experiments are those involving human health.

If the mental experience of a doctor naturally leads to philosophy, the moral tends to make him a philanthropist. He is familiar with all the ills that flesh is heir to. The mystery of birth, the solemnity of death, the anxiety of disease, the devotion of faith, the agony of despair, are phases of life daily open to his view; and their contemplation, if there is in his nature a particle either of reflection or sensibility, must lead to a sense of human brotherhood, excite the impulse of benevolence, and awaken the spirit of humanity. Warren's "Diary of a Physician" gives us an inkling of what varieties of human experience are exposed to his gaze. Vigils at the couch of genius and beauty, full of the stern romance of reality, or imbued with tenderness and inspiration, are recorded in his heart. He is admitted into sanctums where no other feet but those of kindred enter. He becomes the inevitable auditor and spectator where no other stranger looks or listens. Human nature, stripped of its conventionalities, lies exposed before him; the secrets of conscience, the aspirations of intellect, the devotedness of love, all that exalts and all that debases the soul, he beholds in the hour of weakness, solitude, or dismay; and hard and unthinking must he be, if such lessons make no enduring impression, and excite no comprehensive sympathies.

"The corner-stone of health," says a German writer, "is to maintain our individuality intact;" and while the hygienic reformer has lessened the bills of mortality, personal culture has emancipated society from much of the ignorant dependence and insalubrious habits of less enlightened times.

HOLIDAYS.

"And here I must have leave, in the fulness of my soul, to regret the abolition and doing-away with altogether of those consolatory interstices and sprinklings of freedom, through the four seasons — the *red-letter days*, now become to all intents and purposes dead-*letter* days." — CHARLES LAMB.

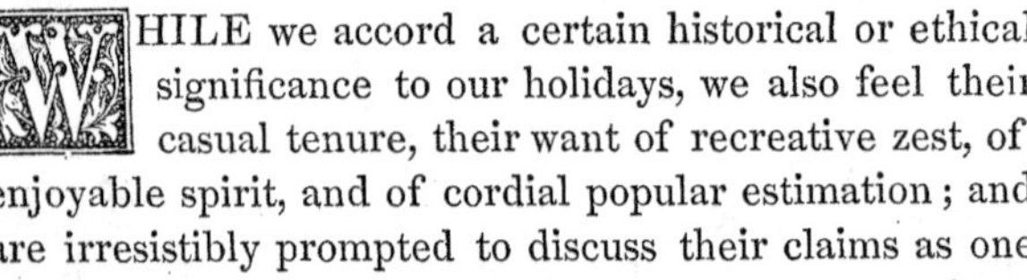

WHILE we accord a certain historical or ethical significance to our holidays, we also feel their casual tenure, their want of recreative zest, of enjoyable spirit, and of cordial popular estimation; and are irresistibly prompted to discuss their claims as one of the neglected elements of our national life. It is an anomalous fact in our civilization, that we have no one holiday, the observance of which is unanimous. It is an exceptional trait in our nationality that its sentiment finds no annual occasion when the hearts of the people thrill with an identical emotion, absorbing in patriotic instinct and mutual reminiscence all personal interests and local prejudice. It is an unfortunate circumstance that no American festival, absolutely consecrated and universally acknowledged, hallows the calendar to the imagination of our people. Anniversaries enough, we boast, of historical importance, but they are casually observed; events of glorious memory crowd our brief annals, but they are not consciously identified with recurring periods; universal celebrities are included in the roll of our country's benefactors, but the dates of their birth, services, and decease, form no saints' days for the Republic. How often in the crises of sectional passion does the moral necessity of a common shrine, a national feast, a place, a time, or a memory sacred to fraternal sympathies of general observance, appal the patriotic heart with regret, or warm it with desire! How much of sectional misunderstanding, hatred, and barbarism culminating in a base and savage mutiny, will the future historian trace in the last analysis to the absence of a common sentiment and occasion of mutual pleasure and faith. Were such a nucleus for popular enthusiasm, such a goal for a nation's pilgrimage, such a day for reciprocal gratulation our own, — a time when the oath of fealty could be renewed at the same altar, the voice of encouragement be echoed from every section of the Union, the memory of what has been, the appreciation of what is, and the hope of what may be, simultaneously felt, what a bond of union, a motive to forbearance, and a pledge of nationality would be secured! Were there not in us sentiments as well as appetites, reflection as well as passion, humanity might rest content with such "note of time" as is marked on a sun-dial or in the almanac; but constituted as we are, a profound and universal instinct prompts observances wherewith faith, hope, and memory may keep register of the fleeting hours and months. In accordance with this instinct, periodical sacrifice, song, prayer, and banquet, in all countries and ages, have inscribed with heartfelt ceremony the shadowy lapse of being. Without law or art, the savage thus identifies his consciousness with the seasons and their transition; anniversaries typifying vicissitude; the wheel of custom stops a while; events, convictions, reminiscences, and aspirations are personified in the calendar; and that reason which "looks before and after," asserts itself under every guise from the barbarian rite to the Christian festival, and begets the Holiday as an institution natural to man. If the ballads of a people are the essence of its history, holidays are, on similar grounds, the free utterance of its character; and as such, of great interest to the philosopher, and fraught with endearing associations to the philanthropist.

The spontaneous in nations as well as individuals is attractive to the eye of philosophy, because it is eminently characteristic. The great charm of biography is its revelation of the play of mind and the aspect of character, when freed from conventional restraints. And, in the life of nations, how inadequate are the records of diplomacy, legislation, and war — the official and economical development — to indicate what is instinctive and typical in character! It is when the armor of daily toil, the insignia of office, the prosaic routine of life, are laid aside, that what is peculiar in form and graceful in movement become evident. In the glee or solemnity of the festival, the soul breaks forth; in the fusion of a common idea, the heart of a country becomes freely manifest.

Accordingly, the manner, the spirit, and the object of festal observances are among the most significant illustrations of history. An accurate chart of these from the earliest time, would afford a reliable index to the progress of humanity; and suggest a remarkable identity of natural wants, tendencies, and aspirations. There is, for instance, a singular affinity between the Saturnalia of the ancient and the Carnival of the modern Romans, the sports of the ancient circus and bull-fights of Spain; while so closely parallel, in some respects, are Druidical and Monastic vows and fanaticism, that one of the most popular of modern Italian operas, which revived the picturesque costume and sylvan rites of the Druids, was threatened with prohibition, as a satire upon the Church. It would, indeed, well repay antiquarian investigation, to trace the germ of holiday customs from the crude superstitions of barbarians, through the usages incident to a more refined mythology, to their modified reappearance in the Catholic temples, where Pagan rites are invested with Christian meaning, or the statue of Jupiter transformed into St. Peter, and the sarcophagus of a heathen becomes the font of holy baptism. Gibbon tells us how shrewd Pope Boniface professed but to rehabilitate old customs, when he revived the secular games in Rome. Not only are traces of Pagan forms discoverable in the modern holidays, but the mediæval taste for exhibitions of animal courage and vigor still lives in the love of prize-fights and horse-racing so prevalent in England, and the ring and the cockpit minister to the same brutal passions which of old filled the Flavian amphitheatre with eager spectators, and gave a relish to the ordeal of blood. In the abuses of the modern pastime we behold the relics of barbarism, and the perpetuity of such national tastes is evident in the combative instinct which once sustained the orders of chivalry, and in our day, has lured thousands to the destructive battle-fields of the Crimea and Virginia.

Not only do the social organizations devoted to popular amusements and economies, thus give the best tokens of local manners and average taste, but they directly minister to the culture they illustrate. The gladiator "butchered to make a Roman holiday," nurtured with his lifeblood and dying agonies the ferocious propensities and military hardihood of the imperial cohorts. The graceful posture and fine muscular display of the wrestler, and discus-player of Athens, reappeared in the statues which peopled her squares and temples. The equine beauty and swiftness exhibited at Derby and Ascot, keep alive the emulation which renders England famous for breeds of horses, and her gentry healthful by equestrian exercise. The custom of musical accompaniments at every German symposium has, in a great measure, bred a nation of vocal and instrumental performers. The dance became a versatile art in France, because it was, as it still is, the national pastime. The Circassian is expert with steed and rifle from the habit of dexterity acquired in the festive trials of skill, excellence in which is the qualification for leadership. The compass, flexibility, and sweetness of the human voice so characteristic of the people of Italy, have been attained through ages of vocal practice in ecclesiastical and rural festivals; and the copious melody of their language gradually arose through the *canzoni* of troubadours and the rhythmical feats of *improvisatori*. The deafening clang of gongs, the blinding smoke of chowsticks, and the dazzling light of innumerable lanterns, wherewith the Chinese celebrate their national feasts, are to European senses the most oppressive imaginable token of a stagnant and primitive civilization; the festive elements of the semi-barbarism artistically represented by their grotesque figures, ignorance of perspective, interminable alphabet, pinched feet, bare scalps, and implacable hatred of innovation, both in the processes and the forms of advanced taste.

Even the aboriginal feasts of this continent were the best indication of what the American Indians, in their palmy days, could boast of strength, agility, and grace.

Thus, from the most cultivated to the least developed races, what is adopted and expressed in a recreative or holiday manner, — what is thus done and said, sought and felt, — the rallying-point of popular sympathy, the occasion of the universal joy or reverence, is a moral fact of unique and permanent interest, — on the one hand, as illustrative of the kind and degree of civilization attained, and of the instinctive direction of the national mind, and, on the other, as indicative of the means and the processes whereby the wants are met and the ideas realized, which stimulate and mould a nation's genius and faith.

The testimony of observation accords with that of history in this regard. The foreign scenes which haunt the memory as popular illustrations of character, are those of Holidays. The government, literature, art, and society of a country may be individually represented to our minds; but when we discuss national traits, we instinctively refer to the pastimes, the religious ceremonials, and the festivals of a people. Where has the pugilistic hilarity of the Irish scope as at Donnybrook Fair? Is a dull parliamentary speech, or an animated debate at the race-course, most vivid with the spirit of English life? Market-day, and harvest-home, and saintly anniversaries, evoke from its commonplace level the life of the humble and the princely, and they appear before the stranger under a genuine and characteristic guise. We associate the French, as a people, with the rustic groups under the trees of Montmorenci, or the crowds of neatly-dressed and gay *bourgeoise* at the *Jardin d'Hiver*, — finding in the green grass, lights, cheap wine and comfits, a flower in the hair, a waltz and saunter, more real pleasure than a less frugal and mercurial people can extract from a solemn feast, garnished with extravagant upholstery, and loaded with luxurious viands. We recall the Italians and Spaniards by the ceaseless bells of their *festas* vibrating in the air, and the golden necklace and graceful *mezzano* of the peasant's holiday; the tinkle of guitars, the *bolero* and processions, or the lines of stars marking the architecture of illuminated temples, the euphonious greeting, the light-hearted carol, the abundant fruit, the knots of flowers, the gay jerkin and bodice, which render the urbane throng so picturesque in aspect and childlike in enjoyment. The sadness which overhung the very idea of Italy, considered as a political entity, exhaled like magic, before the spectacle of a Tuscan vintage. The heaps of purple and amber fruit, the gray and pensive-eyed oxen, the reeking butts, the yellow vine-leaves waving in the autumn sun, form studies for the pencil; but the human interest of the scene infinitely endears its still life. Kindred and friends, in festal array, celebrate their work, and rejoice over the Falernian, *Lachryma Christi*, or *Vino Nostrale*, with a frank and *naïve* gratitude akin to the mellow smile of productive Nature; the distance between the lord of the soil and the peasant is, for the time, lost in a mutual and innocent triumph; they who are wont to serve become guests; the dance and song, the compliment and repartee, the toast and the smile, are interchanged, on the one side with artless loyalty, and on the other with a condescension merged in graciousness. It seems as if the hand of Nature in yielding her annual tribute, literally imparted to prince and peasant the touch which makes "the whole world kin."

The contrast, in respect of pastime, is felt most keenly

when we observe life at home, with the impressions of the Old World fresh in our minds. We have perhaps joined the laughing group who cluster round Punch and Judy on the Mole of Naples; we have watched the flitting emotions on swarthy listeners who greedily drink in the story-teller's words on the shore of Palermo; we have made an old gondolier chant a stanza of Tasso, at sunset, on the Adriatic; our hostess at Florence has decked the window with a consecrated branch on Palm Sunday; we have seen the poor *contadini* of a Roman village sport their silver knobs and hang out their one bit of crimson tapestry, in honor of some local saint; we have examined the last mosaic exhumed from Pompeii, brilliant with festal rites, and thus, as an element both of history and experience, of religion and domesticity, the recreative side of life appears essential and absolute, while the hurrying crowd, hasty salutations, and absorption in affairs around us, seem to repudiate and ignore the inference, and to confirm the opinion of one whose existence was divided between this country and Europe, that "the Americans are practical Stoics."

To appreciate the value of holidays merely as a conservative element of faith, we have but to remember the Jewish festivals. Ages of dispersion, isolation, contempt, and persecution,—all that mortal agencies can effect to chill the zeal or to discredit the traditions of the Hebrews,—have not, in the slightest degree, lessened the sanction or diminished the observance of that festival, to keep which the Divine Founder of our religion, nineteen centuries ago, went up to Jerusalem with his disciples. And it is difficult to conceive a more sublime idea than is involved in this fact. On the day of the Passover, in the Austrian banker's splendid palace, in the miserable Ghetto of Rome, under the shadow of Syrian mosques, in the wretched by-way hostel of Poland, at the foot of Egyptian pyramids, beside the Holy Sepulchre, among the money-changers of Paris and the pawnbrokers of London, along the canals of Holland, in Siberia, Denmark, Calcutta, and New York, in every nook of the civilized world, the Jew celebrates his holy national feast; and who can estimate how much this and similar rites have to do with the eternal marvel of that nation's survival?

The conservatism inherent in traditional festivals not only binds together and keeps intact the scattered communities of a dispersed race, but saves from extinction many local and inherited characteristics. I was never so impressed with this thought as on the occasion of an annual village fête in Sicily. Perhaps no territory of the same limits comprehends such a variety of elements in the basis of its existent population, as that luxuriant and beautiful but ill-fated island. Its surface is venerable with the architectural remains of successive races. Here a Grecian temple, there a Saracenic dome; now a Roman fortification, again a Norman tower; and often a mediæval ruin of some incongruous order, attracts the traveller's gaze from broad valleys rich with grain, olive-orchards, and citron-groves, vineyards planted in decomposed lava, hedges of aloe, meadows of wild-flowers, a torrent's arid path, a holly-crowned mountain, a cork forest, or seaward landscape. But the more flexible materials left by the receding tide of invasion are so blended in the physiognomies, the customs, and the *patois* of the inhabitants, that only nice investigation can trace them amid the generic phenomena of nationality now recognized as Sicilian. Yet the people of a village but a few miles from the Capital, have so identified their Greek origin with the costume of a holiday, that, as one scans their festal array, it is easy to imagine that the unmixed blood of their classic progenitors flushes in the dark eyes and mantles in the olive cheeks. This ancestral dress is the endeared heirloom in the homes of the peasantry, assumed with conscious pride and gayety, to meet the wondering eyes of neighboring *contadini*, curious Palermitans, and delighted strangers, who flock to the spectacle.

The love of power is a great teacher of human instincts; and despotism, both civil and spiritual, has, in all ages, availed itself of the natural instinct for festivals, to multiply and enhance shows, amusements, and holidays, in a manner which yields profitable lessons to free communities intent on adapting the same means to nobler ends. The stated pilgrimage to the tomb of the Prophet is an important part of the superstitious machinery of the Mahommedan tyranny over the will and conscience; and it is difficult to conceive now to what an extent the zeal and unity of the early Christians were enforced by specific days of ceremonial, and by such a hallowed goal as Jerusalem.

Imperial authority in France is upheld by festive seductions adapted to a vivacious populace, and by masque balls, municipal banquets, showers of bonbons, and ascent of balloons, contrives to win attention from republican discontent. Mercenary rulers of petty States, by the gift of stars and red ribbons, and liberal contributions to the opera, obtain an economical safeguard. The policy of the Romish Church is nowhere more striking than in her holiday institutions, appealing to native sentiment through pageantry, music, and impressive rites in honor of saints, martyrs, and departed friends, to propitiate their intercession or to endear their memories.

While the pastimes in vogue typify the national mind, and are to serious avocations what the efflorescence of the tree is to its fruit, — a bountiful pledge and augury of prolific energy, — it is only when kept as holidays, set apart by law and usage, consecrated by time and sympathy, that such observances attain their legitimate meaning; and to this end, a certain affinity with character, a spontaneous and not conventional impulse is essential. The Tournament, for instance, was the natural and appropriate pastime of the age of chivalry; it fostered knightly prowess, and made patent the twin-born inspiration of love and valor. As described in Ivanhoe, it accords intimately with the spirit of the age and the history of the times; as exhibited to the utilitarian vision and mercantile habits of our own day, in Virginia, it comes no nearer our associations than any theatrical pageant chosen at hap-hazard. What other species of grown men could, in this age, enact every year, in the neighborhood of Rome, the scenes which make the artists' holiday? As a profession, they retain the instincts of childhood, with little warping from the world around. But imagine a set of mechanics or merchants attempting such a masquerade. The invention, the fancy, the independence, and the *abandon* congenial with artist-life, gives unity, picturesqueness, and grace to the pageant; and the speeches, costumes, feasting, and drollery, are preëminently those of an artist's carnival. It is indispensable that the spirit of a holiday should be native to the scene and the people; and hence all endeavors to graft local pastimes upon foreign communities, signally fail. This is illustrated in our immediate vicinity. The genial fellowship and exuberant hospitality with which the first day of the year is celebrated in New York were characteristic among the Dutch colonists, and have been transmitted to their posterity; while the tone of New England society, though more intellectual, is less urbane and companionable; accordingly, the few enthusiasts who have attempted it have been unable, either by precept or example, to make a Boston New Year's day the complete and hearty festival which renders it *par excellence* the holiday of the Knickerbockers. Charitable enterprise, for several years past, in the Puritan city has distinguished May-day as a children's floral anniversary; but who that is familiar with the peasant-songs that hail this advent of summer in the south of Europe, ever beheld the shivering infants and the wilted leaves, paraded in the teeth of an east wind, without a conscious recoil from the anomalous *fête?* The facts of habit, public sentiment, natural taste, local association, and of climate, cannot be ignored in holiday institutions, which, like eloquence, as defined by Webster, must spring directly from the men, the subject, and the occasion. Any other source is unstable and factitious. Of all affectations, those of diversion are the least endurable; and there is no phase of social life more open to satire, nor any that has provoked it to more legitimate purpose, than the affectation of a taste for art, sporting, the ball-room, the bivouac, the gymnasium, foreign travel, country life, nautical adventure, and literary amusements; an affectation yielding, as we know, food for the most spicy irony, from Goldoni's *Filosofo Inglese* to Hood's cockney ruralist and Punch's amateur sportsman or verdant tourist. And what is true of personal incongruities, is only the more conspicuous in social and national life.

When our literary pioneer sought to waken the fraternal sentiment of his countrymen towards their ancestral land, he described with sympathetic zest an English Christmas in an old family mansion; and the most popular of modern novelists can find no more potent spell whereby to excite a charitable glow in two hemispheres than a "Christmas Carol." In New as well as in Old England, the once absolute sway of this greatest of Christian festivals has been checked by Puritan zeal. We must look to the ancient ballads, obsolete plays, and musty Church traditions, to ascertain what this hallowed season was in the British Islands, when wassail and the yule-log, largess and the Lord of Misrule, the mistletoe bough, boars' heads, holly wreaths, midnight chimes, the feast of kindred, the anthem, the prayer, the games of children, the good cheer of the poor, forgiveness, gratulation, worship, — all that revelry hails and religion consecrates, — made holiday in palace, manor, and cottage, throughout the land; winter's robe of ermine everywhere vividly contrasting with evergreen decorations, the frosty air with the warmth of household fires, the cold sky with the incense of hospitable hearths; when King Charles acted, Ben Jonson wrote a masque, Milton a hymn, lords and peasants flocked to the altar, parents and children gathered round the board, and church, home, wayside, town and country bore witness to one mingled and hearty sentiment of festivity. Identical in season with the Roman Saturnalia, and the time when the Scalds let "wildly loose their red locks fly," Christmas is sanctioned by all that is venerable in association as well as tender and joyous in faith. It is deeply to be regretted that with us its observance is almost exclusively confined to the Romanists and Episcopalians. The sentiment of all Christian denominations is equally identified with its commemoration, the event it celebrates being essentially memorable alike to all who profess Christianity; and although the forlorn description by Pepys of a Puritan Christmas will not apply to the occasion here, its comparative neglect, which followed Bloody Mary's reign, continues among too many of the sects that found refuge in America. There are abundant indications that if the clergy would initiate the movement, the laity are prepared to make Christmas among us the universal religious holiday which every consideration of piety, domestic affection, and traditional reverence unite to proclaim it.

The humanities of time, if we may so designate the periods consecrated to repose and festivity, were thoroughly appreciated by the most quaint and genial of English essayists. The boon of leisure, the amenities of social intercourse, the sacredness and the humors of old-fashioned holidays, have found their most loving interpreter, in our day, in Charles Lamb. Hear him: —

"I must have leave, in the fulness of my soul, to regret the abolition and doing-away-with-altogether of those *consolatory interstices* and *sprinklings of freedom* through the four seasons, the *red-letter-days*, now become, to all intents and purposes, *dead-letter-days*. There was Paul and Stephen and Barnabas, Andrew and John, men famous in old times, — we used to keep all their days holy, as long back as when I was at school at Christ's. I remember their effigies by the same token, in the old Basket Prayer-Book. I honored them all, and could almost have wept the defalcation of Iscariot, so much did we love to keep holy memories sacred; only methought I a little grudged at the coalition of the *better Jude* with *Simon*,—clubbing (as it were) their sanctities together to make up one poor gaudy-day between them, as an economy unworthy of the dispensation. These were bright visitations in a scholar's and a clerk's life,—'far-off their coming shone.' I was as good as an almanac in those days." *

And who has written, like Lamb, of the forlorn pathos of the charity boy's "objectless holiday"; of the "most touching peal which rings out the old year"; of "the safety which a palpable hallucination warrants" on All-Fools'; and the "Immortal Go-between," St. Valentine?

The devotion to the immediate, the thrift, the enterprise, and the material activity which pertain to a new country, and especially to our own, distinguish American holidays from those of the Old World. Not a few of them are consecrated to the future, many spring from the triumphs of the present, and nearly all hint progress rather than retrospection. We inaugurate civil and local improvements; glorify the achievements of mechanical skill and of social reform; pay honor by feasts, processions, and rhetoric, to public men; give a municipal ovation to a foreign patriot, or a funeral pageant to a native statesman. Our festivals are chiefly on occasions of economic interest. Daily toil is suspended, and gala assemblies convene, to rejoice over the completion of an aqueduct or a railroad, or the launching of an ocean steamer. One of the earliest of these economical displays—in New York, memorable equally from the great principle it initiated and the felicitous auguries of the holiday itself—was the celebration of the opening of the Erie Canal, the first of a series of grand internal improvements which have since advanced our national prosperity beyond all historical precedent; and

* *Essays of Elia.*

one of the last was the grand excursion which signalized the union by railroads of the Atlantic sea-coast and the Mississippi River. The two celebrations were but festive landmarks in one magnificent system. The enterprise initiated in Western New York, in 1825, was consummated in Illinois, in 1854, when the last link was riveted to the chain which binds the vast line of eastern sea-coast to the great river of the West, and the genius of communication, so essential to our unity and prosperity, brought permanently together the boundless harvest-fields of the interior and the mighty fleets of the sea-board. To European eyes the sight of the thousand invited guests conveyed from New York to the Falls of St. Anthony would yield a thrilling impression of the scale of festal arrangements in this Republic; and were they to scan the reports of popular anniversaries and conventions in our journals, embracing every class and vocation, representative of every art, trade, and interest, a conviction would inevitably arise that we are the most social and holiday nation in the world; on the constant *qui vive* for any plausible excuse for public dinners, speeches, processions, songs, toasts, and other republican divertisements. One month brings round the anniversary banquet of the Printers, when Franklin's memory is invoked and his story rehearsed; another is marked by the annual symposium and contributions of the Dramatic Fund; a Temperance jubilee is announced to-day, a picnic of Spiritualists to-morrow; here we encounter a long train of Sunday-scholars, and there are invited to a Publishers' feast in a "crystal palace"; the triumph of the "Yacht America" must be celebrated this week, and the anniversary of Clay's birth or Webster's death the next; a clerk delivers a poem before a Mercantile Library Association, a mechanic addresses his fellows; exhibitions of fruit, of fowls, of cattle, of machines, of horses, ploughing-matches, schools, and pictures, lead to social gatherings and volunteer discourses, and make a holiday now for the farmer and now for the artisan, so that the programme of festivals, such as they are, is coextensive with the land and the calendar. All this proves that there is no lack of holiday instinct among us, but it also demonstrates that the spirit of utility, the pride of occupation, and the ambition of success, interfuse the recreative as they do the serious life of America. The American enters into festivity as if it were a serious business; he cannot take pleasure naturally like the European, and is pursued with a half-conscious remorse if he dedicates time to amusement; so that even our holidays seem rather an ordeal to be gone through with than an occasion to be enjoyed. At many of these *fêtes*, too, we are painfully conscious of interested motives, which are essentially opposed to genuine recreation. Capital is made of amusement as of every other conceivable element of our national life. It is often to advertise the stock, to introduce the breed, to gain political influence, to win fashionable suffrages to a scheme or a product of art or industry, that these expensive arrangements are made, these hospitalities exercised, these guests convened. Too many of our so-called holidays are tricks of trade; too many are exclusively utilitarian; too many consecrate external success and material well-being; and too few are based on sentiment, taste, and good-fellowship. In a panorama of national holidays, therefore, instead of a crowd of gracefully attired rustics waltzing under trees, an enthusiastic chorus, breathing, as one deep voice, the popular chant, ladies veiled in *tulle* following an imperial infant to a cathedral altar, the garlands and maidens of Old England's May-day, or the splendid evolutions of the continental soldiery, — we should be most aptly represented by a fleet of steamers with crowded decks and gay pennons, sweeping through the lofty and wooded bluffs of the Upper Mississippi, the procession of boats and regiment of marines disembarking in the bay of Jeddo, or the old Hall, in whose sleeping echoes lives the patriotic eloquence of the Revolution, alive with hundreds of children invited by the city authorities to the annual school festival; for these occasions typify the enterprise at home, the exploration abroad, and the system of public instruction, which constitute our specific and absolute distinction in the family of nations. A jovial eclectic could, notwithstanding, gather traces of the partial and isolated festivals of every race and country in America; harvest-songs among the German settlers of Pennsylvania, here a "golden wedding," there a private grape-feast; in the South a tournament, at Hoboken a cricket-match, and an archery club at Sunnyside; a Vienna lager-beer dance in New York, or a vine-dressers' merry-making in Ohio.

If from those holidays which arise from temporary causes, we turn to those which, from annual recurrence, aspire to the dignity of institutions, the first thing which strikes us is their essentially local character. "Pilgrim Day," wherever kept, is a New England festival; "Evacuation Day" belongs to the city of New York; the anniversary of the battle of Bunker Hill is celebrated only in Charlestown; and the victory on Lake Erie, at Newport, where its hero resided. The events thus commemorated, deserve their eminence in our regard; and patriotic sentiment is excited and maintained by such observances. Yet, in many instances, they have dwindled to a lifeless parade, and in others have become a somewhat invidious exaggeration of local self-complacency. The latter is the case, for instance, with the New England Society's annual feast in the commercial metropolis of the Union. It occasionally tries the patience and vexes the liberal sentiment of the considerate son of New England, to hear the reiterated laudation of her schools, her clergy, her women, her codfish, and her granite, at the hospitable board where sits, perhaps, a venerable Knickerbocker, conscious that the glib orators and their people have worked themselves into all places of honor and profit, where the honest burgomaster used to smoke the pipe of peace and comfort in his generous portico, his children now superseded by the restless emigrants from the Eastern States, thus boastfully tracing all that redeems and sustains the republic to the wisdom, foresight, and moral superiority of their own peculiar ancestry. The style of the festival is often in bad taste; there is too little recognition of the hospitality of their adopted home, too little respect for Manhattan blood; an exuberance of language too conspicuously triumphant over a race which the best of comic histories illustrates by the reign of Peter the Silent, so that, at length, a jocose reproof was administered by the toast of a humorist present, who gave, with irresistible nasal emphasis, — "Plymouth Rock, — the Blarney-Stone of New England."

It is, however, an appropriate illustration of the cosmopolitan population of New York, that every year her English, Scotch, Welsh, Irish, French, German, and

Dutch children, after their own fashion, recall their respective national associations. In point of oratory the New England Society carries the day, inasmuch as it usually presses into its service some distinguished speaker from abroad; in geniality, antique customs, and long-drawn reminiscences, the St. Nicholas excels; at St. Andrew's board the memory of Burns is revived in song; Monsieur extols his vanished *Republique;* Welsh harps tinkle at St. David's; "God save the Queen" echoes under the banner of St. George; green sprigs and uncouth garments mark the Irish procession of St. Patrick;" and the Germans multiply their festivals by summer picnics, at which lager-beer, waltzing, and fine instrumental music recall the gardens of Vienna. "Thanksgiving-Day" is of Puritan origin, and was designed to combine family reunions with a grateful recognition of the autumnal harvest. The former beautiful feature is not as salient now as when the absence of locomotive facilities made it a rare privilege for the scattered members of a household to come together around the paternal hearth. The occasion has also diminished in value as one of clerical emancipation from Sabbath themes, when the preacher could expatiate unreproved on the questions of the day and the aspects of the times, — that privilege being now exercised, at will, on the regular day of weekly religious service. "Fast-Day" has also become anomalous; its abolition or identification with Good-Friday has been repeatedly advocated; strictly speaking, its title is a misnomer, and the actual observance of it is too partial and ineffective to have any true significance.

An old town on the north-eastern extremity of an

island, the nearest approach to which overland is from the southern shore of Cape Cod, was eagerly visited annually until within a few years, by those who delight in primitive character and local festivals. The broad plain beyond the town, was long held in common property by the inhabitants, as a sheep-pasture. It may be that the maritime occupations of the natives, their insular position and frugal habits imparted, by contrast, a singular relish to the rural episode thus secured in their lives of hazardous toil and dreary absence, as sailors and whalemen; but it is remarkable that amid the sands of that island flourished one of the heartiest and most characteristic of New England festivals. Simplicity of manners, hardihood, frankness, the genial spirit of the mariner, and the unsophisticated energy and kindliness of the sailor's wife, gave to the Nantucket "Sheep-shearing" a rare and permanent freshness and charm. Unfortunately discord, arising from the conflicting interests of these primitive islanders, at length made it desirable to restore peace by sacrificing the flocks,—innocent provocations of this domestic feud;—the sheep were sold, and the unique festival to which they gave occasion vanished with them. We must turn to that most available resource, an old newspaper, for a description of this now obsolete holiday:—

"*Sheep-shearing.*— This patriarchal festival was celebrated on Monday and Tuesday last, in this place, with more than ordinary interest. For some days previous, the sheep-drivers had been busily employed in collecting from all quarters of the Island the dispersed members of the several flocks; and committing them to the great sheepfold, about two miles from town, preparatory to the ceremonies of ablution and *devestment.*

"The principal enclosure contains three hundred acres; towards one side of this area, and near the margin of a considerable pond, are four or five circular fences, one within the other,— like Captain Symmes's concentric curves,— and about twenty feet apart, forming a sort of labyrinth. Into these circuits the sheep are gradually driven, so as to be designated by their "ear-marks," and secured for their proper owners in sheep-cotes arranged laterally, or nearly so, around the exterior circle. Contiguous to these smaller pens, each of which is calculated to contain about one hundred sheep, the respective owners had erected temporary tents, wherein the operation of shearing was usually performed. The number of hands engaged in this service may be imagined from the fact that one gentleman is the owner of about 1000 sheep, another of 700, and numerous others of smaller flocks, varying in number from three or four hundred down to a single dozen. The business of identifying, seizing, and yarding the sheep, creates a degree of bustle that adds no small amusement to the general activity of the scene. The whole number of sheep and lambs brought within the great enclosure is said to be 16,000. There are also several large flocks commonly sheared at other parts of the Island.

"As these are the only important holidays which the inhabitants of Nantucket have ever been accustomed to observe, it is not to be marvelled at that all other business should on such occasions be suspended; and that the labors attendant thereon should be mingled with a due share of recreation. Accordingly, the fancies of the juvenile portion of our community are, for a long time prior to the annual "Shearing," occupied in dreams of fun and schemes of frolic. With the mind's eye, they behold the long array of tents, surmounted with motley banners flaunting in the breeze, and stored with tempting titbits, candidates for money and for mastication. With the mind's ear they distinguish the spirit-stirring screak of the fiddle, the gruff jangling of the drum, the somniferous *smorzando* of the jews-harp, and the enlivening scuffle of little feet in a helter-skelter jig upon a deal platform. And their visions, unlike those of riper mortals, are always realized. For be it known, that independent of the preparations made by persons actually concerned in the mechanical duties of the day, there are erected on a rising ground in the vicinity of the sheep-field, some twenty pole and sail-cloth edifices, furnished with seats, and tables, and casks, and dishes, severally filled with jocund faces, baked pigs, punch, and cakes, and surrounded with divers savory concomitants in the premises, courteously dispensed by the changeful master of ceremonies, studious of custom and emulous of cash. For the accommodation of those merry urchins and youngsters who choose to 'trip it on the light fantastic toe,' a floor is laid at one corner, over which presides some African genius of melody, brandishing a cracked violin, and drawing most moving notes from its agonized intestines, by dint of griping fingers and right-angled elbows.

"We know of no parallel for this section of the entertainment, other than what the Boston boys were wont to denominate '*Nigger 'Lection*,' — so called in contradistinction from '*Artillery Election*.' At the former anniversary, which is the day on which 'who is Governor' is officially announced, the blacks and blackees are permitted to perambulate the Mall and Common, to buy gingerbread and beer with the best of folks, and to mingle in the mysteries of pawpaw. But on the latter day, when that grave and chivalrous corps, known as the Ancient and Honorable Artillery Company, parade for choice of officers, — which officers are to receive their diplomas directly from the hands of His Excellency the Governor and Commander-in-Chief, in open day, and in the august presence of all sorts of civil and martial dignitaries, — why, woe to the sable imp that shall *then* adventure his woolly poll and tarnished cuticle within the hallowed neighborhood of nobility!

"On previous days the sheep had been collected from every quarter of the Island, driven into the great fold at Miacomet (the site of an ancient Indian settlement, about a mile from town), selected and identified by their respective owners, placed in separate pens, and subjected to the somewhat arduous process of *washing*, in the large pond contiguous. After this preparatory ablution, they were then ready to 'throw off this muddy vesture of decay' by the aid of some hundreds of shearers, who began to ply their vocation on Monday morning, seated in rude booths, or beneath umbrageous awnings ranged around the circular labyrinth of enclosures, wherein the panting animals awaited the divestment of their uncomfortable jackets. The space partially occupied by the unshorn and their contented lambs, and in other spots exhibiting multitudes stripped of their fleece and clamorously seeking their wandering young, presented to the eye and ear of the stranger sights and sounds somewhat rare."

We have sometimes been tempted to believe that all illustrious occasions, men, and things in this republic must inevitably be profaned, — that, as a compensatory balance to the "greatest good of the greatest number," secured by democratic institutions, there must exist a sacrifice of the hallowed, aspiring, and consecrated elements of national feeling and achievement. If there is an anniversary which should compel respect, excite eternal gratitude, and win unhackneyed observance, it is that of the day when, for the first time in the world's history, the select intelligences of a country proclaimed to the nations, with deliberate and resolved wisdom, the principles of human equality and the right of self-government, pledged thereto their lives, fortunes, and honor, and consistently redeemed the heroically prophetic pledge. Subsequent events have only deepened the significance of that act and extended its agency; every succeeding year has increased its moral value and its material fruits; the career of other and less happy nations has given more and more relief to its isolated grandeur; and not a day fraught with more hope and glory lives in the calendar. Yet what is the actual observance, the average estimation, it boasts among us? In our large cities, especially in New York, "Independence" is, by universal consent, a nuisance. It is most auspicious to the Chinese, from increasing the importation of fire-crackers. The municipal authorities provide for it, as for a lawless saturnalia; the fire-department dread its approach as indicative of conflagrations; physicians, as hazardous to such unfortunate patients as cannot be removed into the country; quiet citizens, as insufferable from incessant detonation; the prudent, as fraught with reckless tomfoolery; and the respectable, as desecrated by rowdyism. John Adams, when he prophesied that the Fourth of July would be hailed, in all after-time, by the ringing of bells, the blaze of bonfires, and the roar of cannon, was far from intending, by this programme of Anglo-Saxon methods of popular rejoicing, to indicate the exclusive and ultimate style of our national holiday. On its earlier recurrence, when many of the actors in the scenes it commemorates still lived, there was an interest and a meaning in the ceremonies which time has lessened. Yet it is difficult to account for the absence of all that high civilization presupposes, in the celebration of our only holiday which can strictly be called national; and if the sympathies of the most intelligent of our citizens could be enlisted, so as to make the occasion a genuine patriotic jubilee, instead of a noisy carnival, or a time for political animosity to assert itself with special emphasis, much would be gained on the score of rational enjoyment and American fraternity. As it is, although the "Hundred Boston Orators" nobly vindicate the talent and good taste of one city in regard to this anniversary, and is a most pleasing historical memorial of the occasion, it cannot be denied that our usual synonyme for bombast and mere rhetorical patriotism is "a Fourth of July Oration," and that Pickwickian sentiment, pyrotechnic flashes, torpedoes, arrests, bursting cannon, draggled flags, crowded steamboats, the retiracy of the educated, and the uproar of the multitude, make up the confused and wearisome details of what should and might be a sacred feast, a pious memory, a hallowed consecration, a "Sabbath-day of Freedom." Perhaps the real zest of this holiday is felt only abroad, when, under some remote consular flag, at the board of private and munificent hospitality in London, or at an American *reunion* in the French capital, distance from home, the ties of common nativity in a foreign land, and the contrast of uneducated masses or despotic insignia around, with the prosperous, free, and enlightened population of our own favored country, to say nothing of superior festal arrangements, render the occasion at once charming and memorable.

One of the most noticeable features of American life to a stranger's eye is the prevalent habit of travel, and, although the incessant and huge caravans that rush along the numerous railways which make an iron network over this Union, are, for the most part, impelled by motives of enterprise and thrift, yet the common idea of recreation is associated with a "trip." Whether the facilities or the temperament of our country, or both, be the reason of this locomotive propensity, it is a characteristic which at once distinguishes the American from the home-tethered German, the Paris-bound Frenchman, and the locally-patriotic Italian. The schoolboy in vacation, the college graduate, the bridegroom, the overtasked professional man, — all Americans who give themselves a "holiday," are wont to dedicate it to a journey. But even this resource has lost much of its original charm from the catastrophes which have associated some of the most beautiful scenery of the land with the most agonizing of human tragedies. In the crystal waters of Lake George, by the picturesque banks of the Hudson, amid the fertile valleys of the Connecticut, on the teeming currents of Long Island Sound, have perished, often through reckless hardihood, always by more or less reprehensible negligence, some of the fairest and the noblest of our citizens. The statistics of these melancholy events which have so often appalled the public, have yet to be written; but their moral effect may be divined by a mere glance at the mercenary hardihood and soulless haste that mark our civilization. "Les dangers personnels," says an acute writer, "quand ils attegnent un certain limite, bouleversent tous les rapports et l'oublie de l'esperance changé presque notre nature." The zest, too, of a journey in America is much diminished by the monotonous character of the people, and by the gregarious habits, the rapid transits, and the business motives of the *voyageurs*, so that it is only at the *terminus* that we enjoy our pilgrimage; there the sight of a magnificent prairie or mountain range, cataract or mammoth cave, may, indeed, vindicate our locomotive taste, and the wonders of Nature make for the imaginative and reverential, a glorious holiday.

A pleasing feature in the recreative aspect of American life is the literary festival. It is a beautiful custom of our scholars annually to meet amid the scenes of their academical education and renew youthful friendships, while they listen to the orator and poet, who dwell upon those problems of the times which challenge an intellectual solution and identify the duties of the citizen with the offices of learning. Within the memory of almost all, there is probably at least one of these occasions, when the interest of the performances or the circumstances of the hour, lent a memorable charm to the collegiate holiday; when, under the shade of venerable elms, that witnessed the first outpouring of mental enthusiasm or the earliest honors of genius and attainment, they who parted as boys meet as men, and the classic dreamer felt himself a recognized and practical thinker for the people; when the language of eloquent wisdom or poetic beauty came warm from lips hallowed by the chalice of fame. Who that listened ever can forget the anniversary graced by the chaste eloquence of Buckminster, that on which Bryant recited "The Ages," or Everett's musical periods welcomed Lafayette to the oldest seat of American learning? What New England scholar, after years of professional labor in a distant State, ever found himself, once more, within the charmed precincts of his *alma mater*, and surrounded by the companions of his youthful studies, without a thrill of happy reminiscence? Yet even these rational opportunities for what should be a genuine holiday to mind and heart are but casually appreciated. The sultry period of their occurrence, the irregularity of attendance, and the precarious quality of the "feast of reason" provided, have caused them gradually to lose a tenacious hold upon the affections, while there are few *habitués*, the majority, especially those who live at a distance from the scene, and whose presence is, therefore, especially desirable, — are not loyal pilgrims to the shrine where their virgin distinction was earned and their intellectual armor forged. To many, our literary festivals are but technical ceremonies; to not a few, wearisome forms; associated rather with fans, didactics, perspiration, and cold viands, than with any social or intellectual refreshment. The "lean annuitant" who loved to visit "Oxford in vacation," and fancy himself a gownsman, and the ingenious "Opium Eater" who has recorded the enduring claims of those venerable cloisters to the scholar's gratitude, enjoyed speculatively more of the real luxury of academic repose and triumph than is often attained by those who ostensibly participate in our college festivals; and seldom do her children go up to the altars of wisdom consecrated by the pious zeal of our ancestors, with the faithful recognition of the venerable pastor, so long the statistical oracle of the surviving graduates, who, while his strength sufficed, cheerily walked from his rural parish to Old Harvard, to lead off the anniversary psalm, with genial pride and honest self-gratulation.

Of our purely social holidays, New Year's Day, as observed in the city of New York, bears the palm. Initiated by the hospitable instinct of the Dutch colonists, neither the heterogeneous population which has succeeded them, nor the annually enlarged circuit of the metropolis, has diminished the universality or the heartiness of its observance. When the snow is massed in the thoroughfares, and the sunshine tempers a clear, frosty atmosphere, a more cheerful scene, on a large scale, it is impossible to imagine. From morning to midnight, sleighs, freighted with gay companions and drawn by handsome steeds, dash merrily along, — the tinkle of their bells and the scarlet lining of their buffalo-robes redolent of a *fête;* the sidewalks are alive with hurrying pedestrians who exchange cordial greetings as they pass one another; doors incessantly fly open; guests come and go; every one looks prosperous and happy; business is totally suspended; in warm parlors radiant with comfort or splendid with luxury, sit the wives, daughters, sisters, or fair favorites of these innumerable visitors, the queens of the day; the neglects of the past are forgiven and forgotten in the welcome of the present; kindred, friends, and acquaintances all meet and begin the year with mutual good wishes; in every dwelling a little feast stands ready, encompassed with smiles; and all varieties of fortune, all degrees of intimacy, all tastes in dress, entertainment, and manners, on this one day, are consecrated by the liberal and kindly spirit of a social carnival.

Of associations expressly instituted for the observance of holidays there is no lack; of days technically devoted to festivity, in the aggregate, our proportion equals that of older communities; and the legitimate occasions for pastime and ceremony, social pleasure, or historical commemoration, are as numerous as is consistent with the industrious habits and the civic prosperity of the land. The traveller who should make it his speciality to discover and note the ostensible merry-makings and pageants of America would find the list neither brief nor monotonous. In the summer he would light upon many an excursion on our beautiful lakes, many a chowder-party to the seaside, and picnic in the grove; and in the winter would catch the shrill echo of the skating frolic. Here, through pillared trunks, he would behold the smoke-wreaths of the sugar-camp;

there watch laughing groups clustered round the cider-mill or hop-field; and in woods radiant with autumnal tints, or prairies balmy with a million flowers, would sounds of merriment announce to him the cheerful bivouac. Nor have American holidays, even in their most primitive aspect, been devoid of use and beauty. The once renowned "musters" fostered military taste, and the cattle-shows encouraged agricultural science; with the increase of horticultural festivals, our fruits and flowers have constantly improved; regattas and yacht-clubs have indirectly promoted nautical architecture; school festivals attest the superiority of our system of popular education; family gatherings, on the large scale observed in several instances, have induced genealogical research; historical celebrations have led to the collection and preservation of local archives and memorials; the Cincinnati Society annually renews the noblest patriotic sympathies; and the genius for mechanical invention is proclaimed by the Fairs which, every October, bring together so many trophies of skilful handiwork and husbandry, and recognize so emphatically the dignity and scientific amelioration of labor. Yet these facts do not invalidate the general truth that our festivals are too much tinctured with utilitarian aims to breathe earnestness and hilarity; that they are so specific as to represent the division rather than the social triumphs of human toil; that they are too partial in their scope, too sectional in their objects, and too isolated in their arrangements to meet the claims of popular and permanent interests. Our harvests are songless. Reaping-machines have diminished the zest of autumn's golden largess, as destructive inventions have lessened the miracles of chivalry. Here and there may yet convene a quilting-party, but locomotive facilities have deprived rural gatherings, in sparse neighborhoods, of their marvel and their joy; and the hilarious huskings of old chiefly survive in Barlow's neglected verse: —

"The days grow short; but though the fallen sun
To the glad swain proclaims his day's work done;
Night's pleasant shades his various tasks prolong,
And yield new subjects to my various song.
For now, the corn-house filled, the harvest home,
The invited neighbors to the *husking* come;
A frolic scene, where work and mirth and play,
Unite their charms to chase the hours away.
Where the huge heap lies centred in the hall,
The lamp suspended from the cheerful wall,
Brown, corn-fed nymphs, and strong, hard-handed beaux,
Alternate ranged, extend in circling rows,
Assume their seats, the solid mass attack;
The dry husks rustle, and the corn-cobs crack;
The song, the laugh, alternate notes resound,
And the sweet cider trips in silence round.
The laws of husking every wight can tell,
And sure no laws he ever keeps so well:
For each red ear a general kiss he gains,
With each smut ear he smuts the luckless swains;
But when to some sweet maid a prize is cast,
Red as her lips and taper as her waist,
She walks the round and culls one favored beau,
Who leaps the luscious tribute to bestow.
Various the sports, as are the wits and brains
Of well-pleased lasses and contending swains;
Till the vast mound of corn is swept away,
And he that gets the last ear wins the day."

Progress in taste and sentiment, however, is already obvious in our recreative arrangements. There is vastly more of intellectual dignity and permanent use in the *fêtes* of the Lyceum than in those of the training-days and election-jubilees which formerly were the chief holidays of our rural population; exhibitions of flowers mark a notable advance upon the coarse diversions of the ring and the race-ground; and, within a few years, statues by native artists, worthy of their illustrious subjects, have been inaugurated by public rites and noble eloquence.

A radical cause of the inefficiency, and therefore of the indifferent observance of our holidays, may be found in our national inadequacy of expression, in the want of those modes of popular rejoicing and ceremonial that win and triumph, from their intrinsic beauty. As a general truth, it may be asserted that but two methods of representing holiday sentiment are native to the average taste of our people, — military display and oral discourse. These exhaust our festal resources. Our citizens have an extraordinary facility in making occasional speeches, and the love of soldiership is so prevalent that it is the favorite sport of children, and all classes indulge in costly uniforms and volunteer parades. But the language of art, which in the Old World lends such a permanent attraction to holidays, with us hardly finds voice. Had we requiems conceived with the eternal pathos of Mozart, harmonious embodiments of rural pastime, like that which Beethoven caught while sitting on a stile amid the subdued murmurs of a summer evening; melodious invocations to freedom, such as Bellini's thrilling *duo;* were a symphony as readily composed in America as an oration; tableaux, costumes, and processions as artistically invented here as in France; were dance and song as spontaneously expressive as among the European peasantry; had we vast, open, magnificent temples, free gardens, statues to crown, shrines to frequent, palatial balconies, fields Elysian for both rich and poor, a sensibility to music, and a sense of the appropriate and beautiful, as wide and as instinctive as our appreciation of the useful, the practical, and the comfortable, — it would no longer be requisite to resort exclusively to drums, fifes, powder, substantial viands, and speechifying, to give utterance to the common sentiment, which would find vent in tones, forms, hues, combinations, and sympathies, that respond to the heart, through the imagination, and conform "the show of things to the desires of the mind."

Other causes of our deficient holidays are obvious. The primary are to be found in the absorption in business and the dominion of practical habits, both of thought and action. Enterprise holds Carnival while Poetry keeps Lent. The facts of to-day shut out of view the perspective of time, or, at best, lure the gaze forward with boundless expectancy. To rehearse the fortunate achievements of the past gratifies our national egotism; but the sensibility and meditation which consecrate historical associations find no room amid the rush and eagerness of the passing hour. Content to point to the heroic episode of the Revolution, to the wisdom and justice of our Constitution, to the caravans that sweep on iron tracks over leagues of what a few years ago was a pathless forest, — to the swiftest keels and most graceful models that traverse the ocean, — to the aerial viaducts that span dizzy heights and impetuous torrents, — to the exquisite vignettes of a limitless paper currency, — to the dignified and consistent maintenance of usurped law in younger States of the Union, and to the continually increasing resources of its older members; we are disposed to sneer at the childish love of amusement which beguiles the inhabitants of European capitals, and to pity the superstition and idleness which retain, in this enlightened age, the melodramatic church shows of Romanism. In all this there is doubtless a certain manly intelligence; but there is also an inauspicious moral hardihood. If, as a people, we cultivated more heartily the social instincts and humane sentiments expressed in holiday rites, life would be more valued, the whole nature would find congenial play, and our taskwork and duty, our citizenship and our natural advantages, would be adorned by gracefulness, alacrity, and repose. Quantity would not be so grossly estimated above quality, speed above security, routine above enjoyment. We need to win from time what is denied to us in material. Other nations have in Art a permanent and accessible refreshment, which prevents life from being wholly prosaic; the humblest dweller on English soil can enter a time-hallowed and beautiful cathedral; the poorest rustic in Italy can feel the honest pride of a distinctive festal attire; the veriest clodhopper in Germany can soften the rigors of poverty by music; the London apprentice may wander once a week amid the venerable beauties of Hampton Court; and the Parisian shopkeeper may kindle pride of country by reading the pictorial history of France at Versailles. It is not the expensive arrangements, but the national provision, and, above all, the personal sentiment, which makes the holiday. There was more holy rapture in the low cadence of the hymn stealing from the Roman Catacombs, where the hunted Christians of old kept holy the Sabbath-day, than there is in the gorgeous display and complex melody under the magnificent dome of St. Peter's. There was more of the grace of festivity in such a dance as poor Goldsmith's flute enlivened on the banks of the Loire, than there is in the grand ball which marks the season's climax at an American watering-place. In public not less than private banquets, the scriptural maxim holds true: "Better is a dinner of herbs *where love is*." Our national life is too diffusive to yield the best social fruits. The extent of territory, the nomadic habits of our people, the alternations of climate, the vicissitudes of trade, the prevalence of spasmodic and superficial excitements, the boundless passion for gain, the local changes, the family separations, and the incessant fevers of opinion, scatter the holy fire of love, reverence, self-respect, contemplation, and faith. What a senseless boast, that the United States has thirty-five thousand miles of railroad,* while England claims but ninety-two hundred, France forty-eight hundred, if, against the American overplus are to be arrayed countless hetacombs of murdered fellow-citizens, and desolating frauds unparalleled in the history of finance! What a mockery the distinction of having accumulated a fortune in a few years, by sagacity and toil, if, to complete the record, it is added that mercenary ambition risked and lost it in as many months, or the want of self-control, and mental resources made its possession a life-long curse from *ennui* or tasteless extravagance! It is as a check to the whirl of inconsiderate speculation, an antidote to the bane of material luxury, an interval in the hurried march of executive life, that holidays should "give us pause," and might prove a means of refinement and of disinterestedness. We could thus infuse a better spirit into our work-day experience, refresh and warm the nation's heart, and gradually concentrate what of higher taste and more genial sympathy under-

* In 1860.

lies the restless and cold tide that hurries us onward, unmindful of the beauty and indifferent to the sanctities with which God and Nature have invested our existence.

Of natal anniversaries we have in our national calendar one which it would augur well for the Republic to observe as a universal holiday. Every sentiment of gratitude, veneration, and patriotism has already consecrated it to the private heart, and every consideration of unity, good faith, and American feeling, designates its celebration as the most sacred civic *fête* of the land. Recent demonstrations in literature, art, and oratory, indicate that the obligation and importance of keeping before the eyes, minds, and affections of the people the memory of Washington, are emphatically recognized by genius and popular sentiment. Within a few years, the pen of our most endeared author, the eloquence of our most finished orator, and the chisel of our best sculptors, have combined to exhibit, in the most authentic and impressive forms of literary and plastic art, the character and image of the Father of his Country. Copies of Stuart's masterly portrait have multiplied. A monument bearing the revered name is slowly rising at the Capital, the materials of which are gathered from every part of the globe. One of the last and most noble efforts to renew the waning national sentiment ere its lapse brought on civil war, was that of a New England scholar, patriot, and orator who, despite the allurements of prosperity and the claims of age and long service, traversed the length and breadth of the Republic, eloquently expatiating on the character of Washington, retracing his spotless and great career and evoking his sacred memory as a talisman to quicken and combine a people's love. With the large contributions thus secured, and those gathered by the daughters of the Republic, the home and grave of Washington has been redeemed as national property. Let the first homage of a free people be paid at that shrine; and alienated fellow-citizens gather there as at a common altar: his tomb is thus doubly hallowed. In Virginia is a sculptured memorial of enduring beauty and historical significance. A new and admirable biography, with all the elements of standard popularity, makes his peerless career familiar to every citizen from the woods of Maine to the shores of the Pacific. One effective statue already ornaments the commercial emporium, and another is about to be erected in the city of Boston. These, and many other signs of the times, prove that the fanaticism of party strife has awakened the wise and loyal to a consciousness of the inestimable value of that great example and canonized name, as a bond of union, a conciliating memory, and a glorious watchword. Desecrated as has been his native State by rebels against the government he founded and the nation he inaugurated, profaned as has been his memory, now that Peace smiles upon the land his august image will reappear to every true, loyal and patriotic heart with renewed authority, and hallowed by a deeper love. The present, therefore, is a favorable moment to institute the birthday of Washington,—hitherto but partially and ineffectually honored — as a solemn National Festival. Around his tomb let us annually gather; let eloquence and song, leisure and remembrance, trophies of art, ceremonies of piety, and sentiments of gratitude and admiration, consecrate that day with an unanimity of feeling and of rites, which shall fuse and mould into one pervasive emotion, the divided hearts of the country, until the discordant cries of faction are lost in the anthems of benediction and of love; and, before the august spirit of a people's homage, sectional animosity is awed into universal reverence.

LAWYERS.

"To vindicate the majesty of the law." — JUDGE'S CHARGE.

"Why may not this be a lawyer's skull? Why does he suffer this rude knave to knock him about the sconce with a dirty shovel, and will not tell him of his action for battery?" — HAMLET.

HE miniature effigy of a town-crier, with a little placard on his bell, inscribed "*Lost — a Lawyer's conscience!*" was a favorite toy for children not many years ago; and, about the same time, a song was in vogue, warbled by a whole generation of young misses, "all about the L-A-W," in which that venerable profession was made the subject of a warning chant, whose dolorous refrain, doubtless, yet lingers in many an ear. Thus early is law associated with uncertainty and shamelessness; Messrs. Roe and Doe become the most dreaded of apocryphal characters; red-tape the clew of an endless labyrinth; Justice Shallow, with all his imbecility, a dangerous personage, and human beings, even a friend, transformed by the mysterious perspective of this anomalous element to a "party." The most popular of modern novelists have found these associations sufficiently universal to yield good material in "dead suitors broken, heart and soul, on the wheel of chancery;" and Flite, Gridley, and Rick, are fresh and permanent scarecrows in the harvest-field of the law.

From the Mosaic code, enrolled on tables of stone, to the convention which inaugurated that of the modern conqueror of Europe, law has been a field for the noblest triumphs and most gross perversions of the human intellect. No profession offers such extremes of glory and shame. From the most wretched sophistry to the grandest inference, from a quibble to a principle, from the august minister of justice to the low pettifogger, how great the distance; yet all are included within a common pale.

In every social circle and family group, there is an oracle — some individual whose age, wit, or force of character, gives an intellectual ascendency — and there are always Bunsbys to "give an opinion" among the ignorant, to which the others spontaneously defer; and thus instinctively arises the lawgiver, sometimes ruling with the rude dogmatism of Dr. Johnson, and at others, through the humorous good sense of Sydney Smith, or the endearing tact of Madame Recamier. These authorities, in the sphere of opinion and companionship, indicate how natural to human society is a recognized head, whence emanates that controlling influence to which we give the name of law. Like every other element of life, this loses somewhat of its native beauty, when organized and made professional. To every vocation there belong master-spirits who have established precedents, and there are natural lawgivers; as in art, Michael Angelo and Raphael; in oratory, Demosthenes; in philosophy, Bacon. The endowments of each not only justify, but originate their authority; they interpret truth through their superior insight and wisdom in their respective departments of action and of thought; but of the vast number who undertake to illustrate, maintain, or apply the laws which govern States, a small minority are gifted for the task, or aspire to its higher functions; hence the proverbial abuse of the profession, its few glorious ornaments, and its herd of perverted slaves.

From this primary condition, it is impossible for any human being to escape; if he goes into the desert, he is still subject to the laws of Nature, and, however retired he may live amid his race, the laws of society press upon him at some point; if his own opinion is his law in matters of fancy or politics, he must still obey the law of the road: in one country the law of primogeniture; in another, that of conscription; in one circle, a law of taste; in another, of custom; and in a third, of privilege, reacts upon his free agency; at his club is sumptuary law; over his game of whist, Hoyle; in his drawing-room, Chesterfield; now *l'esprit du corps;* and again, the claims of rank; in Maine, the liquor law; in California, lynch law; in Paris, a *gens d'armes;* at Rome, a permission of residence; on an English domain, the game laws; in the fields of Connecticut, a pound; everywhere turnpikes, sheriffs' sales, marriage certificates, prisons, courts, passports, and policemen, thrust before the eyes of the most peaceable and reserved cosmopolite — insignia that assure him that law is everywhere unavoidable. His physician discourses to him of the laws of health; his military friends, of tactics; the beaux, of etiquette; the belles, of *la mode;* the authors, of tasteful precedents; the reformer, of social systems; and thus all recognize and yield to some code.

If he have nothing to bequeath, no tax to pay, no creditor to sue, or libeller to prosecute, he yet must walk the streets, and thereby realize the influence or neglect of municipal law in the enjoyment of "right of way," or the nausea from some neglected offal; the accidents incident to travel in this country assure him of the slight tenure of corporate responsibility under republican law; and the facility of divorce, the removal of old landmarks, the incessant subdivision and dispersion of estates, indicate that devotion to the immediate which a French philosopher ascribes to free institutions, and which affects legal as well as social phenomena. In a tour abroad, he discovers new majesty in the ruins of the Forum, from their association with the ancient Roman law, upon which modern jurisprudence is founded; and a curious interest attaches to the picturesque beauty of Amalfi, because the Pandects were there discovered. Westminster revives the tragic memories of the State trials, and seems yet to echo the Oriental rhetoric that made the trial of Hastings a Parliamentary romance. At Bologna, amid the old drooping towers, under the pensive arcades, in the radiant silence of the picture-gallery, comes back the traditionary beauty of the fair lecturer, who taught the students juridical lore from behind a curtain, that her loveliness might not bewilder the minds her words informed; and at Venice every dark-robed, graceful figure that glides by the porticos of San Marco's moonlit square, revives the noble Portia's image, and that "same scrubbed boy, the doctor's clerk."

No inconsiderable legal knowledge has been traced in Shakspeare. His Justice Shallow and Dogberry are types of imbecile magistracy; in the historical plays, the law of legitimacy is defined; and not a little judicial lore is embodied in the "Merchant of Venice" and "Taming the Shrew." Lord Campbell wrote a book to prove that Shakspeare, in his youth, must have been, at least, an attorney's clerk. One of the characters in a popular novel is made to say that he is never in company with a lawyer but he fancies himself in a witness-box. This hit at the interrogative propensity of the class is by no means an exaggerated view of a use to which they are specially inclined to put conversation; and, if we compare the ordeal of inquiry to which we are thus subjected, it will be found more thorough, and better fitted to test our knowledge than that of any other social catechism; so that, perhaps, we gain in discipline what we lose in patience. It is to be acknowledged, also, that few men are better stocked with ideas, or more fluent in imparting them, than well-educated lawyers. There is often a singular zest in their anecdotes, a precision in their statement of facts, and a dramatic style of narrative, which render them the pleasantest of companions. In all clever coteries of which we have any genial record, there usually figures a lawyer, as a wit, a boon companion, an entertaining dogmatist, or an intellectual champion. In literature, the claims and demerits of the profession are emphatically recognized; and it is curious to note the varied inferences of philosophers and authors. Thus, Dr. Johnson says to Boswell: "Sir, a lawyer has no business with the justice or injustice of the cause he undertakes;" and "everybody knows you are paid for affecting a warmth for your client." "Justice," observes Sydney Smith, "is found, experimentally, to be best promoted by the opposite efforts of practiced and ingenious men, presenting to an impartial judge the best argument for the establishment and explanation of truth." "Some are allured to the trade of law," says Milton, "by litigiousness and fat fees;" one authoritative writer describes a lawyer as a man whose understanding is on the town; another declares no man departs more from justice; Sancho Panza said his master would prattle more than three attorneys; and Coleridge thought that, "upon the whole, the advocate is placed in a position unfavorable to his moral being, and, indeed, to his intellect also, in its higher powers;" while it was a maxim of Wilkes, that scoundrel and lawyer are synonymous terms. Our pioneer *littérateur*, Brockden Brown, whose imaginative mind revolted at the dry formalities of the law, for which he was originally intended, defined it as "a tissue of shreds and remnants of a barbarous antiquity, patched by the stupidity of modern workmen into new deformity." "In the study of law," remarks the poet Gray, "the labor is long, and the elements dry and uninteresting, nor was there ever any one not disgusted at the beginning." Foote, the comic writer and actor, feigned surprise to a farmer that attorneys were buried, in the country, like other men; in town, he declared, it was the custom to place the body in a chamber, with an open window, and it was sure to disappear during the night, leaving a smell of brimstone. A portrait-painter assures us he is never mistaken in a lawyer's face; the avocation is betrayed to his observant eye by a certain *inscrutable* expression; and Dickens has given this not exaggerated picture of a class in the profession: "Smoke-dried and faded, dwelling among mankind, but not consorting with them, aged without experience of genial youth, and so long used to make his cramped nest in holes and corners of human nature that he has forgotten its broader and better range."

A French writer defines a lawyer as "un marchand de phrases, un fabricant de paradoxes, qui ment pour l' argent et vend ses paroles" ; and another remarks of the profession that it is a "vaste champ, ouvert aux ambitions des honnêtes ; une tribune offerte aux subtilités de la pensée et l' abus de la parole ;" while Arthur Helps declares that, "Law affords a notable example of loss of time, of heart, of love, of leisure. I observe," he adds, "that the first Spanish colonists in America wrote home to Government, begging them not to allow lawyers to come to the colony." * On the other hand, what an eloquent tribute to the possible actual beneficence of law is the close of Lord Brougham's memorable speech in its defence: —

> "You saw the greatest warrior of the age, — conqueror of Italy, humbler of Germany, terror of the North, — saw him account all his matchless victories poor, compared with the triumph you are now in a condition to win, — saw him contemn the fickleness of Fortune, while in despite of her he could pronounce his memorable boast, 'I shall go down to posterity with the Code in my hand!' You have vanquished him in the field; strive now to rival him in the sacred arts of peace. Outstrip him as a lawgiver whom in arms you overcame. The lustre of the Regency will be eclipsed by the more solid and enduring splendor of the Reign. It was the boast of Augustus — it formed part of the glare in which the perfidies of his earlier years were lost — that he found Rome of brick, and left it of marble. But how much nobler will be the Sovereign's boast, when he shall have it to say, that he found law dear and left it cheap; found it a sealed book, left it a living letter; found it the patrimony of the rich, left it the inheritance of the poor; found it the two-edged sword of craft and oppression, left it the staff of honesty and the shield of innocence!"

"Why may not this be a lawyer's skull?" muses Hamlet, in the graveyard; "where be his quiddets now,

* *Friends in Council.*

his quillets, his cases, his tenures, and his tricks? Humph! this fellow might be in 's time a greater buyer of land, with his statutes, his recognizances, his fines, his double-vouchers, his recoveries; and this, the fine of his fines, and the recovery of his recoveries, to have his fine poll full of dirt! The very conveyances of his lands will hardly lie in this box; and must the inheritor himself have no more?"

The diversities of the profession in England and America are curious and suggestive. Already is the obligation mutual; for if in the old country there are more profound and elaborate resources, in the new the science has received brilliant elucidations, and its forms and processes been simplified. There routine is apt to dwarf, and here variety to dissipate the lawyer's ability; there he is too often a mere drudge, and here his vocation regarded as the vestibule only of political life. In England, the advocate's knowledge is frequently limited to his special department; and in America, while it is less complete and accurate, he is versed in many other subjects, and apt at many vocations. "The Americans," says Sidney Smith, "are the first persons who have discarded, in the administration of justice, the tailor, and his auxiliary the barber, — two persons of endless importance in the codes and pandects of Europe. A judge administers justice without a calorific wig and parti-colored gown; — in a coat and pantaloons; he is obeyed, however, and life and property are not badly protected in the United States."

There can be no more striking contrast than that between the lives of the English chancellors and the American chief justices: in the former, regal splendor, the vicissitudes of kingcraft and succession, of religious transition, of courts, war, the people and the nobility, lend a kind of feudal splendor, or tragic interest, or deep intrigue, to the career of the minister of justice; he is surrounded with the insignia of his office; big wigs, scarlet robes, ermine mantles, the great seal, interviews with royalty, the trappings and the awe of power invest his person; his career is identified with the national annals; the lapse of time and historic associations lend a mysterious interest to his name; in the background, there is the martyrdom of Thomas á Becket, the speech of the fallen Wolsey, the scaffold of Sir Thomas More, the inductive system and low ambition of Bacon, and the literary fame of Clarendon. Yet, in intellectual dignity, our young republic need not shrink from the comparison. The Virginia stripling, who drilled regulars in a hunting-shirt, is a high legal authority in both hemispheres. "Where," says one of Marshall's intelligent eulogists, "in English history, is the judge whose mind was at once so enlarged and so systematic; who had so thoroughly reduced professional science to general reason; in whose disciplined intellect technical learning had so completely passed into native sense?" And now that Kent's Commentaries have become the indispensable guide and reference of the entire profession, who remembers, except with pride, that, on his first circuit, the Court was often held in a barn, with the hay-loft for a bench, a stall for a bar, and the shade of a neighboring apple-tree for a jury-room? The majesty of justice, the intellectual superiority of law as a pursuit, is herein most evident; disrobed of all external magnificence, with no lofty and venerable halls, imposing costume, or array of officials, the law yet borrows from the learning, the fidelity, and the genius of its votaries, essential dignity and memorable triumphs. "Of law, no less can be said," grandly observes Hooker, "than that her seat is the bosom of God, her voice the harmony of the world."

The most celebrated English lawyers have their American prototypes; thus, Marshall has been compared to Lord Mansfield, Pinkney to Erskine, and Wirt to Sheridan (who was a student of the Middle Temple, though not called to the bar); imperfect as are such analogies, they yet indicate, with truth, a similarity of endowment, or style of advocacy. The diverse influence of the respective institutions of the two countries is, however, none the less apparent because of an occasional resemblance in the genius of eminent barristers. The genuine British lawyer is recognized by the technical cast of his expression and habit of mind, to a degree seldom obvious in this country. Indeed, no small portion of the graduates of our colleges who select the law as a pursuit, do so without any strong bias for the profession, but with a view to the facilities it affords for entrance into public life. Some of these aspirants thus become useful servants of the State; a few, statesmen, but the majority mere politicians; and from the predominance of the latter class originate half the errors of American legislation; for, however much profound legal training may fit a man of ability for the higher functions of representative government, a superficial knowledge and practice of law renders him only an adept in chicanery and the "gift of the gab"; and it is easy to imagine how a mob of such adroit and ambitious partisans — especially when brought together from the narrow sphere of village life — may pervert the great ends of legislative action. They make the laws according to their own interests; and there is no prospect of the reformation demanded in juridical practice, while such a corps form the speaking and voting majority, and act on what has been justly called the one great principle of English law, — "*to make business for itself.*" *

Two names appear on the roll of English lawyers which are identified with the worst characteristics of the race, — impious, wild, and brow-beating arrogance, — that of Jeffreys, whose ferocious persecution of those suspected of complicity with Monmouth's Rebellion forms one of the most scandalous chapters in the history of British courts; and Lord Thurlow, who, in a more refined age, won the alias of Tiger, for his rudeness, inflexibility, oaths, and ill-manners, his black brows, and audible growls. In beautiful contrast shine forth the Law Reformers of England, whose benign eloquence and unwearied labor mitigated the sanguinary rigors of the criminal code, and pressed the Common Law into the service of humanity. Romilly and Erskine have gained a renown more enduring than that of learned and gifted advocates; their professional glory is heightened and mellowed by the sacred cause it illustrates.

The trial by jury and *habeas corpus* are the grand privileges of England and our own country; the integrity of the former has been invaded among us, by the abuse incident to making judgeships elective, and by the lawless spirit of the western communities; while the conviction of such eminent criminals as Earl Ferrers,

* "By the working of the apparatus for the administration of justice, they make their profits; and their welfare depends on its being so worked as to bring them profits, rather than on its being so worked as to administer justice." — *Herbert Spencer.*

Dr. Dodd, and Fauntleroy, prove how it has been, and is respected by the public sentiment of England.

"The great expense of the simplest lawsuit," writes an English lawyer, in a popular magazine, "and the droll laws which force all English subjects into a court of Equity for their sole redress, in an immense number of cases, lead, at this present day, to a very entertaining class of practical jokes. I mean that ludicrous class, in which the joke consists of a man's taking and keeping possession of money or other property to which he even pretends to have no shadow of right, but which he seizes because he knows that the whole will be swallowed up if the rightful owner should seek to assert his claim." The instances which are cited are rather fitted to excite a sense of humiliation than of fun, at the cruel injustice of a legal system which expressly organizes and protects robbery.

The legal treatises produced in England in modern times, are wonderful monuments of erudition, research, and analytical power. The intelligent lawyer who examines Spence's two volumes on Equity, does not wonder his brain gave way when thus far advanced on his gigantic task. It is this patient study, this complete learning, which distinguishes the English lawyer; in point of eloquence, he is confessedly inferior to his Irish and American brethren, as they are to him in profundity; in the careful and persistent application of common sense to the hoarded legal acquisitions of centuries, the great minds of the English bar stand unrivalled. It is, indeed, the most certain professional avenue to official power. "Rely upon it," says a brilliant novelist, "the barrister's gown is the wedding-garment to the British feast of fat things;" and Veron declares that "en France, mais en France seulement, un avocat est propre à tout, tandis qu'un mèdecin n'est jugé propre à rien qu'à hanter les hôpitaux."

In this country, the lawyers of each State have a characteristic reputation; the Bar of Boston, as a whole, is more English, that of the South more Irish, in its general merits. Marshall was an exception to the eloquent fame of American lawyers born and bred south of the Potomac; his superiority was logical: "aim exclusively at strength," was his maxim; and "close, compact, simple, but irresistible logic," his great distinction. Wheaton's labors in behalf of International, and Hamilton's in that of Constitutional law, have laid the civilized world, as well as their native country, under high and lasting obligations.

The popular estimate of a profession is dependent on circumstances; and this, like every other human pursuit, takes its range and tone from the character of its votary, and the existent relation it holds to public sentiment; not so much from what it technically demands, but from the spirit in which it is followed, comes the dignity and the shame of the law. The erudite generalizations of Savigny belong to the most difficult and enlarged sphere of thought, while the cunning tergiversations of the legal adventurer identify him with sharpers and roguery. How characteristic of Aaron Burr, that he should sarcastically define law as "whatever is boldly asserted and plausibly maintained." In the first cycle of our Republic, when a liberal education was rare, the best lawyers were ornaments of society, and the intellectual benefactors of the country. In that study were disciplined the chivalrous minds of Marshall, Hamilton, Adams, Morris, and other statesmen of the Revolution. A trial, which afforded the least scope for their remarkable powers, was attended by the intelligent citizens with very much the same kind of interest as filled the Athenian theatre — a mental banquet was confidently expected and deeply enjoyed. To have a great legal reputation, then, implied all that is noble in intellect, graceful in manner, and courteous in spirit — it bespoke the scholar, the gentleman, and the wit, as well as the advocate. When Emmet came hither with the *prestige* of inherited patriotism and talents, as well as the claims of an exile, he found men at the bar whose eloquence rivalled the fame of Curran and Grattan.

In Scotland, lawyers are eminently identified with social distinction and arrangements. "The fact of the substitution of the legal profession for the old Scottish aristocracy," says a late Review, "in the chief place in Edinburgh society, is typified by the circumstance that the so-called Parliament House, which is on the site of the ancient hall where the Estates of the Kingdom sat when the nation made its own laws, is now the seat of the Scottish law-courts and the daily resort of the interpreters of the land. The general hour of breakfast in Edinburgh is determined by the time when the Courts open in the morning; and dispersed through their homes or at dinner-parties in the evening it is the members of the legal profession that lead the social talk."

The equality of free institutions was never more aptly illustrated than by a scene which occurred in a Court-House we used to frequent, in boyhood, in order to hear the impassioned rhetoric of a gifted criminal lawyer. A trial of peculiar interest was to come on; the room was crowded with spectators and officials; the judge, a venerable specimen of the stern and dignified magistrate, took his seat; the sheriff announced the opening of the court, and the clerk called over the names of those summoned to act as jurors. We were startled to hear, among those of grocers, draymen, and mechanics, the well-known name of an aristocratic millionaire. It was thrice repeated and no answer given. "Has that juror been duly summoned," inquired the judge. "Yes, your honor," was the reply. "Let two constables instantly bring him before us," said the magistrate. One can imagine the vexation of the rich gentleman of leisure, when dawdling, in a flowered *robe de chambre*, over his sumptuous breakfast, to be disturbed by those rude minions of the law; however, there was no alternative, and he was obliged to dispatch his meal and accompany the distasteful escort. He entered the court, where a deep silence prevailed, with a supercilious smile and complacent air of well-bred annoyance. "How dare you keep the court waiting, sir?" was the indignant salutation of the judge, who, perhaps, when last in the gentleman's company, had sipped a glass of delectable old Madeira to his health. "I intended to pay my fine and not serve," stammered the millionaire. "And do you suppose, sir, that wealth exonerates you from the duties of a citizen, and is any apology for your gross incivility in thus detaining the court for over an hour? No excuse will be accepted; either take your seat in the jury-box or stand committed." Through the silent crowd, the luxurious man of fortune threaded his way, and sat down between a currier and wood-merchant, with whom he had to listen to the law and the evidence for a fortnight.

The author of the "Lives of the English Chancellors" refers to the usual explanation of the origin of the term "wool-sack," as intended in compliment to the staple product of the realm; and adds his own belief that, in "the rude simplicity of early times, a sack of wool was frequently used as a sofa." In the colonial era of our history, when ceremony and etiquette ruled the public hall as well as the private drawing-room, American judges wore the robe and wig still used in the Old Country. These insignia of authority inspired an awe, before the era of legal reform and of philosophical jurisprudence, which comported with the tyrannous exercise of juridical power, when it was little more than the medium of despotism, and when the calm reproach of Stafford was a literal truth: "It is better to be without laws altogether, than to persuade ourselves that we have laws by which to regulate our conduct, and to find that they consist only in the enmity and arbitrary will of our accusers."

The Conveyancer, Writer to the Signet, Attorney, Barrister, and other divisions of the legal profession, indicate how, in this, as in other vocations, the division of labor operates in England; while on this side of the water, the contrary principle not only assigns to the lawyer a degree of knowledge and aptitude in each branch of his calling, but lays him under contribution in every political and social exigency, as an interpreter or advocate of public sentiment; hence his remarkable versatility and comparatively superficial attainments. In the history of English law, the early struggles and profound acquirements of her disciples form the salient points, while in that of America, they are to be found rather in the primitive resources of justice and the varied career of her ministers. With regard to the former, our many racy descriptions of the process of

Western colonization, abound in remarkable anecdotes of the unlicensed administration of justice. After the Pioneer comes the Ranger, a kind of border police, then the Regulator, and finally the Justice of the Peace. In the primitive communities, when a flagrant wrong is committed, a public meeting is called, perhaps, under an oak-clump, or in a green hollow, the oldest settler is invited to the chair, which is probably the trunk of a fallen tree; the offence is discussed; the offender identified; volunteers scour the woods; he is arraigned, and, if found guilty, hung, banished, or reprimanded, as the case may be, with a dispatch which is not less remarkable than the fair hearing he is allowed, and the cool decision with which he is condemned.

There is a peculiar kind of impudence exhibited by the lawyer — it is sometimes called "badgering a witness" — and consists essentially of a mean abuse of that power which is legally vested in judge and advocate, whereby they can, at pleasure, insult and torment each other, and all exposed to their queries, with impunity. It is easy to imagine the relish with which unprofessional victims behold the mutual exercise of this legal tyranny. A venerable Justice, in one of our cities, was remarkable for the frequent reproofs he administered to young practitioners in his court, and the formal harangues with which he wore out the patience of those so unfortunate as to give testimony in his presence. On one occasion, it happened that he was summoned as a witness, in a case to be defended by one of the juvenile members of the bar, whom he had often called to order, with needless severity. This hopeful limb of the law was gifted with more than a common share of the cool assurance so requisite in the profession, and determined to improve the opportunity, to make his "learned friend" of the bench feel the sting he had so often inflicted. Accordingly, when his Honor took the stand, the counsel gravely inquired his name, occupation, place of residence, and sundry other facts of his personal history — though all were as familiar to himself and every one present as the old church, or main street of their native town. The queries were put in a voice and with a manner so exactly imitated from that of the judge himself, as to convulse the audience with laughter; every unnecessary word the hampered witness used was reprimanded as "beyond the question;" he was continually adjured to "tell the truth, the whole truth, and nothing but the truth;" his expressions were captiously objected to; he was tantalized with repetitions and cross-questioning about the veriest trifles; and, finally, his tormentor, with a face of the utmost gravity, pretended to discover in the witness a levity of bearing, and equivocal replies, which called for a lecture on "the responsibility of an oath;" this was delivered with a pedantic solemnity, in words, accent, and gesture, so like one of his own addresses from the bench, that judge, jury, and spectators, burst forth into irresistible peals of laughter; and the subject of this clever retaliation lost all self-possession, grew red and pale by turns, fumed, and at last protested, until his young adversary wound up the farce, by a threat to commit him for contempt of court.

When Chief Justice Coleridge retired from the bench, his farewell address deeply affected the members of the bar present: "These are not your severest trials," said he, referring to the more familiar difficulties of the profession; "they are those which are most insidious;

which beset you in the ordinary path of your daily duty; those which spring from the excitement of contest, from the love of intellectual display, and even from an exaggerated sense of duty to your clients. Gentlemen, — especially my younger friends, — suffer me, without offence, to put you on your guard against these. We can well afford to bear traditional pleasantries upon us from without, but we cannot afford that, underlying these, there should exist among thoughtful persons a feeling that our professional standard of honor is questionable, — that we, as advocates, will say and do in court what we, as gentlemen, would scorn to do in the common walks of life. Sometimes, I confess, it seems to me that we lend support to such a feeling by the lightness with which we impute ungenerous conduct or practices to each other. Surely no case is so sacred, no client so dear, that ever an advocate should be called upon to barter his own self-respect. If that be our duty, our great and glorious profession is no calling for a gentleman."

The relation of law to poetry is proverbially antagonistic; and the attempt to bind imagination to technicalities has usually proved a hopeless experiment; and yet it is curious to note how many of the brotherhood of song were originally destined for this profession, and how similar their confessions are, of a struggle, a compromise, and finally, an abandonment of jurisprudence for the sake of the Muses. Ovid, Petrarch, Tasso, Milton, Cowper, Ariosto, and others, are examples; Scott was faithful awhile to a branch of the law; Blackstone's only known poem is a "Farewell to the Muse;" Marshall and Story wooed the Nine, in their youth; Talfourd deemed it requisite to declare, in the preface to

"Ion," that he "left no duty for this idle trade," and Procter only weaves a song in the intervals of his stern task as a Commissioner of Lunacy. With philosophy the law is more congenial: Bacon and Mackintosh are illustrious examples of their united pursuit. Sir Thomas More wrote verses on the wall of his prison with a coal, and Addison compliments Somers on his poetry in his dedication of the "Campaign." Lord Mansfield's name appears in history a successful competitor for the Oxford prize poem. Lyndhurst and Denham were given to rhyme, and Sir William Jones is popularly known by his nervous lines on "What constitutes a State." Lord Jeffrey is one of the most characteristic modern examples of the union of legal and literary success, — his taste of the latter kind having, with the aid of a felicitous style, made him the most famous reviewer of his day, while the mental traits of the advocate unfitted him to appreciate the ideal, as they rendered him expert and brilliant in the discussion of rhetoric, facts, and philosophy.

Its connection with the most adventurous and tragic realities of life often brings law into the sphere of the dramatic and imaginative. Popular fiction has found in its annals all the material for profound human interest and artistic effect. Scott's most pathetic tale, the "Heart of Mid-Lothian," "Ten Thousand a-Year," and "Bleak House," are memorable examples. The trials of Russell, Strafford, Vane, and other noble prisoners charged with high treason, have furnished both plot and incidents for popular novelists. Uriah Heep, Oily Gammon, and Gilbert Glossin, are familiar types of legal villainy. Thackeray's best work, artistically speaking,— "Henry Esmond," — is largely indebted to the State

Trials of Queen Anne's time for its material. Have you ever seen Portia enacted by a woman of genius? Then has the romance of law been impersonated forever to your mind. That demoniac plaintiff, so memorably represented by Kean, with his haunting expression and voice, — the noble wife of Bassanio, uttering, in tones of musical entreaty, her immortal plea for Mercy, and, when it failed to touch the Jew's heart of adamant, cleaving his hope of vengeance by a subtle evasion, — the joy of Antonio, the fiat of the judge, the merry reunion and gay bridal talk at Belmont that night, whose moonlit gladness lives forever in the page of Shakspeare; — Queen Katherine's defence, and Othello's argument before their judges, equally show how effective is a tribunal under the hand of the poet of Nature; and every barrister of long experience can relate episodes in his career "stranger than fiction."

Although one would naturally turn to the State Trials, *Causes Célèbres*, "Memoirs of Vidocq," and similar works, for the dramatic materials developed by process of law, yet, to the initiated, there is an equal fund of interest in those researches of the profession which appear to deal only with technicalities. How many effective situations have playwrights, and such observers of human nature as Hogarth, drawn from, or grouped around the formal act of making or reading a Will! There is positive romance in the task of the Conveyancer, when he traces the title of an estate far back through the ramifications of family history, often bringing to light the most curious historical facts and remarkable personal incidents. Questions of property, of heirship, of fraud, and of divorce, involve manifold relative facts, that only require the sequence and arrangement of literary art, to make them dramas. Perhaps no field of character has yielded types as memorable to the writers of modern fiction as that of the Law. Think of Balzac's diagnosis of the French statutes regulating burial and marriage settlements, in his psychological Tales; of Brass, Tulkinghorn, and Peyton. Libel cases vie with police reports in unveiling the tragedy and comedy of life. That a trial involves scope for the broadest humor, or the most facetious invention, is evident from the Moot Court having become a permanent form of public entertainment in London.

No profession affords better opportunities for the study of human nature; indeed, an acute insight of motives is a prerequisite of success; but unfortunately it is the dark side of character, the selfish instincts, that are most frequently displayed in litigation, and hence the exclusive recognition of these which many a practised lawyer manifests. In its ideal phase, among the noblest — in its possible actuality, among the lowest — of human pursuits, we can scarcely wonder that popular sentiment and literature exhibit such apparently irreconcilable estimates of its value and tendencies. English lawyers of the first class are scholars and gentlemen. Classical knowledge and familiarity with standard modern literature are indispensable to their equipment; and such attainments are usually conducive to a humane and refined character. In the programme suggested by eminent lawyers, for a general training for the Bar, there is, however, an amusing diversity of opinion as to the best literary culture; one writer recommends the Bible, another Shakspeare, one English history, and another Joe Miller, as the best resource for apt quotation and discipline in the art of efficient rhetoric. Coke was remarkable for his citations from Virgil. But there is no doubt that general knowledge is an essential advantage to the lawyer, if he understand the rare art of using it with tact. The mere fact that the highest political distinction and official duty are open to the lawyer, ought to incline him to liberal studies and comprehensive acquaintance with literature, science, and philosophy.

How distinctly in social life the phases of the legal mind have become, is evident from such allusion as that of a Quarterly Reviewer, who, in a political discussion, remarks that "Mr. Percival was only a poorish *nisi prius* lawyer, and there is no kind of human being so disagreeable to the gross Tory nation;" while De Quincey, with that philosophic benignity which sometimes inspires his weird pen, observes that, "he had often thought that the influence of a portion of the acrid humors, which seem an element in the human mental constitution, being drained off, as it were, in forensic disputation, raised the lawyer above the average of mankind, in the qualities that give enjoyment to society."

The trial of Aaron Burr elicited the most characteristic eloquence of Clay and Wirt; that of Knapp, the tragic force of statement in which Webster excelled. Emmet's address to his judges has become a charter to his countrymen. Patrick Henry's remarkable powers of argument and appeal, which fanned the embers of Revolutionary zeal into a flame, originally exhibited themselves in a Virginia court-house. And, if eloquence has been justly described as existing "in the man, in the subject, and in the occasion," we can easily imagine why the legal profession affords it such frequent and extensive scope.

The intellectual process by which the advocate seeks

his ends is observable in the best conversation and writing. Almost all good talkers are essentially pleaders; they espouse, defend, illustrate, or maintain a question. Many of Lord Jeffrey's reviews are little else but special pleadings, and Macaulay's most brilliant articles are digests executed with taste and eloquence; the subject is first thoroughly explored, then its presentation systematized, and afterwards stated, argued, and summed up, after the manner of a charge or plea, with the addition of rhetorical graces inadmissible in a legal case. There is nothing, therefore, in the peculiar exercise of the faculties which renders law a profession apt to pervert second-rate minds; the evil lies in the predetermined side, the logic aforethought, — if we may so say, — the interested choice and dogmatical assumption of a certain view undertaken "for a consideration." "I know some barristers," observes Thackeray, "who mistake you and I for jury-boxes when they address us; but these are not your modest barristers, not your true gentlemen."

The special pleading and judicial complacency of Jeffrey — in other words his lawyer's mind — prevented his recognition of the highest and best poetical merit. It has been said of the conversation of his circle at Edinburgh, that it was, "in a very great measure, made up of brilliant disquisition, of sharp word-catching, ingenious thinking, and parrying of dialectics, and all the quips and quiddities of bar-pleading. It was the talk of a society to which lawyers and lecturers had, for at least a hundred years, given the tone." *

When from the advocate we pass to the bench, and from the feed barrister to the philosophical jurist, a new

* Lockhart's *Life of Scott.*

and majestic vista opens to the view. As in literature, two great divisions mark the legal character: there is the narrow but thoroughly informed practitioner, and the comprehensive judicial mind, — the first only distinguished within a limited bound of immediate utility and respectable adherence to precedent, and the other a pioneer in the realm of truth, a brave and original minister at the altar of justice. Lord Brougham, in his "Sketches of English Statesmen," has admirably indicated these two classes. To the former he says, "The precise dictates of English statutes, and the dictates of English judges and English text-writers, are the standard of justice. They are extremely suspicious of any enlarged or general views upon so serious a subject as law." The second and higher order of lawyers are well described in his portrait of Lord Grant, of whose charges he remarks: "Forth came a strain of clear, unbroken fluency, disposing, in the most luminous order, all the facts and all the arguments in the cause; reducing into clear and simple arrangement the most entangled masses of broken, conflicting statement; settling one doubt by a parenthetical remark, passing over another only more decisive that it was condensed; and giving out the whole impression of the case upon the judge's mind, — the material view, with argument enough to show why he so thought, and to prove him right, and without so much reasoning as to make you forget that it was a judgment you were hearing, and not a speech." Do we not often find, in literature and in life, counterparts of this picture of a judicial mind? Add to it discovery, and we have the legal philosopher; intrepid love of right, and we recognize the legal reformer. To this noble category belong such lawyers as

Mansfield and Marshall, Romilly, Erskine, and Webster. Genius for the bar is as varied, in its character, as that for poetry or art. In one man the gift is acuteness, in another felicity of language; here extraordinary perspicuity of statement, there singular ingenuity of argument. It is rhetoric, manner, force of purpose, a glamour that subdues, or a charm that wins; so that no precise rules, irrespective of individual endowments, can be laid down to secure forensic triumph. Doubtless, however, the union of a sympathetic temperament and an attractive manner with logical power and native eloquence form the ideal equipment of the pleader. Erskine seems to have combined these qualities in perfection, and to have woven a spell both for soul and sense. He magnetized, physically and intellectually, his audience. "Juries," says his biographer, "declared that they felt it impossible to remove their looks from him when he had riveted, and, as it were, fascinated them by his first glance; and it used to be a common remark of men who observed his motions, that they resembled those of a blood-horse."

The tendency to subterfuge in the less highly endowed, is but an incidental liability; in general, law-practice seems to harden and make sceptical the mind absorbed in its details. One can almost invariably detect the keen look of distrust or the smile of incredulity in the physiognomy of the barrister. Everything like sentiment, disinterestedness, and frank demonstration, is apt to be regarded without faith or sympathy. Most lawyers confess that they place no reliance on the statements of their clients. If you introduce a spiritual hypothesis or a practical view of any topic, it is treated by this class of men with ill-concealed scorn.

The habit of their minds is logical; they usually ignore and repudiate those instincts which experience seldom reveals to them, and observation of life in its coarser phases leads them to doubt and contemn. But, while thus less open to the gentler and more sacred sympathies, they often possess the distinction of manliness, of courage, and generosity. The very process which so exclusively develops the understanding, and makes their ideal of intellectual greatness to consist in aptitude, subtlety, and reasoning power, tends to give a certain vigor and alertness to the thinking faculty, and to emancipate it from morbid influences. One of Ben Jonson's characters thus defines the lawyer: —

> " I oft have heard him say how he admired
> Men of your law-profession, that could speak
> To every cause and things mere contraries,
> Till they were hoarse again, yet all be law.
> That, with most quick agility, could turn
> And return, make knots and undo them,
> Give forked counsel, take provoking gold
> On either hand, — and put it up."

And one of Balzac's characters says: — " Savez-vous, mon cher, qu'il existe dans notre société trois hommes: le prêtre, le médecin, et l'homme de justice, qui ne peuvent pas estimer le monde? Ils ont des robes noires, peut-être parce qu'ils portent le deuil de toutes les vertus, de toutes les illusions. *Le plus malheureux des trois est l'avoué.*" When the question at issue is purely utilitarian, and the interest discussed one of outward and practical relations, this legal training comes into eminent efficiency; in a word, it is applicable to affairs, but not to sentiment, to fact, but not to abstract truth. How evanescent is often a great lawyer's fame; often as intangible as that of a great vocalist or actor. Even their eloquence is now rare. Great lawyers are uniformly distrustful of rhetoric, and their power is based on knowledge. We learn from the son and biographer of Chief Justice Parsons that a special reason of his eminent superiority was that accident gave him early and undisturbed access to the best law library in America. It has been truly said, that the eloquence of the bar has become a tradition; "it is suspected as impugning sense and knowledge," and is opposed to the practical spirit of the age. Yet, the advocate, like the poet, is occasionally born, not made, notwithstanding the maxim *orator fit*. A mind fertile in expedients, warmed by a temperament which instinctively seizes upon, and, we had almost said, incarnates, a cause, is a phenomenon that sometimes renders law an inspiration instead of a dogma. Such a pleader lately lived in one of the Eastern States. Not only the grasp of his thought, but his elocution, announced that he had literally thrown himself into the case. It would be more strictly correct to say that he had absorbed it. The gesture, the eye, the tone of his voice, the quiver of the muscle, nay, each lock of his long steel-gray hair, that he tossed back from his dripping brow, in the excitement of his fluent harangue, seemed alive and overflowing with the rationale and the sentiment of the cause; his enthusiasm was real, however it may have originated; and, by identifying himself with his client, he espoused the argument as if it were vital to his own interest. Such instances, however, are exceptional; few are the lawyers thus constituted. Accepting their cases objectively, and maintaining them by formula, the usual effect is that which Burke describes in his character of Greville: "He was bred to the law, which is, in my opinion, one of the first and noblest of human sciences — a science which does more to quicken and invigorate the understanding than all other kinds of learning put together; but it is not apt, except in persons very happily born, to open and liberalize the mind exactly in the same proportion."

Why is the poet's function the noblest? Because it is inspired, not arbitrarily decreed by the will. Mental activity is grand and beautiful in proportion as it is disinterested; and it is on account of the almost inevitable forcing, by circumstances, of a lawyer's mind from the line of honest conviction into that of determined casuistry, that the moral objection to the pursuit is so often urged. "The indiscriminate defence of right and wrong," says Junius, "contracts the understanding while it corrupts the heart." Some men, in conversation, affect us as unreal. We attach no vital interest to what they say, because the mind appears to act wholly apart — the fusion of sense and feeling, which we call soul, is wanting; there is no conviction, no personal sentiment, no unselfish love of truth in what they say; and yet it may be intelligent, erudite, and void of positive falsity — still it is mechanical, the intellect is *used*, not *inspired*, willed to act, not moved thereto: this is the characteristic of legal training, unmodified by the higher sentiments; it makes intellectual machines, logical grist-mills, talkers by rote; the rational powers, from long slavery to temporary and interested aims, seem to have lost magnanimity; their spontaneous, genuine, and earnest action has yielded to a conventional and predetermined habit. Yet at the other extreme, we see the most lofty and permanent intellectual results. It has been justly said that the Code Napoleon is even now the sole embodiment of Lord Bacon's thought — "put them (the laws) into shape, inform them with philosophy, reduce them in bulk, give them into every man's hand. Laws are made to guard the rights of the people, not to feed the lawyers."

Whoever, in the freshness of youthful emotions, has been present at the tribunal of a free country, where the character of the judge, the integrity of the jury, and the learning and eloquence of the advocates have equalled the moral exigencies and the ideal dignity of the scene, and when the case has possessed a high tragic or social interest, can never lose the impression thus derived of the majesty of the law. No public scene of human life can surpass it to the apprehension of a thoughtful spectator. He seems to behold the principle of justice as it exists in the very elements of humanity, and to stand on the primeval foundation of civil society; the searching struggle for truth, the conscientious application of law to evidence, the stern recital of the prosecutor, the appeal of the defence, the constant test of inquiry, of reference to statutes and precedents, the luminous arrangement of conflicting facts by the judge, his impartial deductions and clear final statement, the interval of suspense and the solemn verdict, combine to present a calm, reflective, almost sublime exercise of the intellect and moral sentiments, in order to conform authority to their highest dictates, which elevates and widens the function and the glory of human life and duty. Compare, with such a picture, the base mockery of justice exhibited by the Inquisition of old, and an Austrian court-martial of our own day; the arbitrary fiat of an Eastern official, and the murderous ordeal of the provisional bodies that ruled during the first French revolution, and it is easy to appreciate the identity of justly-administered law with civilization and freedom. "Justice," says Webster, "is the great interest of man on earth. It is the ligament which holds civilized beings and civilized nations together. Wherever her temple stands, and as long as it is duly honored, there is a foundation for social security, general happiness, and the improvement and progress of our race. And whoever labors on this edifice, with usefulness and distinction, whoever clears its foundations, strengthens its pillars, adorns its entablatures, or contributes to raise its august dome still higher in the skies, connects himself, in name and fame and character, with that which is, and must be, as durable as the frame of human society."

SEPULCHRES.

"The hills,
Rock-ribbed and ancient as the sun; the vales,
Stretching in pensive quietness between;
The venerable woods; rivers that move
In majesty, and the complaining brooks
That make the meadow green; and poured round all
Old ocean's gray and melancholy waste,
Are but the solemn decorations all
Of the great tomb of man." — BRYANT.

HE comparatively recent and widely diffused interest in the establishment of rural cemeteries in this country is an auspicious reaction of popular feeling. Never did a Christian nation manifest so little conservative and exalted sentiment, apart from its direct religious scope, as our own. This patent defect is owing, in a measure, to the absence of the venerable, the time-hallowed, and the contemplative in the scenes and the life of our country; it is, however, confirmed by the busy competition, the hurried, experimental, and ambitious spirit of the people. Local change is the rule, not the exception; scorn of wise delay, moderation, and philosophic content, the prevalent feeling; impatience, temerity, and self-confidence, the characteristic impulse; houses are locomotive, church edifices turned into post-offices, and even theatres; ancestral domains are bartered away in the second generation; old trees bow to the axe; the very sea is encroached upon, and landmarks are removed almost as soon as they grow familiar; change, which is the life

of Nature, seems to be regarded as not less the vital element of what is called local improvement and prosperity; the future is almost exclusively regarded, and the past contemned.

If a man cites the precedents of experience, he is sneered at as a "fogy"; if he has a competence, he risks it in speculation; newspapers usurp the attention once given to standard lore; the picturesque rocks of the rural wayside are defiled by quack advertisements, the arcana of spirituality degraded by legerdemain, the dignity of reputation sullied by partisan brutality, the graces of social refinement abrogated by a mercenary standard, the lofty aims of science levelled by charlatan tricks, and independence of character sacrificed to debasing conformity; observation is lost in locomotion, thought in action, ideality in materialism. Against this perversion of life, the sanctity of death protests, often vainly, to the general mind, but not ineffectually to the individual heart.

When it was attempted to secure the collection of Egyptian antiquities brought hither by Dr. Abbott of Cairo, for a future scientific museum to be established in New York, the representatives commercial, professional, and speculative of "Young America" scorned the bare idea of exchanging gold for mummies, sepulchral lamps, papyrus, and ancient utensils and inscriptions; yet, within a twelvemonth, a celebrated German philologist, a native biblical scholar, and a lecturer on the History of Art, eagerly availed themselves of these contemned relics to prove and illustrate their respective subjects; and the enlightened of Gotham's utilitarian citizens acknowledged that the trophies of the past were essential to elucidate and confirm the wisdom of the present. It is this idolatry of the immediate which stultifies republican perception. Offer a manuscript to a publisher, and he instantly inquires if it relates to the questions of the day; if not, it is almost certain to be rejected without examination. The conservative element of social life is merged in gregarious intercourse; the youth looks not up to age; the maiden's susceptibilities are hardened by premature and promiscuous association; external success is glorified, private consistency unhonored; art becomes a trade, literature an expedient, reform fanaticism; aspiration is chilled, romance outgrown, life unappreciated; and all because the vista of departed time is cut off from our theory of moral perspective, and existence itself is regarded merely as an opportunity for instant and outward success, not a link in an eternal chain reaching "before and after."

Sentiment is the great conservative principle of society; those instincts of patriotism, local attachment, family affection, human sympathy, reverence for truth, age, valor, and wisdom, so often alive and conscious in the child and overlaid or perverted in the man, — for the culture of which our educational systems, habitual vocations, domestic and social life, make so little provision, — are, in the last analysis, the elements of whatever is noble, efficient, and individual in character; in every moral crisis we appeal to them, as the channels whereby we are linked to God and humanity, and through which alone we can realize just views or lawful action. In our normal condition they may not be often exhibited; yet none the less they constitute the latent force of civil society. To depend upon intelligence and will is, indeed, the creed of the age, and especially of this republic; but these powers, when unhallowed by the primal and better instincts, react and fail of their end. It is so in individual experience and in national affairs. The absence of the sentiments which the pride of intellect and the brutality of self-will thus repudiate, is the occasion of our greatest errors; to them is the final appeal, through them the only safety; and their violation was the precursor of base and bloody treason; their vindication but the renewal through sacrifice of a normal and vital interest of human society. The war for the Union has been expiatory not less than patriotic. And the great lesson taught by these and similar errors is, that the life, the spirit, the faith of the country had, by a long course of national prosperity and a blind worship of outward success, become gradually but inevitably material; so that motives of patriotism, of reverence, of courtesy, of generous sympathy, — in a word, the sentiments as distinguished from the passions and the will, had ceased to be recognized as legitimate, and the reliable springs of action and guides of life. It was the repudiation of these which horrified Burke at the outbreak of the French Revolution; he augured the worst from that event, at the best hour of its triumph, because it stripped Humanity of her divine attribute of sentiment, and left her to shiver naked in the cold light of reason and will, unredeemed by the sense of justice, of beauty, of compassion, of honorable pride, which under the name of Chivalry, he lamented as extinct. He spoke and felt as a man whose brain was kindled by his heart, and whose heart retained the pure impulse of these sacred instincts and knew their value as the medium of all truth and the basis of civil order. They were temporarily quenched in France by the frenzy of want; they are inactive and in abeyance here, through the gross pressure of material prosperity and mercenary ambition. Hence whatever effectively appeals to them, and whoever sincerely recognizes them, whether by example or precept, in a life or a poem, through art or rhetoric, in respect for the past, love of nature, or devotion to truth and beauty, excites our cordial sympathy. In this age and land, no man is a greater benefactor than he who scorns the worldly and narrow philosophy of life which degrades to a material, unaspiring level the tone of mind and the tendency of the affections. If he invent a character, lay out a domain, erect a statue, weave a stanza, write a paragraph, utter a word, or chant a melody which stirs in any breast the love of the beautiful, admiration for the heroic, or the chastening sense of awe, — any sentiment, in truth, which partakes of disinterestedness, and merges self "in an idea dearer than self," — uplifts, expands, fortifies, intensifies, and therefore inspires, — he is essentially and absolutely a benefactor to society, a genuine though perhaps unrecognized champion of what is "highest in man's nature" against what is "lowest in man's destiny." And not the least because the most universal of these higher and holier feelings is the sentiment of Death, consecrating its symbols, guarding its relics, and keeping fresh and sacred its memories.

The disposition of the mortal remains was and is, to a considerable extent, in England, an ecclesiastical function; in Catholic lands it is a priestly interest. Indignity to the body, after death, was one of the most dreaded punishments of heresy and crime; to scatter human ashes to the winds, expose the skulls of malefactors in iron gratings over city portals, refuse interment in ground consecrated by the Church, and disinter and insult the body of an unpopular ruler, were among the barbarous reprisals of offended power. And yet, in these same twilight eras, in the heathen customs and the mediæval laws, under the sway of Odin and the Franks, the sentiment of respect for the dead was acted upon in a manner to shame the indifference and hardihood of later and more civilized times. With the emigration to America, this sentiment looked for its legal vindication entirely to the civic authority. With their reaction from spiritual tyranny, our ancestors transferred this, with other social interests, to popular legislation and private inclination. Hence the compar atively indefinite enactments on the subject, and the need of a uniform code, applicable to all the States, and organized so as clearly to establish the rights both of the living and the dead, and to preserve inviolable the choice of disposition, and the place of deposit, of human remains.

The practical treatment of this subject is anomalous. Amid the scenes of horror, outraging humanity in every form, which characterized the anarchy incident to the first dethronement of legitimate authority in France, how startling to read, among the first decrees of the Convention, provisions for the dead, while pitiless destruction awaited the living! And in this country, while motives of hygiene limit intermural interments, and a higher impulse sets apart and adorns rural cemeteries, our rail-tracks, still often ruthlessly intersect the fields of the dead, and ancestral tombs are annually broken up to make way for streets and warehouses. The tomb of Washington was long dilapidated; the bones of Revolutionary martyrs are neglected, and half the graveyards of the country desecrated by indifference or misuse. The conservative piety of the Hebrews reproaches our inconsiderate neglect, in the faithfully tended cemetery of their race at Newport, R. I., where not a Jew remains to guard the ashes of his fathers, thus carefully preserved by a testamentary fund. Of late years elaborate monuments in rural cemeteries have done much to redeem this once proverbial neglect. They constitute the most sacred adornment of the environs of our principal cities.

Both the modes and places of burial have an historical significance. The pyre of the Greeks and Romans, the embalming process of the Egyptians, the funeral piles of Hindoo superstition, and those bark stagings, curiously regarded by Mississippi voyagers, where Indian corpses are exposed to the elements, — the old cross-road interment of the suicide, — the inhumation of the early patriarchs and Christians, — all symbolize eras and creeds. The lying-in-state of the royal defunct, the sable catafalque of the Catholic temples, the salutes over the warrior's grave, the "Day of the Dead" celebrated in Southern Europe, the eulogies in French cemeteries, the sublime ritual of the Establishment, and the silent prayer of the Friends, requiems, processions, emblems, inscriptions, badges, and funereal garlands mark faith, nation, rank, and profession at the very gates of the sepulchre. Vain is the sceptic's sneer, useless the utilitarian's protest; by these poor tributes the heart utters its undying regret and its immortal prophecies, though "mummy has become merchandise," and to be "but pyramidically extant is a fallacy in duration"; for, as the same religious philosopher * of Norwich declared, "it is the heaviest stone that melan-

* Sir T. Browne.

choly can throw at a man, to tell him he is at the end of his nature"; and therefore, in the grim Tuscan's Hell, the souls of those who denied their immortality when in the flesh, are shut up through eternity in living tombs. How the idea of a local abode for the mortal remains is hallowed to our nature, is realized in the pathos which closes the noble and sacred life of the Hebrew lawgiver: "And he buried him in a valley of the land of Moab, over against Beth-peor; but no man knoweth of his selpuchre unto this day."* Etruria's best relics are sepulchral urns; social distinctions are as obvious in the tombs of the ancients as in their palaces: witness the Columbarium in ruins and the fresh pit of the plebeians, the sandy isles of the Venetian cemetery, and Pompeii's street of tombs. Byron thought "*Implora pace*" the most affecting of epitaphs; and the visitor at Coppet recognizes a melancholy appropriateness in the garden-grave of its gifted mistress.

Natural, therefore, and human is the consoling thought of the poet, of the ship bringing home for burial all of earth that remains of his lamented friend: —

> "I hear the noise about thy keel;
> I hear the bell struck in the night;
> I see the cabin-window bright;
> I see the sailor at the wheel.
>
> "Thou bringest the sailor to his wife,
> And travelled men from foreign lands;
> And letters unto trembling hands;
> And thy dark freight, a vanished life.
>
> "So bring him: we have idle dreams:
> This look of quiet flatters thus
> Our home-bred fancies; O, to us,
> The fools of habit, sweeter seems

* Deut. xxxiv. 6.

14

'To rest beneath the clover sod,
That takes the sunshine and the rains,
Or where the kneeling hamlet drains
The chalice of the grapes of God,

"Than if with thee the roaring wells
Should gulf him fathom deep in brine;
And hands so often clasped in mine
Should toss with tangle and with shells." *

Doubtless many of the processes adopted by blind affection and superstitious homage, to rescue the poor human casket from destruction, are grotesque and undesirable. Had Segato, the discoverer of a chemical method of petrifying flesh, survived to publish the secret, it would be chiefly for anatomical purposes that we should appreciate his invention; there is something revolting in the artificial conservation of what, by the law of Nature, should undergo elemental dissolution; and it is but a senseless homage to cling to the shattered chrysalis when the winged embryo has soared away:

"All' ombra de' cipressi e dentro l'urne
Confortate di pianto, è forse il sonno
Della morte men duro?" †

Nature sometimes is a conservative mother even of mortal lineaments; in glacier or tarn, in *tuffo* and limestone fossils, she keeps for ages the entire relics of humanity. The fantastic array of human bones in the Capuchin cells at Palermo and Rome; the eyeless, shrunken face of Carlo Borromeo embedded in crystal, jewels, and silk, beneath the Milan cathedral; the fleshless figure of old Jeremy Bentham in the raiment of this working-day world; the thousand spicy wrappings

* Tennyson's *In Memoriam.*

† *Dei Sepolchri,* di Ugo Foscolo.

which enfold the exhumed mummy whose exhibition provoked Horace Smith's facetious rhymes, — these, and such as these, poor attempts to do vain honor to our clay, are not less repugnant to the sentiment of death, in its religious and enlightened manifestation, than the promiscuous and careless putting out of sight of the dead after battle and in the reign of pestilence, or the brutal and irreverent disposal of the bodies of the poor in the diurnal pits of the Naples Campo Santo. More accordant with our sense of respect to what once enshrined an immortal spirit, and stood erect and free, even in barbaric manhood, is the adjuration of the bard: —

> " Gather him to his grave again,
> And solemnly and softly lay,
> Beneath the verdure of the plain,
> The warrior's scattered bones away;
> The soul hath quickened every part, —
> That remnant of a martial brow,
> Those ribs that held the mighty heart,
> That strong arm, — strong no longer now!
> Spare them, each mouldering relic spare,
> Of God's own image; let them rest,
> Till not a trace shall speak of where
> The awful likeness was impressed."

Yet there are many and judicious reasons for preferring cremation to inhumation; the prejudice against the former having doubtless originated among the early Christians, in their respect for patriarchal entombment, practised by the Jews, and their natural horror at any custom which savored of heathenism. But there is actually no religious obstacle, and, under proper arrangement, no public inconvenience, in the burning of the dead. It is, too, a process which singularly attracts those who would save the remains of those they love from the possibility of desecration, and anticipate the ultimate fate of the mortal coil "to mix forever with the elements"; at all events, there can be no rational objection to the exercise of private taste, and the gratification of personal feeling on this point. "I bequeath my soul to God," said Michael Angelo, in his terse will, "my body to the earth, and my possessions to my nearest kin"; — and this right to dispose of one's mortal remains appears to be instinctive; though the indignation excited by any departure from custom would indicate that, in popular apprehension, the privilege so rarely exercised is illegally usurped.

The outcry in a Western town, a few years ago, when cremation was resorted to, at the earnest desire of a deceased wife, and the offence taken and expressed in an Eastern city, when it became known that a distinguished surgeon, from respect to science, had bequeathed his skeleton to a medical college, evidence how little, among us, is recognized the right of the living to dispose of their remains, and the extent to which popular ignorance and individual prejudice are allowed to interfere in what good sense and good feeling declare an especial matter of private concern. Yet that other than the ordinary modes of disposing of human relics are not absolutely repugnant to endearing associations, may be inferred from the poetic interest which sanctions to the imagination the obsequies of Shelley. Although it was from convenience that the body of that ideal bard, so misunderstood, so humane, so "cradled into poesy by wrong," was burned, yet the lover of his spiritual muse beholds in that lonely pyre, blazing on the shores of the Mediterranean, an elemental destruction of the material shrine of a lofty and loving soul, accordant with his aspiring, isolated, and imaginative career.*

Vain, indeed, have proved the studious precautions of Egyptians to conserve from decay and sacrilege the relics of their dead. Not only has "mummy become merchandise," in the limited sense of the English moralist; the traffic of the Jews in their gums and spices, the distribution of their exhumed forms in museums, and the use of their cases for fuel, is now superseded by commerce in their cerements for the manufacture of paper; and it is a startling evidence of that human vicissitude from which even the shrouds of ancient kings are not exempt, that recently, in one of the new towns of this continent, a newspaper was printed on sheets made from the imported rags of Egyptian mummies.

Of primitive and casual landmarks, encountered on solitary moors and hills, the cairn and the Alpine cross affect the imagination with a sense alike of mortality and tributary sentiment, even more vividly than the elaborate mausoleum, from the rude expedients and the solemn isolation; while the beauty of cathedral archi-

* A recent advocate for cremation thus suggests the process: "On a gentle eminence, surrounded by pleasant grounds, stands a convenient, well-ventilated chapel, with a high spire or steeple. At the entrance, where some of the mourners might prefer to take leave of the body, are chambers for their accommodation. Within the edifice are seats for those who follow the remains to the last; there is also an organ and a gallery for choristers. In the centre of the chapel, embellished with appropriate emblems and devices, is erected a shrine of marble, somewhat like those which cover the ashes of the great and mighty in our old cathedrals, the openings being filled with prepared glass. Within this — a sufficient space intervening — is an inner shrine, covered with bright, non-radiating metal, and within this again is a covered sarcophagus of tempered fire-clay, with one or more longitudinal slits near the top, extending its whole length. As soon as the body is

tecture is hallowed by ancestral monuments. Of all Scott's characters, the one that most deeply enlists our sympathies, through that quaint pathos whereby the Past is made eloquent both to fancy and affection, is Old Mortality renewing the half-obliterated inscriptions on the gravestones of the Covenanters, his white hair fluttering in the wind as he stoops to his melancholy task, and his aged pony feeding on the grassy mounds. Even our practical Franklin seized the first leisure from patriotic duties, on his visit to England, in order to examine the sepulchral tablets which bear the names of his progenitors.

A cursory glance at the most cherished trophies of literature indicates how deeply the sentiment of death is wrought into the mind and imagination, — how it invests with awe, love, pity, and hope, thoughtful and gifted spirits, inspires their art, elevates their conceptions, and casts over life and consciousness a sacred mystery. The most finished and suggestive piece of modern English verse is elegiac, — its theme a country churchyard, and so instinct are its melancholy numbers with pathos and reflection, embalmed in rhythmical music, that its lines have passed into household words. Our national poet, who has sung of Nature in all her

deposited therein, sheets of flame at an immensely high temperature, rush through the long apertures from end to end; and acting as a combination of a modified oxyhydrogen blow-pipe, with the reverberatory furnace, utterly and completely consume and decompose the body in an incredibly short space of time; even the large quantity of water it contains is decomposed by the extreme heat, and its elements, instead of retarding, aid combustion, as is the case in fierce conflagrations. The gaseous products of combustion are conveyed away by flues, and means being adopted to consume anything like smoke, all that is observed from the outside is occasionally a quivering transparent ether floating away from the high steeple to mingle with the atmosphere."

characteristic phases on this continent, next to those ever-renewed glories of the universe has found his chief inspiration in the same reverent contemplation: "Thanatopsis" was his first grand offering to the Muses, and "The Disinterred Warrior," the "Hymn to Death," and "The Old Man's Funeral," are but pious variations of a strain worthy to be chanted in the temple of humanity. Shakspeare in no instance comes nearer what is highest in our common nature and miraculous in our experience, than when he makes the philosophic Dane question his soul and confront mortality. The once popular and ever-memorable "Night Thoughts" of Young elaborate kindred ideas in the light of Christian truth; the most quaintly eloquent of early speculative writings in English prose is Sir Thomas Browne's treatise on Urn-Burial. The most thoughtful and earnest of modern Italian poems is Foscolo's "Sepolchri;" the Monody on Sir John Moore, Shelley's Elegy on Keats, Tickell's on Addison, Byron's on Sheridan, and Tennyson's "In Memoriam," contain the most sincere and harmonious utterances of their authors. Not the least affecting pages of "The Sketch Book" are those which describe the "Village Funeral" and the "Widow's Son"; and the endeared author has marked his own sense of the local sanctity of the grave by selecting that of his family in "Sleepy Hollow," in the midst of scenes endeared by his abode and his fame. Halleck has given lyrical immortality to the warrior's death in the cause of freedom; and Wordsworth, in perhaps his most quoted ballad, has recorded with exquisite simplicity childhood's unconsciousness of death; even the most analytical of French novelists found in the laws and ceremonial of a Parisian interment, material for his keenest diagnosis of the scenes of life in that marvellous capital. Hope's best descriptive powers were enlisted in his sketch of burial-places near Constantinople, so pensively contrasting with the more adventurous chapters of Anastasius. If in popular literature this sentiment is so constantly appealed to, and so enshrined in the poet's dream and the philosopher's speculation, classic and Hebrew authors have inscribed its memorials in outlines of majestic and graceful import; around it the picturesque and the moralizing, the vivacious and the grandly simple expressions of the Roman, the Greek, and the Jewish writers seem to hover with the significant plaint, — heroism or faith, — which invokes us, with the voice of ages, to

> "Pay the deep reverence taught of old,
> The homage of man's heart to death;
> Nor dare to trifle with the mould
> Once hallowed by the Almighty's breath."

Perhaps there is no instance of this vague and awful interest more memorable to the American than when he reads, on some ancient tablet in the Old World, the burial record of his ancestors.

The monitory and reminiscent influence of the churchyard, apart from all personal associations, cannot, indeed, be over-estimated; doubtless in a spirit of propriety and good taste, it is now more frequently suburban, made attractive by trees, flowers, a wide landscape, and rural peace, and rendered comparatively safe from desecration by distance from the so-called march of improvement, which annually changes the aspect of our growing towns. Yet, wherever situated, the homes of the dead, when made eloquent by art, and kept fresh by reverent care, breathe a chastening and holy lesson, perhaps the more impressive when uttered beside the teeming camp of life. To the traveller in Europe it is a pathetic sight to watch the Norwegian peasants strew flowers, every Sabbath, on the graves of their kindred, and gives a living interest to the memorials of Scandinavian antiquity gathered in the museums, whereby, through the weapons and drinking-cups of stone, bronze, and iron, exhumed from graves, he traces the origin and growth of that remote civilization. And when time has softened the most acute and bitter memories of the War for the Union, what monument to individual prowess, what trophy of patriotic self-sacrifice will compare, in solemn and elevating pathos, with the impression derived from the "national cemeteries" of the battle-field and the hospital? As Lincoln said of Gettysburg, — "they will dedicate us afresh to our country, to humanity, and to God."

When the traveller gazes on the marble effigy of the warrior at Ravenna, and then treads the plain where Gaston de Foix fell in battle, the fixed lineaments and obsolete armor bring home to his mind the very life of the Middle Ages, solemnized by youthful heroism and early death; when he scans the vast city beneath its smoky veil, — thick with roofs and dotted with spires,— from an elevated point of Père la Chaise, the humble and garlanded cross, and the chiselled names of the wise and brave that surround him, cause the parallel and inwoven mysteries of life and death to stir the fountains of his heart with awe, and make his lips tremble into prayer; and, familiar as is the spectacle, the more thoughtful of the throng in New York's bustling thoroughfare will sometimes pause and cast a salutary glance from the hurrying crowd to the monuments of the heroic Lawrence, the eloquent Emmet, the gallant Montgomery, and the patriotic Hamilton. Those associations which form at once the culture and the romance of travel are identified with the same eternal sentiment. Next in interest to the monuments of genius and character are those of death; or rather, the inspiration of the former are everywhere consecrated by the latter.

"Take the wings
Of morning, and the Barcan desert pierce,
Or lose thyself in the continuous woods
Where rolls the Oregon, and hears no sound
Save his own dashings, — yet the dead are there!"

Nero dug his own grave, lest he should be denied burial, and Shakspeare guarded his own ashes by an imprecatory epitaph; David praises the men of Jabez Gilead who rescue the bones of their king from the enemy. It is a sweet custom, — that of making little excavations in sepulchral slabs to catch the rain, that birds may be lured thither to drink and sing. The Chinese sell themselves in order to obtain means to bury their parents.

We enter a city of antiquity — memorable Syracuse or disinterred Pompeii — through a street of tombs; the majestic relics of Egyptian civilization are the cenotaphs of kings; the Escurial is Spain's architectural elegy; Abelard's philosophy is superseded, but his love and death live daily to the vision of the mourners who go from the gay capital of France, to place chaplets on the graves of departed friends; * the grandeurs of West-

* "How can we reconcile this pious and faithful remembrance with the character of a nation generally thought so frivolous and inconstant? Let this amiable, affectionate, but slandered people send the stranger and the traveller to this place. These carefully tended flowers, these tombs, will speak their defence." — *Memoir of Harriet Preble*, p. 70.

minster Abbey are sublimated by the effigies of bards and statesmen, and the rare music of St. George's choir made solemn by the dust of royalty; deserted Ravenna is peopled with intense life by the creations of Dante which haunt his sepulchre; Arqua is the shrine of affectionate pilgrims; the radiant hues and graceful shapes of Titian and Canova become ethereal to the fancy, when viewed beside their monuments; St. Peter's is but a magnificent apostolic tomb; and the shadow of mortality is incarnated in Lorenzo's brooding figure in the jewelled temple of the dead Medici. Even the dim, half-explored catacombs of Rome yield significant testimony to the Christian's heart to-day. "The works of painting found within them," well says a recent writer, "their construction, the inscriptions on the graves, — all unite in bearing witness to the simplicity of the faith, the purity of the doctrine, the strength of the feeling, the change in the lives of the vast mass of the members of the early Church of Christ." *

What resorts are Santa Croce, Mount Vernon, Saint Paul's, and Saint Onofrio! What a goal, through ages, the Holy Sepulchre! How the dim escutcheons sanctify cathedrals, and sunken headstones the rural cemetery! How sacred the mystery of the Campagna hid in that "stern round tower of other days," which bears the name of a Roman matron! The beautiful sarcophagus of Scipio, the feudal crypt of Theodric, the silent soldier of the Invalides, the mossy cone of Caius Cæstus, in whose shadow two English poets † yet speak in grace-

* *Atlantic Monthly*, vol. ii. p. 139.

† "I am now engaged," wrote Mr. Severn, the artist-friend who watched over Keats in his last hours, "on a picture of the poet's grave. The classical story of 'Endymion' being the subject of his principal

ful epitaphs, Thorwaldsen's grand mausoleum at Copenhagen, composed of his own trophies, — what objects are these to win the mind back into the lapsing ages and upward with "immortal longings"! We turn from brilliant thoroughfares, alive with creatures of a day, to catacombs obscure with the impalpable dust of bygone generations; we pass from the vociferous piazza to the hushed and frescoed cloister, and walk on mural tablets whose inscriptions are worn by the feet of vanished multitudes; we steal from the cheerful highway to the field of mounds, where a shaft, a cross, or a garland breathes of surviving tenderness; we handle the cloudy lachrymal, quaint depository of long-evaporated tears, or admire the sculptured urn, the casket of what was unutterably precious, even in mortality; and thereby life is solemnized, consciousness deepened, and we feel, above the tyrannous present, and through the casual occupation of the hour, the "electric chain wherewith we 're darkly bound." "When I look upon the tombs of the great," says Addison, "every emotion of envy dies in me; when I read the epitaphs of the beautiful, every inordinate desire goes out; when I meet with the grief of parents upon a tombstone, my heart melts with compassion; when I see the tombs of the parents themselves, I consider the vanity of grieving for those whom we must quickly follow. When I see kings lying by those who deposed them, when I consider rival wits placed side by side, or the holy men that divided the

poem, I have introduced a young shepherd sleeping against the headstone, with his flock about him; while the moon from behind the pyramid illuminates his figure, and serves to realize the poet's favorite theme, in the presence of his grave. This interesting incident is not fanciful, but is what I actually saw, one autumn evening, at Monte Tertanio, the year following the poet's death."

world with their contests and disputes, I reflect with sorrow and astonishment on the little competitions, fractions, and debates of mankind. When I read the several dates of the tombs, of some that died yesterday, and some six hundred years ago, I consider that great day when we shall all of us be contemporaries, and make our appearance together." Thus perpetual is the hymn of death, thus ubiquitous its memorials, — attesting not only an inevitable destiny, but a universal sentiment; under whatever name, — God's Acre, Pantheon, Campo Santo, Valhalla, Potter's Field, Greenwood, or Mount Auburn, — the last resting-place of the body, the last earthly shrine of human love, fame, and sorrow, claims — by the pious instinct which originates, the holy rites which consecrate, the blessed hopes which glorify it — respect, protection, and sanctity.

There is, indeed, no spot of earth so hallowed to the contemplative as that which holds the ashes of an intellectual benefactor. What a grateful tribute does the transatlantic pilgrim instinctively offer at the sepulchre of Roscoe at Liverpool, of Lafayette in France, of Berkeley at Oxford, of Burns at Alloway Kirk, and of Keats and Goldsmith, — of all the bards, philosophers, and reformers whose conceptions warmed and exalted his dawning intelligence, and became thereby sacred to his memory forever! How fruitful the hours—snatched from less serene pleasure — devoted to Stratford, Melrose, and the Abbey! To realize the value of these opportunities, the spirit of humanity enshrined in such "Meccas of the mind," we must fancy the barrenness of earth stripped of these landmarks of the gifted and the lost. How denuded of its most tender light would be Olney, Stoke Pogis, the vale of Florence, the cypress groves of Rome, and the park at Weimar, unconsecrated by the sepulchres of Cowper and Gray, Michael Angelo, Tasso, and Schiller, whose sweet and lofty remembrance links meadow and stream, mountain and sunset, with the thought of all that is most pensive, beautiful, and sublime in genius and in woe.

ACTORS.

"All the world 's a stage,
And all the men and women merely players."
HAMLET.

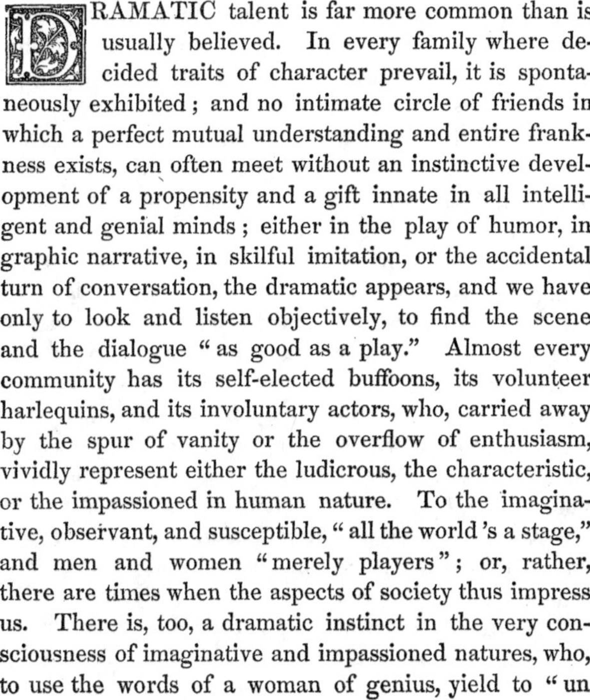

DRAMATIC talent is far more common than is usually believed. In every family where decided traits of character prevail, it is spontaneously exhibited; and no intimate circle of friends in which a perfect mutual understanding and entire frankness exists, can often meet without an instinctive development of a propensity and a gift innate in all intelligent and genial minds; either in the play of humor, in graphic narrative, in skilful imitation, or the accidental turn of conversation, the dramatic appears, and we have only to look and listen objectively, to find the scene and the dialogue "as good as a play." Almost every community has its self-elected buffoons, its volunteer harlequins, and its involuntary actors, who, carried away by the spur of vanity or the overflow of enthusiasm, vividly represent either the ludicrous, the characteristic, or the impassioned in human nature. To the imaginative, observant, and susceptible, "all the world 's a stage," and men and women "merely players"; or, rather, there are times when the aspects of society thus impress us. There is, too, a dramatic instinct in the very consciousness of imaginative and impassioned natures, who, to use the words of a woman of genius, yield to "un besoin inné qu'elles éprouvent de dramatiser leur existence à leurs propres yeux." A national dramatic language has ever been recognized in the responsive vivacity of the Italian manners, the theatrical bearing of the French, and the proud reticence of the Spaniard; these traits are infinitely modified to the eye of scientific observation; and are the direct and significant language of temperament, race, and character. It is, perhaps, because the elements of the dramatic art are thus universal, that its professors are so little esteemed, unless of the very highest order. It is certainly true of most of the celebrated performers that they have been unhappy, and averse to their children adopting the vocation.

To appreciate the significance of elocutionary art, we have but to consider that all poetry and rhetoric need interpretation. To the multitude, in its printed or written form, the word of genius is often as much a sealed book as the notes of a fine musical composition to one uninitiated as to the meaning of those occult signs of harmony. Wordsworth gained many converts to his poetical theory by the impressive manner in which he recited his verses, who would have remained insensible to their worth if only the force of reasoning had been used. The popularity of many English lyrics and dramatic scenes is owing to the emphasis given them, in the memory, by felicitous declaimers. How different is the Church Service, an old ballad, an oration, the sentiment of Tennyson, the chivalry of Campbell, or the ardent gloom of Byron, when melodiously and intelligently uttered: only those who really feel the sense or pathos of a poem, win others adequately to receive it; and there now lie neglected heaps of noble verse, the latent music of which has not been vocally eliminated. In this view, the requisite combination of voice, sensibility, and intelligence that constitute a good elocutionist is an endowment of inestimable value. Lee, the dramatist, used to read his plays so effectively that it discouraged the actors from undertaking them; and the crowds that listen attentively to an able reader of Shakspeare, indicate the extent of public taste for this unappreciated and rarely cultivated accomplishment. Kean gave "a local habitation," in the minds of thousands, to Shaksperian inspiration; his surviving auditors are yet haunted by his tones; his inflections and emphasis sculptured, as it were, with a breath, upon memory, words that had previously left only a transient impression. Had we, in our Western civilization, a profession analogous to the improvisatore of the South, or the story-teller of the East, to make familiar and impressive the utterance of our poets, they need not fear comparison with the ancient bards of the people. Tasso and Ariosto are read to this day, in squares and on quays in Italy, to swarthy and tattered groups, who applaud a good line as if it were a new candidate for fame; and, notwithstanding the aversion of the highly intellectual to the theatre, Shakspeare became domesticated in the English mind through the interpretation of histrionic genius. It is on account of this vital connection between literature and elocution, this absolute need of a popular exposition of what otherwise would never penetrate the common mind, that the decadence of the Stage is to be regretted, and the recognition of elocution as a high, graceful, and useful art is desirable. We have an abundance of critics; we need expositors, artists to embody in clear, emphatic, and justly modulated tones, the graces and the thoughts which minstrel and philosopher have elaborated; this would awaken moral sympathy, give a social interest to the pleasures of literature, and wing words of truth and beauty over the world. It is in view of such an office that the actor rises to dignity; and that such a "great simple being" as Mrs. Siddons, was consoled, when insulted by an audience, for her "consciousness of a humiliating vocation;" and that Kean, wayward and dissolute, recklessly leaping the barrier of civilization, like Freneau's Indian boy who ran from college to the woods, reappears to the fancy as a genuine minister at the altar of humanity. Talma's life was coincident with some of the greatest events of the century; and his social position is a noble vindication of histrionic genius in alliance with superior character. Associated with the literary men of his country, and befriended by her statesmen, his reminiscences were quite as interesting as his professional triumphs. Intimate with Chenier, David, and Danton, he was admired and cherished by Napoleon. Like Kean his earliest attempts failed, and like Garrick he was a reformer in his art. The philosophy of dramatic personation as regarded by such a man has a peculiar interest. "Acting," he said, "is a complete paradox; we must possess the power of strong feeling, or we could never command and carry with us the sympathy of a mixed audience in a crowded theatre; but we must, at the same time, control our sensations on the stage, for their indulgence would enfeeble execution. The skilful actor calculates his effects beforehand; the voice, gesture, and look which pass for inspiration, have been rehearsed a hundred times. On the other hand, a dull, composed, phlegmatic nature can never make a great actor." Talma's introduction of Kemble's toga in the Roman plays, his teaching Bonaparte to play king, according to the famous *on-dit*, his matchless dignity and elocution, his English affinities, his charming talk, his select circle of friends, his prosperous style of living, and the new rank he gave his vocation, combine to endear and elevate his memory.

In an historical view the relation of actors to society, art, letters, and religion, offers many curious problems: *protéges* of the State in the palmy days of Greece, with the purely secular interest attached to the stage under the Romans, it degenerated; yet Cicero profited by the instructions of Roscius, and gained for him an important suit; and while Augustus decreed that "players were exempt from stripes," later edicts declared, "that no senators should enter the houses of pantomimes, and that Roman knights should not attend them in the streets." Excommunicated by the Church of Rome in the Middle Ages, they gave vital scope and character to Spanish literature by evoking the rich and national materials of that extraordinary drama of which Calderon and Lope de Vega are the permanent expositors. Its history shows how, from religious comedies to historical and social plays, the representatives of the stage in Spain fostered her intellectual development and only popular culture, "until there was hardly a village that did not possess some kind of a theatre." The actors at Madrid "constituted no less than forty companies," and "secular comedies of a very equivocal complexion were represented in some of the principal monasteries of the kingdom." The conduct of the Spanish actors, however, according to the same testimony,* "did more than

* Ticknor's *Spanish Literature.*

anything else to endanger the privileges of the drama." Their personal lot seems to have been as hard as the worst of their successors; "slaves in Algiers were better off." In France, political, social, and literary life and labor are often so related to or influenced by the renowned *artistes* of the stage, that they figure as an inevitable element in popular memoirs; nowhere is the influence of the profession so direct and absolute; and while the rise of German literature and liberalism is identified with the advent of dramatic genius and the national revival of the theatre, in England the most distinctive and pervading glory of her intellectual character and fame is the offspring of this form of letters and this phase of social recreative art. The biographies of the most celebrated and endeared authors, from Alfieri to Irving, and from Goethe to Wilson, indicate that dramatic entertainments, whether Italian opera or the English stage in its prime, court-plays at Weimar, or Terry at Edinburgh, are to them the most available recuperative and inspiring of pastimes.

It is alike instructive and amusing to trace the dramatic element, so instinctive and versatile, from the natural language of races and individuals, through social manners to its organized culmination in art; and thus to realize its historical significance. The Greek drama has afforded philosophical scholars the most inspiring theme whereby to illustrate the culture of classic antiquity. In the mellifluous verses of Metastasio, the stern emphasis of Alfieri, and the comedies of Goldoni, we have a perfect reflection of the lyrical taste, the free aspiration, and the colloquial geniality of the Italians. From Molière to Scribe what vivid and true pictures of human life and nature as modified by French character; while the essential facts of the origin and development of the British stage, so fully recorded by Dr. Doran, brings it into intimate and sympathetic contact with all the phases and crises of literature, society, and politics. In the days of the first Charles the stage "suffered with the throne and the church." Around Blackfriars, Whitefriars, the Globe, the Rose, Drury Lane, Covent Garden, and the Haymarket, crystallize the most salient associations of court and authorship; on this vantage-ground Puritan and Cavalier alternately triumphed; and the genius of England bore its consummate flower in Shakspeare. Now denounced and now cherished, to-day patronized by kings, and to-morrow denounced by clergy, the memoirs and annals of each epoch include the fortunes and the fame of the drama as one of the most suggestive tests of social transitions. Queen Henrietta was "well-affected towards plays," while South vigorously assailed, and Bossuet consigned their personators to the infernal regions. The play-houses declared a public nuisance by the Middlesex grand jury of 1700, at an earlier and later period were shrines of fashion, nurseries of talent, and haunts of courtiers. The representative men and women of the day were dramatic authors, actors, and actresses; each succeeding generation of poets essayed in this arena, so that a familiar designation of the ages is borrowed from their leading playwrights, whose works faithfully mirror the moral tone, the social spirit, and the public taste. In Alphra Behn's "Oronooko," Mrs. Centlivres' "Busy-Body," Addison's "Cato," Steele's "Tender Husband," Dr. Young's "Revenge," Gay's "Beggar's Opera," Sheridan's "School for Scandal," Goldsmith's "She Stoops to Conquer," Rowe's "Jane

Shore," Farquhar's "Beaux' Stratagem," and many other popular plays, we have, as it were, the living voice of ideas, passions, and sentiments which agitated or charmed the town; and the robust, earnest individuality of the English race forever lives in the profound, impassioned utterance of the old dramatists, as its emasculated tone is embodied in the comic muse of the Restoration. How vivid the glimpses of stage influence in the memoirs and correspondence of each era, in the art and the annals of the nation. Evelyn and Pepys note Betterton's triumphs; Tillotson learned from him his effective elocution; Kneller painted, and Pope loved him. The "Tatler" comments on "haughty George Powell"; Jack Lacy still lives in his portrait at Hampton Court. "The great Mrs. Barry" is buried in Westminster cloisters; and Mrs. Pritchard's bust looms up from among those of poets and statesmen in the Abbey, and recalls Churchill's metrical tribute. Burke, Johnson, Walpole, and Chesterfield, expatiate on Garrick with critical zest or personal sympathy. Each great performer creates an epoch of taste or fashion, feeling or fame. Betterton, Quin, Barry, Foote, Cibber, Garrick, Kemble, Cooke, and Kean, are names whose mention brings to mind not a transient histrionic reputation, but a reign, a social, literary, or national period, crowded with interesting characters, remarkable achievements, or special traits of life and manners. Each theatre has its memorable traditions; each school its great illustrators; audiences, criticisms, the court, the coffee-house, the journal, derive from and impart to the theatre a specific influence. The gallantry, the wit, the local manners, the style of writing, the fashion that prevail at a given period, are associated with the stage, the annals whereof, whether in Paris, London, or Vienna, are therefore invaluable as a reference to historian, novelist, and artist. "The Garrick fever," we are told, "extended to St. Petersburg"; "a dissenting, one-eyed jeweller" in George Barnwell, brought the domestic drama into vogue; the "Beggar's Opera" "made highwaymen fashionable," and Ross is still remembered in Edinburgh "as the founder of the legal stage."

There is this great difference between the British and the French stage, that while the former has achieved the grandest triumphs of tragic genius, both literary and histrionic, the comedy of the latter has proved a permanent school of manners, of language, and of art. The patronage of the government, and the most strict artistic methods and discipline, have established a standard of acting through the Théâtre Français. Accordingly, instead of one superlatively clever and a score of inefficient performers, all the French actors and actresses work together for a harmonious result; unity of art and of effect, exquisite finish, scientific aptitude, graces of manner, of utterance, and of expression, often combine to make the modern French drama the perfection of artificial triumphs.

The lyric drama has greatly diminished the influence and modified the character of the stage; and its personal records and associations abound in romantic and artistic triumphs. The rare and delicate gift of a voice adapted to this sphere, the temperament, talent, and beauty of the queens of song, the individuality and power of musical composition, the vast expense and varied attractions of the Italian opera, its fashionable sway, and the genius and social interest identified with its history, all combine to throw a special and significant charm around its votaries and its record. What a world of emotional and artistic meaning the very names of Purcell, Pergolesi, Bach, Cherubini, Mozart, and Rossini, Bellini, Donizetti, Verdi, Beethoven, Mercandante, and other eminent composers, awakens; and how the memory of their great interpreters haunts the imagination! Perhaps, in our material age, there is no sphere where fancy and feeling have found such scope. From the memoirs of Alfieri to those of our own Irving, it is evident that the most available of inspiring recreations, for men of thought and sensibility, is the lyric drama; and from the days of Metastasio at the court of Vienna, to those of Felice Romani's libretto of "La Norma," words and melody have reproduced, in vivid and vital grace, the tragic and the naive in history, sentiment, and life. Even around imperial careers flit the vocal victors of the hour. Joseph of Austria, the great Frederic, and the first Napoleon, had their authoritative or conciliatory skirmishes with a *prima donna*, or an *impresario;* operatic alternate with diplomatic episodes. Nor is the social charm and prestige of the lyric drama less apparent in the annals of kindred genius. At Sophia Arnould's *salon* the illustrious writers and statesmen of Paris gladly convened. Goethe celebrated in verse the eighty-third birthday of Mara. Sir Joshua painted Mrs. Billington as St. Cecilia; and Catalani made English tars, rowing her to a frigate, weep as she warbled the national anthem. The amours, rivalries, luxury, disasters, adventures, courtly favor, social influence, conjugal quarrels, noble charities, and artistic triumphs, of vocalists, add a new and marvellous chapter to the annals of dramatic character and fortunes. Lavinia Fanton's "Polly Peachum" secured the triumph of Gay's

"Beggar's Opera," and the heart of a duke; of kindred significance is that scene, so exceptional in English conventional life, and well described by Dr. Burney, where Anastasia Robinson was acknowledged by Lord Peterborough as his wife. A cardinal and a cook were the parents of Gabrielli; Pasta's "Medea" was an epoch in histrionic art; Malibran's brief and brilliant career revealed the most versatile woman, as well as original *cantatrice* of her day; Sontag's death was a public calamity; Catalani's marvellous vocalization lacked pathos, because "she had not suffered;" while Mrs. Woods gained the same quality from a contrary experience. Madame Devrient was called the Siddons of Germany; Jenny Lind's *naive* song won thousands for the indigent; and Braham's triumphant tones in singing the triumphs of Israel, made the audience appear to Lamb, as Egyptians over whose necks the Hebrew chanter rode.

From the time Burbage was lessee of the Globe Theatre, and Shakspeare performed in his own characters, the morality of an actor's profession and the stage have been discussed; but that there is no inevitable degradation in the theatre, is evident from the late wholly suc cessful though temporary revival of its glory under the auspices of Macready; by magnificent and complete scenic arrangements, the restoration of mutilated Shakspearian dramas, efficient companies, the reformation of the house itself, and especially by combining with the best dramatic authors of the day, and rigidly maintaining his own self-respect as a member of society, Macready once more brought together the scattered elements upon which the character and utility of the stage is based, invested it with the highest interest, and raised it above the cavils both of severe intellectual taste and of pure morality. For a brief period it was the centre of graceful ministries, a high school of art, the handmaid of literature, and the means of elevating public sentiment and refreshing the most toilsome minds; works of real dramatic genius were elicited; latent artistic resources suggested; and the noblest drama in the world adequately represented. Financial difficulties, incident to the monopoly enjoyed by patentees, soon put a stop to the laudable enterprise; but the experiment is as memorable as it was satisfactory. Ronzi shed tears of pleasure when she found herself the only guest at a nobleman's villa near Florence to which she had been invited to a *fête* sumptuously and tastefully arranged; it was so rare an exception to the rule of making professional vocalists contribute to, instead of receiving, private entertainment; and it is a curious fact, in the social history of theatrical characters, that the English, notwithstanding their prudery and exclusiveness, first recognized actors and actresses of merit as companions. Miss Farren is not the only performer married to one of the nobility. The Earl of Craven espoused Miss Bromton; Lord Peterborough, Anastasia Robinson; a nephew of Lord Thurlow, Miss Bolton; and Sir William Becher, Miss O'Neil. One can readily understand how an intellectual bachelor like James Smith, accustomed to solace himself for domestic privations by cultivating a sympathy for the heroines of the mimic world, should lament, as he did, in apt verse, their appropriation even by noble lovers. He closes a pathetic record of the kind with this allusion to the union between his prime favorite, Miss Stevens, and Lord Essex, who seems to have acted on the advice of the author of "Matrimonial Maxims," who says, "If you marry an actress, the singing-girls are the best":

"Last of the dear, delightful list,
Most followed, wonder'd at, and miss'd
In Hymen's odds and evens; —
Old Essex caged our nightingale,
And finished thy dramatic tale,
Enchanting Kitty Stevens!"

Boswell's reason for his partiality to players and soldiers was that they excelled "in animation and relish of existence." There is a striking illustration of the personal sympathy awakened by the profession in conflict with the judgment that condemns it, as a career, in the life of Scott. On one of the last days of Sir Walter's life, when in a bath-chair at Abbotsford, he was wheeled to a shady place by Lockhart and Laidlaw, he asked the former to read him something from Crabbe. Lockhart read the description of the arrival of the Players at the Borough. Sir Walter cried "Capital!" at the poet's sarcasms on that way of life, but asked penitently, "How will poor Terry endure those cuts?" and when Lockhart reached the summing up —

"Sad, happy race! soon raised and soon depressed,
Your days all past in jeopardy and jest;
Poor without prudence, with afflictions, vain,
Not warned by misery, nor enriched by gain ——"

"Shut the book," said Scott; "I can't stand more of this: it will touch Terry to the quick." A different but significant tribute to the actual personal worth of the profession occurs in one of those genial "imaginary conversations," vital with reality of reminiscence and rhapsody, wherein Christopher North and the Ettrick Shepherd discourse so memorably. The conduct of Kean in appearing on the stage immediately after a scandalous intrigue had become public, is reprobated by "Tickler" as "an insult to humanity"; to which the Shepherd replies: "What can ye expec' fráe a play-actor?" "What can I expect, James?" is the reply; "Why, look at Terry, Young, Matthews, Charles Kemble, and your friend Vandenhoff; and then I say that you expect good players to be good men as men go; and likewise gentlemen."

This sympathy with the profession, and vivid interest in some phase or period of the drama, is an almost universal fact in the experience of intelligent and sensitive persons. Thackeray's picture of Pendennis enamored of an actress in boyhood, is typical of a common episode of youth; if not in this form it takes the shape of enthusiasm for a certain actor or class of plays, or a mania defined as the condition of being "stage-struck"; while to the philosophical as well as sympathetic of these early votaries, the literature of the drama is a perennial storehouse of psychological data, and the most vital connecting link between written lore and actual life — the source of the highest poetry and the most universal human truth.

In literary biography, the accounts of the manner in which the plays of Goldsmith, Sheridan, Byron, Mrs. Hemans, Joanna Baillie, Procter, Talfourd, Hunt, Lamb, and other poets, were brought on the stage, — the reciprocal good offices of actors and authors — mutually acknowledged, the array of intellectual friends convened to grace the occasion, and the anecdotes and criticism thence resulting — form some of the most agreeable episodes in literary biography. Farquhar, Holcraft, Mrs. Inchbald, Knowles, and others, combined the author and actor; and it was a genial and noble custom for distinguished writers to contribute prologues and epilogues; — the interchange of such kindly offices gave, as we have said, a wide and elevated social interest to the theatre which had, in a great measure, passed away before the advent of Kean. Besides the comparative indifference of the public, he was obliged to contend against both the prejudices and the refinements of taste — the one opposing all innovation as to style, and the other repudiating the intensity and boldness of his conceptions.

The Spagnoletto style of Sandford, and the "cordage" visible in old Macklin's face, are traditional. The inimitable pathos of Miss O'Neil, the tragic beauty of Pasta, the heroic manner of Siddons, the irresistible humor of Matthews, and Liston's comic genius, had each their distinctive character; they respectively individualized the art, and, if we range over the entire gallery of histrionic celebrities, we shall find their fame based upon as peculiar traits of excellence as that of renowned authors and painters; and their genius consisting in some quality emphatically their own — where imitation and art became subservient to, or illustrative of, an idiosyncrasy.

Impulsive genius seldom receives the credit of artistic study, and its most effective points are often ascribed to chance inspiration. This is an error of frequent occurrence in judging of actors; and it is one almost perversely indulged by the bigoted opponents of the romantic or natural school. The most effective touches, however, in Garrick, Kean, and other eminent performers, are easily traced to careful observation or a personal idiosyncrasy or association. In the very first instruction the latter received in his art, recourse was had to natural sympathy in order to perfect his imitative skill. The pathetic intonation with which, even as a boy, he exclaimed, "Alas, poor Yorick!" in Hamlet, was derived from the manner in which he habitually spoke of an unfortunate relative who constantly excited his commiseration; he was instructed to transfer the tone awakened by real to the expression of imaginary grief: his manner of falling on his face was derived from the figure on Abercrombie's monument, and his fighting with a weaponless arm in Richard was borrowed from the death-scene of an officer in Spain. The play of Bertram, by Maturin, he is said to have rendered memorable by a single touching benison: all who once heard his "God bless the child," recall it with emotion; it was a favorite mode of uttering his paternal tenderness at home; hence its reality. Garrick made a study of an old crazy friend of his in order to enact Lear with truth to nature; and when Kean was playing in New York, he accompanied his physician to Bloomingdale asylum for the express purpose of obtaining hints for the same part, from the manner and expression of the insane patients. Indeed, those most intimate with Kean in his best days, unite in the opinion that he was never surpassed for the intense and original study of his characters; he brooded over them in the quiet fields, observed life and nature, conversed with discerning men, and acutely examined books and his own consciousness, for the purpose of attaining an harmonious and artistic conception; he tried experiments in elocution before his wife, and was in the habit of rehearsing, for hours, without any auditor. So elaborate were his studies, that having once decided on a course, he never modified it without great self-dissatisfaction, and on one occasion when he yielded his judgment, on a special point, to please Mrs. Garrick, the inharmonious effect was obvious to all.

"What the bank is to the credit of the nation," said Steele, "the playhouse is to its politeness and good manners." And although this maxim is scarcely applicable now, the instinct and the sympathy by virtue of which the stage instructs and refines, forever obtain in humanity. Among recent illustrations, is the genial influence of dramatic pastimes upon the isolated and dark sojourn of ice-bound Arctic voyagers, as described by the intrepid and philosophic Kane and his predecessors. The gallery of human portraits, conserved even by the minor English drama, are among the most genuine illustrations of life and character; Sir Peter Teazle and Joseph Surface, Sir Pertinax and Tony Lumpkin, Sylvester Daggerwood and Mawworm, are emphatic types with which we could ill dispense. One of the remarkable intellectual phenomena of the age in which we live, however, is the gradual encroachment of literature upon dramatic art. The best modern characters which genius has created exist in masterpieces of fiction and poetry; in a measure they have superseded in popular favor dramatic ideals, except the highest and most endeared. Scott, Dickens, and their contemporaries or successors, have given the world a new gallery of living portraits such as of old were only to be found in the drama. Well said Wilson in the "Noctes": "I think the good novels that are published, come in place of new dramas." The Italian opera has by its affluent artistic attractions, overshadowed, and in a great measure superseded, the "legitimate drama." Even in Italy the opportunity is comparatively rare to enjoy fine acting apart from music and the ballet; yet there is no better lesson for the novice in that "soft bastard Latin" that Byron loved, than to listen to one of Goldoni's old-fashioned colloquial plays as clearly and with admirable emphasis, recited by such a company as that of which Internari was so long the ornament; by melodious emphasis alone commonplace maxims seemed to attain the sparkle of wit; and the mere tone of voice is fraught with infectious merriment. From Arlechino's broad jokes to Ristori's majestic pathos, the natural dramatic instinct and endowments of the Italians, awaken every shade and subtlety of sympathetic feeling.

Philosophically examined, the stage will be found a compensatory institution, and its actual relation to society intimate or conventional, accòrding to the predominance of real or ideal satisfaction. Thus the free enterprise and speculative range in America makes it merely recreative; the best Italian dramatist wrote when his country's civic life was paralyzed. The sentiment checked by caste and absolutism in Elizabeth's day, burst forth in the old dramatists, and culminated, for all time, in Shakspeare; while the memoirs of Goethe, Schiller, and Korner indicate how near and dear to the popular heart of their country was the art in all its phases and forms, wherein baffled aspirations found scope. The histrionic artists of Germany, and the actresses of Paris, are or have been a vital element of the social economy, impracticable and almost inconceivable to English and Americans. "Wilhelm Meister" is the legitimate romance of its country and era. "L' artiste aimée du public," says Madame Dudevant, "est comme un enfant a qui l' univers est la famille," while the affinity of the dramatic instinct with literary culture and capability is not only evident in the friendships between authors and actors, but in the facility with which the former become amateur performers. Montaigne says, "I played the chief part in the Latin tragedies of Buchanan, Guerente, and Moret, that were acted in our college of Guienne." Dickens is a capital actor and dramatic reader of his own stories; and Washington Irving, when sojourning at Dresden, delectably enacted, in a genial family circle, Sir Charles Rackett.

One proof of the essential individuality of histrionic genius, is that in every celebrated part each renowned actor seems to have excelled in a different phrase. Garrick's Hamlet was inimitable in the words, "I have that within that passeth show;" while the most affecting touch of the elder Wallack was "That undiscovered country from whose bourne no traveller returns." Kean's first soliloquy in Richard is perhaps the best preserved traditional recitation of the English stage; and the power of contrasted intonation in the expression of feeling, never forgotten by those who listened, was evinced in the memorable passage in Othello —

> "Perdition catch my soul but *I do love thee*,
> And when I love thee *not*, chaos is come again."

His conceptions were remarkable for bold earnestness. His discordant voice, insignificant figure, and slightly misshaped feet, seemed to pass miraculously away before the glowing energy of his spirit; to the imaginative spectator he visibly expanded, and filled the stage, and towered over the inferior actors of larger physical dimensions; his action, expression of countenance, intelligent emphasis, and vigor of utterance, lifted, kindled, and glorified, as it were, his merely human attributes, and bore him, and those who gazed and listened, triumphantly onward in a whirl of passion, a concentration of will, or a chaos of emotion.

As far as contemporary memoirs elucidate the subject, it is evident that gross violations of elocutionary taste were habitual both prior to and succeeding the time of Betterton. This actor, with remarkable physical disadvantages, appears to have had the most decided genius — especially for tragedy; we have no accounts of the effects of tragic personation exceeding those recorded of Betterton; so truly did he feel the emotion represented that it is said his color, breathing, accent, and looks betrayed an incessant and absolute sympathy with the part; as Hamlet he turned deadly pale at the sight of the ghost, and Cibber emphatically declares that his tone, accentuation, and the whole management of his voice were faultlessly adapted to each passage he recited. Garrick seems first to have established a taste for the refinements of the art; his style, compared to what had been in vogue, was singularly chaste; he embodied the great idea of unity; and when he first appeared, his manner, expression of countenance, inflection of voice, and whole air instantly revealed the character, of which he did not lose sight for a moment. The Kemble school has been traced to Quin; but its individuality was trenched upon vitally by Kean, although it has been, in many essential features, renewed by the elder Vandenhoff and Macready. It is contended by its ardent votaries that Kean sacrificed the dignity of his art — so ably sustained by John Kemble and his renowned sister, to mere effect; that he substituted impulse for science, and excited sympathy by powerful but illegitimate appeals to emotion. This, however, is a narrow statement, and like the old dispute about Racine and Shakspeare, the classic and romantic, the natural and the artistic — resolves itself into the fact that the principle of a division of labor is applicable to art as well as social economy. In Cato and Coriolanus and Wolsey, the traits of Kemble were perfectly assimilated; in the more complex part of Richard the Third, and the more impetuous one of Othello, the energy, quickness, intense expression, and infectious action of Kean were not only electrical in their immediate effect, but appropriate in the highest degree in the view of reflection and taste. Thus, too, Cooke, as Sir Pertinax McSycophant, Mrs. Siddons as Lady Macbeth, Cooper as Virginius, Kean as Shylock, Macready as Werner, and Booth as Iago, made indelible because highly characteristic impressions. The actor, like the author and artist, has his *forte* — a sphere peculiarly fitted to elicit his powers and give scope and inspiration to his genius; and it is here that we should estimate him, and not according to a comparative and irrelevant standard.

The lives of actors partake of the extreme alternations and varied excitement of their profession. To the philosopher there is nothing anomalous in the frequent contrast between the lessons of virtue they enact and the recklessness of their habits. When we consider how much they are the sport of fortune, and how often poverty and contempt form the background to the picture of love, triumph, or wit in which they figure; and remember the constant draft upon nervous sensibility and the resources of temperament, as well as intelligence, it is their lot to undergo, we cannot reasonably wonder that extravagances of conduct, vagaries of habit, and a proneness to seek pleasure in the immediate, characterize players. "Players," says Hazlett, "are the only honest hypocrites." It is proved by judicial statistics, that "of all classes they are the freest from crime"; while their charitable sympathies are proverbial; in marriage and finance, however, they are the reverse of precisians; yet few more pleasing examples of domestic virtue and happiness can be found than some recorded in histrionic memoirs. A kindly but acute observer who long fraternized with the craft, Douglas Jerrold, said of the strolling player: "He is the merry preacher of the noblest, grandest lessons of human thought. He is the poet's pilgrim, and in the forlornest by-ways and abodes of men, calls forth new sympathies, sheds upon the cold, dull trade of real life an hour of poetic glory. He informs human clay with thoughts and throbbings that refine it; and for this, he was for centuries a 'rogue and a vagabond,' and is, even now, a long, long day's march from the vantage-ground of respectability." Through the annals of the English stage there may be traced a vein of romantic vicissitude as suggestive as any the written drama affords: — Wilks, generous and spirited, abandoning a profitable engagement in Dublin, with language as noble in its key as one of Fletcher's characters, to allay the conjugal jealousy of a brother actor; Nell Gwinn discouraged in her theatrical ambition by the manager, becoming orange-girl to the theatre in order to be in the line of her aspirations, which, when realized, made her the mistress of a king and the envy of courtiers; Mountfort, killed in an impromptu duel with a noble rival for the love of Mrs. Bracegirdle; the charming Mrs. Woffington disguised as a man, at a country ball, undeceiving the affianced of her disloyal lover; the beautiful Miss Bellamy meditating suicide on the steps of Westminster Bridge; Savage asleep on a street-bunk, and, three days after, the admired guest at a lord's table; the eccentricities of Cibber's daft daughter; Holcraft's affecting story of his boyhood, and the ludicrous self-importance displayed in his account of his trial for treason; the fascinating dialogue of the benevolent Mrs. Jordan with the Quaker in the rain under a shed; Jerrold's father playing in a barn upon an estate that was rightfully his own; and Douglas himself, the future dramatic author, carried on the stage by Kean, as the child in Rolla. Palmer fell dead while personating "The Stranger," in consequence of the excess of sorrow which the situation induced, he having just been stricken by a great domestic bereavement; Williams was killed by Quin; and Mountford and Clive murdered. Quin's memorable jokes, Cooke's lapses from more than Roman dignity and Anglo-Saxon sense, to a worse than Indian sottishness; Grimaldi, whom Hook called "the Garrick of Clowns," and to whom Byron gave a silver snuff-box, leaving buffoonery and harlequin whirls to train pigeons, collect flies, or meet with London robbers; Matthews, after keeping the Park audience in a roar for hours, crossing the river to stroll in pensive thought under the trees at Hoboken; and the versatile and admired Hodgkinson dying at a solitary tavern on the road to Washington, amid the horrors of pestilence, and his body thrown into a field by slaves; Booth's extraordinary fits of contemplative originality, and the grotesque night-adventures in which Kean was the leader, are but incidental glimpses of a world in which the violent, fantastic, and reckless instincts of human nature are wantonly displayed, yielding curious material for the metaphysician, and ample scope for charity. An English poet has brought together many such anecdotes of Kean, — some touching, in the highest degree, some superlatively ridiculous, and others shocking to the heart, — yet all kindled with the forlorn glory of genius, like the scathed form of Milton's fallen angel. And what a mercurial compound was Samuel Foote, London's great source of fun and satire for years, — whose chance observations became proverbs, who used to find a seat for Gray the poet, stand ruefully against the scenes to have his artificial leg attached, and then go forward to set the house in a roar, — as ingenious as Steele in evading "injunctions," who lived by his "takings off," over which the grave Johnson shook with merriment, and whose "wits" were literally his capital, whereby he realized three fortunes! It is no wonder people frequented Macklin's ordinary when he quit the stage; nor that they listened until far into the night to that "perpetual showman of the extraordinary in manners, adventure, sentimentality, and sin," — Elliston, — whose "I 'll never call you Jack, my boy, again," equalled in comic zest the tragic force of Kean's "God bless the child," in "Bertram," who made life itself a comedy, and played the "child of fortune" to the end; exuberant in vagaries, a vagabond by instinct, celebrating "the triumph of abstinence by excess," and with "eccentricity absolutely germain to his being," yet could so perfectly enact the "regal style" in common life, that Charles Lamb declared he should "repose under no inscription but one of pure Latinity." The "Memoirs of Grimaldi" was the first book Dickens published, and in that biography of a harlequin are the smiles and tears of a genuine romance. In the perusal of such an experience, we realize how directly comedy springs from human life; the *piazzas* of Spain and Italy, with their motley crowds and glib dialogue, gave birth to the theatre. What a curious fact in human nature is the relation of seeming to being in the drama. Dr. Shelden, Archbishop of Canterbury, was dining with the celebrated Betterton, and said: "Pray, Mr. Betterton, inform me what is the reason you actors can affect your audiences with speaking of things imaginary as if they were real, while we of the Church speak of things real which our congregations only receive as if they were imaginary." "Why, my Lord," replied the player, "the reason is plain. We actors speak of things imaginary as if they were real, and you in the pulpit speak of things real as if they were imaginary." It has been observed that there are no English lives worth reading except those of players, who, "by the nature of the case, have bidden Respectability good-day"; and a grave literary critic explains on higher ground than this *abandon*, why there is an intrinsic charm in an actor's memoirs, when he remarks that "notwithstanding everything which may be said against the theatrical profession, it certainly does require from those who pursue it, a certain quickness and liveliness of mind."

The very nature of the vocation is inciting to vagrant propensities and thoughtless adventures. The English theatre originated in strollers who performed in inn-yards; and the Greek drama is associated with the "cart of Thespis." I have seen an itinerant company of Italians perform a tragedy in the old Roman amphitheatre at Verona, on a spring afternoon, to a hundred spectators grouped about the lower tiers of that magnificent relic of antiquity, where gladiators once contended in the presence of thousands. It was an impressive evidence of the universality of dramatic taste, which, however modified by circumstances, always re-asserts itself in all nations and climes. The best historians, cognizant of this, make the condition and influence of the theatre a subject of record; and its phases undoubtedly mirror the characteristic in social and national life more truly than any other institution. It was a great bone of contention between the Puritans and Cavaliers; Macaulay finds it needful to revert to the subject to illustrate the reign of Charles II. and the Commonwealth, and Hildreth to mark the difference of public sentiment in New England and the other States after the revolution. Its critical history in England would afford a reliable scale by which to measure the rise, progress, and lapses of civilization and public taste. Upon this arena the great controversy between nature and art, rules and inspiration, eclecticism and adherence to a school, which, under different names, forms an everlasting problem to the votaries of intellectual enjoyment, was boldly fought. And the discussion once inspired by Kemble and Kean has been renewed by the respective advocates of Rachel and Ristori.

The diminished influence of the stage is obvious in its comparative isolation. "The dramatic temperament," observes Mrs. Kemble, "always exceptional in England, is becoming daily more so under the various adverse influences of a civilization and society which fosters a genuine dislike to exhibitions of emotion, and a cynical disbelief in the reality of it, both necessarily depressing, first its expression, and next its existence." This social repudiation of the dramatic instinct undoubtedly affects its professional development; and the stage in Great Britain, of late years, with the exception of the lyric drama, appeals far more to the amusing than the tragic element; the comic muse and the melodrama have long been in the ascendant. The social character which once rendered the stage in England a connecting link between literature and the town, refined circles and the public at large, no longer exists; that such a relation naturally obtains we perceive in the mutual advantages then derived from its recognition; authors and actors, indeed, have a reciprocal interest in the drama, while the tone of society and manners is directly influenced by, and reflected from, the theatre; much, therefore, of the deterioration of the latter is owing to its being in a great degree abandoned by those whose taste, character, and personal influence alone can redeem it from abuse and degradation; for it has been well said that the theatre is respectable only in proportion as it is respected. A traditional charm and intellectual dignity, as well as social attractiveness, lingers around the memory of its palmy days; when Quin so nobly befriended the author of "The Seasons;" when Steele was a patentee, and Mrs. Bracegirdle inspired the best authors to write for her, and received a legacy from Congreve; when Dr. Johnson and Goldsmith discussed new plays and old readings with Garrick, and Mrs. Oldfield remembered poor Savage in her will; or Sheridan vibrated between the greenroom and the dress circle. Similar pleasing associations belong to the era of Mrs. Siddons, when she doffed the majestic air of Lady Macbeth, to mingle with the literati of Edinburgh; and nightly saw Reynolds, Gibbon, Burke, and Fox in the orchestra. Peg Woffington charmed Burke, and incited him to his first successful literary effort; and Archbishop Tillotson profited by the elocution of Betterton. We are told in corresponding memoirs, of Kitty Clive's 'clear laugh,' 'fair Abington with her dove-like looks,' 'charming Mrs. Barry,' and 'womanly Mrs. Pritchard.' There is no vocation so directly inspired by love of approbation; the stimulus of applause is an indispensable encouragement, and popular caprice vents itself without limit in deifying or degrading the children of Thespis. It is not to be wondered at that diseased vanity often results from such adulation as attends the successful actor. "Is it possible," asks Sir Lytton, "that this man so fondled, so shouted to, so dandled by the world, can, at bedtime, take off the whole of Macbeth with his stockings?" The old essayists criticized the stage with efficiency; men of political fame watched, with interest, over its destiny; men of genius proclaimed its worth, and men of birth took an active part in its support and direction. Thus encouraged and inspired, actors of the higher order felt a degree of responsibility to the public, and indulged in aspirations that gave elevation and significance to their art. Its evanescent triumphs, when compared with those of letters, painting, or sculpture, have often been lamented; Cibber is eloquently pathetic on the subject, and Campbell has expressed the sentiment in a memorable stanza. In one respect, however, the fragility of histrionic renown is an advantage; no species of enjoyment from art has been made the theme of such glowing reminiscence; as if inspired by the very consciousness that the merit they celebrated had no permanent memorial, intelligent lovers of the drama describe, in conversation and literature, the traits of favorite performers and the effects they have produced, with a zest, acuteness, and enthusiasm rarely awarded the votaries of other pursuits. What genial emphasis, even in the traditional memory of Wilks' Sir Harry Wildair, Barry's Jaffier, Quin's Falstaff, Henderson's Sir Giles, Yates' Shakspeare's Fools, Macklin's Shylock, Harry Woodworth's Captain Boabdil, Cooke's McSycophant, Siddons' Lady Macbeth, and Kean's Othello! Yet in no art is eclecticism more a desideratum; our great actors proverbially suffer for adequate support in the minor characters; rivalry and division of labor sadly mar the possible perfection of the modern stage. Walpole, who was an epicurean in his dramatic as in his social tastes, sighed for the incarnation in one prodigy of the voice of Mrs. Cibber, the eye of Garrick, and the soul of Mrs. Pritchard. In Cibber's eulogies upon the tragic genius of Betterton, or the inimitable drollery of Nokes, — Hunt's genial memoirs of Jack Bannister, Lamb's account of Munden's acting, Campbell's tribute to Mrs. Siddons, and Barry Cornwall's description of Kean's characters, — there is a relish and earnestness seldom devoted to the limner and the bard, who, we feel, can speak best for themselves to posterity. Indeed, the heartiness of appreciation manifested by literary men towards great actors, is the result of natural affinity. There is something, too, in the mere vocation of the latter, when efficiently realized, that excites intellectual and personal sympathy. The actor seems a noble volunteer in behalf of humanity, — a kind of spontaneous lay-figure upon which the drapery of human life may be arranged at pleasure; — he is the oral interpreter of the individual mind to the hearts of the people; and takes upon himself the passion, wit, and sentiment of types of the race, that all may realize their action and quality.

NEWSPAPERS.

"What is it but a map of busy life?"—COWPER.

 REMEMBER how vivid was the impression of Paris life, in its contrasts and economy, derived from the distribution of the "Entr' Acte" at the Opera Comique, announcing the death of Talleyrand. Cinti Damoreau had just warbled a *finale* in the "Pré Aux Clercs," and the applause had scarcely died away, when a shower of neatly-printed gazettes were seized and pondered. There was a minute description of the last hours of a man associated with dynasties and diplomacy, for half a century, who had been the confidant of the Bourbons and the Bonapartes, and a few moments before bade farewell to earth and Louis Philippe; and all these historical and incongurous memories solemnized by death, filled up the interval of a gay and crowded opera, and the pauses of an exquisite vocalist;—a more bewildering consciousness of the past and present, of art and history, of intrigue and melody, of mortality and pastime, it is difficult to imagine.

The newspaper is not only a map but a test of the age; its history is parallel with civilization, and each new feature introduced is significant of political and social changes; while its tone, style, and opinions, at any given time, indicate the spirit of the times more definitely than any other index. If we scan, with a philosophic eye, these fugitive emanations of the press, from their earliest date to the present hour, we find that they not only record events, but bear indirect, and therefore, authentic testimony to the transitions of society, the formation of opinions and the actual standards of public taste. Hence they are eminently characteristic to the annalist. Compare the single diminutive sheet, which, in the latter part of the sixteenth century, formed the London newspaper, almost wholly occupied with state papers and the statistics of a battle in some distant region, with a copy of the present leading Tory journal in the same latitude; the extent and variety of its contents, the finished rhetoric of its leading article, the scholarly criticism, fully reported debates, thorough detail of news, foreign and domestic, local and universal, personal and social — evince how the resources of the world have multiplied, the refinements of life progressed, and the intellectual demands of society risen. News, like all other desirable things, was, at the origin of newspapers, a monopoly of government; the Gazette a mere instrument of courts: now the daily journal, in free countries, is the legitimate expression of the popular mind; its comparative liberty of utterance is the criterion of political enfranchisement; and where entire scope is afforded, it takes as many forms as there are sects, theories, and interests in a community. Thus from being a mere record it has become an expositor; from heralding royal mandates it has grown into an advocate of individual sentiments; and daguerreotypes civil life in its swiftly moving panorama, with incredible celerity and faithfulness. The improvements in the modern journal are chiefly owing to those in human intercourse. The steam-engine and the electric telegraph, by rapidly concentrating the knowledge of events at central points, give both the motive and the means of vitality and completeness to the newspaper. A remarkable effect, however, of these facilities is that they have diminished what may be called the personal influence of the editor, and reduced the daily journal in a great measure, to its normal state — that of a dispenser of news. The success of the newspapers, for instance, in the commercial metropolis of this country and also in London, is at the present day more the result of enterprise than talent. The paper which collects the earliest and most complete intelligence of passing events is the most successful. When these materials of interest were not so abundant; when days and weeks elapsed between the publication of important news, the vehicle of this evanescent but much desired commodity, were kept alive by the individual talent and information of editors. Their views were earnestly uttered and responded to; and the paper was eagerly seized for the sake of its eloquence, its argument, or its satire. It is true, indeed, that a degree of this *prestige* still belongs to the daily journal; but the *eclat* of the writer is now all but lost in the teeming interest of events; the editor, who, in less exciting times, would have been the idolized lay-preacher or improvisatore of the town, must content himself with judiciously compiling new facts, vividly describing passing events, and making up from his foreign and domestic files, an entertaining summary of news. His comments are necessarily brief; no opportunity is afforded carefully to digest the knowledge he acquires or to compare the occurrence of to-day with its parallel in history. Accordingly he glances at the new book, utters his party dictum on the last legislative act, gives a vague interpretation to the aspects of the political horizon, and refers to the full, varied, and interesting details of "news," for both the attraction and the value of his journal. A curious effect of this modern facility in accumulating news, is that of anticipating the effect of time, or superseding the interest of artificial excitements. So various, incessant, and impressive are the incidents daily brought to our knowledge, so visible now is the drama of the world's life, that we have scarcely time or inclination for illusions. History seems enacting; changes, once the work of years, are effected in as many months, and we are so accustomed to the wonderful that sensibility to it is greatly diminished. Imagine the scientific discoveries, the political revolutions, the memorable facts of the last twenty years, all at once revealed to one of our ancestors, at the epoch when editors used to board vessels at the wharf to glean three months' English news for their weekly readers; when political items, marine disasters, advertisements and marriages were all printed in the same column and type, and notice was formally given that the postman would start on horseback in a week, to convey letters a hundred miles! Compare, too, the terse, emphatic style of the modern press to the old-fashioned prolixity, and the practice of publishing both sides of a public question on the same sheet, with the existent division of newspapers into specific organs; the original extreme deference to authority with the present bold discussion of its claims; and the even tenor of the past with the eventful present. Each period has its advantages; and the enduring intellectual monuments of the earlier somewhat reproach the restlessness, diffuse and fragmentary life of to-day. "The patriarch of a community," says Martineau, "can never be restored to the kind of importance which he possessed in the elder societies of the world; from their prerogatives he is deposed by the journal; whose speechless and impersonal lore coldly but effectually supplies the wants once served by the living voice of elders, kindling with the inspiration of the past."

To discover the public feeling of an epoch as well as its social economy, historians, not less than novelists, wisely resort to a file of old newspapers. In James Franklin's journal, commenced at Boston in 1722, and afterwards removed to Newport, for instance, we find controversies between the clergy and the editors of the province, discussions on the utility of inoculation, advertisements of runaway slaves, and notices of whippings and the pillory — all characteristic facts and landmarks of the progress of civilization. The advanced culture of the Eastern States is evident from the contemporaneous republication in one of their daily prints of the poetry of Shenstone, Collins, and Goldsmith, and in another of Robertson's History; there, too, we find Whitefield's preaching theologically analyzed, and the manner of the "Spectator" and "Tattler" at once imitated. Federalism was incarnated in the "Columbian Centinel"; and in another organ, of the same community, at an earlier period, the contributions of Otis and Quincy prepared the public mind gravely to assert the rights for which the colonies were about to struggle. The financial essays of Morris and others taught them, through a similar medium, the principles of currency, exchange, and credit; Dennie induced, in the same way, a taste for elegant literature; and the journals of Freneau and Bache embodied the spirit of French political fanaticism. History, indeed, records events in their continuity and with reference to what precedes and follows; but the actual state of public sentiment in regard to such exciting affairs as Hamilton's duel, Jefferson's gunboats, Genet's mission, Perry's victory, the Freemason's oath, the death of Washington, California gold, and Kossuth's crusade, is most vividly reflected from the diverse reports, opinions, and chronicles of the newspaper press.

It is impossible to estimate the fusion of knowledge and argument brought about by the press in free countries, whereby public sentiment is formed and concentrated. Truth, even the most sacred, was propagated in the world ages ago, by oral and written communication; perhaps it was then more cherished and better considered; but without modern facilities of intercourse like the press, it is difficult to imagine how a political organization like our own, could be regulated and conserved; how universal reputations could be so speedily created, the discoveries of science made available to all, or charitable and economical enterprise be expanded to their present wide issues. The establishment of prolific and cheap journals in New York in 1830, was an event of incalculable historical importance. The universal interest in public affairs, justifies in this country the greatest editorial enterprise; while the growing value of our journals as means of reference, make it desirable their form should be convenient; the book-shape of Niles' Register is one reason it is so much consulted. The variety of talent and opinion enlisted in American journalism, the fights and flatteries of its conductors, the alacrity and seasonableness which is its chief ideal, are traits which absolutely reflect the normal life of the people; the church and school-house which inaugurate an American settlement, are instantly followed by the newspaper; and as the antiquarian now searches the "Boston-News Letter" or "Pennsylvanian Gazette" for incidents of the Revolutionary war, or statistics of colonial trade, he will, a century hence, find in the journals of to-day the economical questions, the social gauge, the daguerreotyped enterprise, filibusterism, and popular tastes of this era.

The stagnation of business and the lapse of metropolitan fashionable life, which so emphatically marks midsummer in America, make that wonderful chart of life, the daily newspaper, more sought and enjoyed than at any other time. From the merchant in his counting-room, to the stranger in the hotel-parlor, from the passenger in suburban cars and steamboats, to the teamster waiting for a job — there is observable a patience and attention in reading newspapers such as one seldom perceives at more busy periods of the year. And if we were to cite a single characteristic sign of the times, as of universal import, it would be American journalism. The avidity with which the papers are seized at watering places — the habit of making their contents the staple of talk, and the manner in which they are conducted in order to meet the popular demands — are facts indicative of modern civilization which no one can ignore who would rightly appreciate its tendency and traits. These are brought out and made conscious, to a remarkable degree, in the leisure intervals which midsummer alone affords to our active and busy people.

The truth is that newspaper reading is the exclusive mental pabulum of a vast number in this country; and to this circumstance is to be ascribed the amount of general information, and ready, though superficial ideas, on all kinds of subjects, which so astonish foreigners. If you converse with your neighbor in the railway cars, or listen to the remarks at the *table d'hote*, hear what the farmers, mechanics, tradesmen, and gentlemen, so gregariously locomotive now, have to say — you will find that the daily press furnishes nine-tenths of the subject-matter and the speculative inspiration. There never was a time or a country where this "fourth estate," as it has been well called, enacted so broad and vital a function. Every year our press has become more personal and local on the one hand, and more comprehensive on the other. Cowper's idea of seeing life through the "loop-holes of retreat," can now be realized as never before. However sequestered may be the summer home of our citizens, they have but to con the daily journals and know all that goes on in the great world, with a detail, as to events, persons, and places, which not only satisfies curiosity, but imagination. Nothing is too abstract for the discussion, or too trivial for the gossip of the American journal. It concentrates the record of daily life at home and abroad; and has so encroached upon the province of the old essayists, the excitements of fiction and the materials of history, that more or less of the literature of each may be found in every well-conducted newspaper.

And yet so undesirable is the unseasonable or excessive dependence upon newspaper reading, considered with reference to high culture and refined individuality, that, of all indirect benefits of modern travel, perhaps none is more valuable, as a mental experience, than an Eastern tour which cuts off the usual excitements and routine of civilized life, and especially that intense and absolute relation with the Present fostered by the newspaper. Under the palms, on the Nile, and amid the desert, to a thoughtful mind and sensitive organization, it is blissful and auspicious to feel isolated awhile not only from the busy material life of the age, but from its chart and programme — the newspaper; and so be able to live consciously for a season in the Past, and feel the solemn spell of solitude and antiquity. The modern deluge of journalism it has been said with more truth than we can at present quite appreciate, "bereaves life of spirituality, disturbs and overlays individuality, and often becomes a mania and a nuisance, to keep out of which is the only way to keep sacred. It is a sad barbarism," continues the same writer, "when men yield to every impulse from without, with no imperial dignity in the soul which closes its apartments against the virulence of the world and from unworthy intruders." * A Swedish archæologist proves, by relics found in graves in Europe and America, that man in the savage state makes in form, and as far as possible in material, identical utensils and weapons; so in civilized nations the same abuses and traits characterize the periodical press. Crabbe's description of the newspaper in England eighty years ago, finds a curious parallel in that of Sprague in America, fifty years later.

The individual needs an organ in this age wherein and whereby he may record or find reflected his opinions; the great evil is that he who directs this representative medium, may be a "landless resolute," a Bohemian adventurer, without convictions or interests. It is to Burke and the opposition who protected printers from the House of Commons in 1770, that the "Fourth Estate dates its birth;" and Burke was right in his

* W. L. Symonds.

declaration — "posterity will bless this day." Under the ancient *régime* one in a hundred Parisians only could read. After the Revolution, all became interested in battles; to read the news became indispensable; hence it has been well said: — "Napoleon a appris à lire aux Parisiennes. Le professeur leur a coûté cher." The biographer of Volney records that philosopher's testimony against the newspaper as a means of popular culture: — "L'auteur des Ruines, appelé à la chaire d'Histoire, accepté cette charge pénible, mais qui portait avec elle lui offrir les moyens d'être utile: tout en enseignant l'histoire, il voulait chercher à diminuer l'influence journalière qu'elle exerce sur les actions et les opinions des hommes; il la regardàit à juste titre comme l'une des sources les plus fécondes de leurs préjugés et de leurs erreurs." De Tocqueville indicates, in a different way, his sense of the casual adaptation of the newspaper which he describes as "a speech made from a window to the chance passers-by in the street." Among other tests which the rebellion in the United States has thoroughly applied, is that of the press; and it is no exaggeration to say that thereby London and Paris journalism has been completely denuded of the prestige of integrity and humanity save as exceptional traits.

The deliberate protest of an eminent public man like Cobden, is sufficient proof of this fact in regard to the great British organ. He writes: — "A tone of preëminent unscrupulousness in the discussion of political questions, a contempt for the rights and feelings of others, and an unprincipled disregard of the claims of consistency and sincerity on the part of its writers, have long been recognized as the distinguishing characteristics of the *Times*, and placed it in marked contrast with the rest of the periodical press, including the penny journals of the metropolis and the provinces. Its writers are, I believe, betrayed into this tone mainly by their reliance on the shield of an impenetrable secrecy. No gentleman would dream of saying, under the responsibility of his signature, what your writer said of Mr. Bright yesterday. I will not stop to remark on the deterioration of character which follows when a man of education and rare ability thus lowers himself, ay, even in his own eyes, to a condition of moral cowardice. We all know the man whose fortune is derived from the *Times*. We know its manager; its only avowed and responsible editor—he of the semi-official correspondence with Sir Charles Napier in the Baltic, through whose hands, though he never pen a line himself, every slander in its leaders must pass —is as well known to us as the chief official at the Home-Office. Now the question is forced on us whether we, who are behind the scenes, are not bound in the interests of the uninitiated public, and as the only certain mode of abating such outrages as this, to lift the veil and dispel the delusion by which the *Times* is enabled to pursue this game of secrecy to the public and servility to the government—a game (I purposely use the word) which secures for its connections the corrupt advantages, while denying to the public its own boasted benefits of the anonymous system."

The London *Times* has won, and popularly confirmed for itself during the American war for the Union, the name of "Weathercock," only fixed awhile by a *trade* wind, and veering, with shameless alacrity, at every mercenary and malicious breath; while never before in the history of the world, has the line of demarcation between what is true and comprehensive, and what is interested and partisan, been made so emphatically apparent to the common mind as in the vaunts, vagaries, and vacillations of journalism. On the other hand one of the most remarkable evidences of the benefit of popular education as well as an unique contribution to the materials of history, may be found in the letters of the soldiers of the Union army, written from the seat of war to their kindred and printed in the local journals; thousands of them have been collected and arranged, and they naively describe every battle as witnessed and fought by as many individuals. Never before were such materials of history available. In view of the great result — the elimination of vital truth by public discussion — the expression as well as the enlightenment and discipline of public sentiment through the press, we have ample reason to agree with Jefferson, who declared, "If I had to choose between a government without newspapers, or newspapers without a government, I should prefer the latter."

A son of Leigh Hunt, in a voluminous work entitled "The Fourth Estate," has written the annals of the English press; — of which Count Gurowski has well said that it "addresses itself to classes, but seldom, very seldom, to the people itself, as the only national element. The English press mentions the name of the people to be sure, but speaks of it only in generalities, not in that broad and direct sense, as is the case in America. Whole districts, communities, and townships in England, as well as on the Continent, exist without having any newspaper — any organ of publicity. Therein England is under the influence of centralization, as are the other European States. Almost every township and more populous village in the free States in the Union has its organs, whose circulation is independent, and does not interfere with that of those larger papers published in the capitals of States, or in the larger cities."

A philosophical and authentic history of the newspaper, would, however, not only yield the most genuine insight as to public events and the spirit of the age, it would also reveal the most exalted and the lowest traits of humanity. The cowardly hireling who stabs reputations as the *bravo* of the Middle Ages did hearts—for a bribe; and the heroic defender of truth and advocate of reform, loyal with his pen to honest conviction amid the wiles of corruption and the ignominy of abuse — in a word, the holy champion and the base lampooner are both represented in this field. It is one of the conditions of its freedom, that equal rights shall be accorded all; and the wisest men have deemed the possible evils of such latitude more than compensated by the probable good. Perhaps our own country affords the best opportunity to judge this question; and here we cannot but perceive that private judgment continually modifies the influence of the press. We speak habitually of each newspaper as the organ of its editor; and the opinion it advances has precisely as much weight with intelligent readers as the individual is entitled to and no more. The days when the cabalistic "we" inspired awe, have passed away; the venom of a scurrilous print, and the ferocity of a partisan one, only provoke a smile; newspapers here, instead of guiding, follow public opinion; and they have created, by free discussion, an independent habit of thought on the part of their readers, which renders their influence harmless when not useful. Yet the abuses of journalism were so patent and pernicious thirty years ago, that Hillhouse thus entered his wise protest against the growing evil: "Many of our faults, much of our danger, are chargeable to *a reckless press.* No institutions or principles are spared its empiric handling. The most sacred maxims of jurisprudence, the most unblemished public characters, the vital points of constitutional policy and safety, are dragged into discussion and exposed to scorn by presumptuous scribblers, from end to end of the nation." Printers originally issued gazettes, and depended upon contributions for a discussion of public affairs — news whereof they alone furnished: gradually arose the editor; and two conditions soon became apparent as essential to his success — prompt utterance of opinion, and constant re-announcement and advocacy thereof. Cobbett declared the genius of journalism to consist in *re-iteration,* upon which distinction a witty editor improved by substituting *re-irritation.*

As a political element, journalism has entirely changed the position of statesmen, and seems destined to subvert the secret machinery of diplomacy. These results grow out of the enlightenment and circulation of thought on national questions induced by their constant public discussion by the press; their tendency is to break up monopolies of information, to scatter the knowledge of facts, and openly recognize great human interests. By condensing the mists of popular feeling into clear and powerful streams, or shooting them into luminous crystals, the judgment, the sympathies, and the will of mankind are gradually modified. Hence, all who represent the people, are acted upon as they never could have been when authority was less exposed to criticism, and the means of a mutual understanding and comparison of ideas among men less organized and effective. It has been justly observed that no danger can result from the most seductive "leader" on a public question, while the same sheet contains a full report of all the facts relating to it. The pamphlet and gazette of Addison's day, and earlier, are now combined in the newspaper. In great exigencies, however, the immediate promulgation of facts may be a serious national peril; an experienced American editor and careful observer of the phenomena of the Rebellion, thus emphatically testifies to the possible evil of an enterprising press: "I believe most strongly now, that this Rebellion would have been subdued ere this, if, at the outbreak, the Government had suppressed every daily newspaper which contained a line or a word upon the war question, except to give the results of engagements. Our daily journals have kept the Confederates minutely and seasonably informed. The greater the vigilance and accuracy of these journals, the greater their value to the enemy." But a more significant result than this may be found in the test which the Rebellion has proved, not only to social and national, but to professional life, and especially the editorial. How completely has the prestige of newspapers as organs of opinion faded away before the facts of the hour! What poor prophets, reasoners, historical scholars, patriots, and *men* have some of the conductors of the press proved! With what distrust is it now regarded; and how does public confidence refuse any nucleus but that of individual character. The press, therefore, as a popular organ, is unrivalled. It now illustrates every phase, both of reform and conservatism, every religious doctrine, scientific interest, and social tendency. Take up at random any popular newspaper of the day, and what a variety of subjects and scope of vision it covers, superficially indeed, but to the philosophic mind, none the less significantly; — the world is therein pictured in miniature, the world of to-day.

Probably the most universal charm of a newspaper is the gratification it affords what phrenologists call the organ of eventuality. Curiosity is a trait of human nature which belongs to every order of mind, and actuates the infant as well as the sage. To its more common manifestations, the newspaper appeals, and, indeed, originated in this natural craving for incident. In its most sympathetic degree, this feeling is the source of the profound interest which tragedy inspires, and its lower range is the occasion of that pleasure which gossip yields. It is a curious fact, that the same propensity should be at once the cause of the noblest and the meanest exhibitions of character; yet the poetic impulse and reverent inquiry of the highest scientific intelligence — intent upon exploring the wonders of the universe, is but the exalted and ultimate development of this love of the new and desire to penetrate the unknown. The everlasting inquiry for news, which meets us in the street, at the hearthstone, and even beside the bier and in the church, constantly evinces this universal passion. How often does that commonplace question harshly salute the ear of the reflective; what a satire it is upon the glory of the past; how it baffles sentiment, chills enthusiasm, and checks earnestness! The avidity with which fresh intelligence, although of no personal concern, is seized, the eagerness with which it is circulated, and the rapidity with which it is forgotten, are more significant of the transitory conditions of human life, than the data of the calendar or the ruins of Balbec. They prove that we live altogether in the immediate, that our dearest associations may be invaded by the most trivial occurrence, that the mental acquisitions of years do not invalidate a childish love of amusement; and that the mere impertinences of external life have a stronger hold upon our nature than the deepest mysteries of consciousness. "It seems," wrote Fisher Ames, "as if newspaper wares were made to suit a market as much as any other. The starers and wonderers and gapers engross a very large share of the attention of all the sons of the type. I pray the whole honorable craft to banish as many murders, and horrid accidents, and monstrous births, and prodigies from their gazettes, by degrees, as their readers will permit; and by degrees, coax them back to contemplate life and manners, to consider events with some common sense, and to study Nature where she can be known." On the other hand, this curiosity about what does not concern us, is undoubtedly linked with the more generous sympathies, and is, in a degree, prompted by them, so that philanthropy, good-fellowship, and the amenities of social life and benevolent enterprise are more or less the result of the natural interest we feel in the affairs of nations and those of our neighbor. If the newspaper, therefore, considered merely as a vehicle of general information in regard to passing events, has a tendency to diffuse, and render fragmentary our mental life, on the other hand, it keeps the attention fixed upon something besides self, it directs the gaze beyond a narrow circle, and brings home to the heart a sense of universal laws, natural affinities, and progressive interests. But curiosity is not altogether a disinterested passion; and it is amusing to see how newspapers act upon the idiosyncrasy or the interest of readers. The broker unfolds the damp sheet at the stock column; the merchant turns, at once, to the ship-news; the spinster first reads the marriages; the politician, legislative debates; and the author, literary criticisms; while lovers of the marvellous, like Abernethy's patient, enjoy the murders. To how many human propensities does the newspaper thus casually minister! Old gentlemen are, indeed, excusable for losing their temper on a cold morning, when kept waiting for a look into the paper by some spelling reader; and to a benign observer, the comfort of some poor frequenter of a coffee-house oracularly dispensing his gleanings from the journals, is pleasant to consider; — a cheap and harmless gratification, an inoffensive and solacing phase of self-importance. We can easily imagine the anxious expectancy with which the visitors at a gentleman's country-seat in England, before the epoch of journals, awaited the news-letter from town, — destined to pass from house to house, through an isolated neighborhood, and almost worn out in the process of thumbing.

Three traditions exist to account for the origin of newspapers. The first attributes their introduction to the custom prevalent at Venice, about the middle of the fifteenth century, of reading the written intelligence received from the seat of war, then waging by the republic against Solyman II., in Dalmatia, at a fixed time and place, for the benefit of all who chose to hear. French annalists, on the other hand, trace the great invention to a gossiping medical practitioner of Paris, who used to cheer his patients with all the news he could gather, and to save time, had it written out, at intervals, and distributed among them; while an English historian, quoted by D'Israeli the elder, says, "they commenced at the epoch of the Spanish Armada; and that we are indebted to the wisdom of Elizabeth and the prudence of Burleigh for the first newspaper." * The same authority conjectures that the word gazette is derived from *gazzerótta*, a magpie, but it is usually ascribed to *gazet*, a small coin, — the original price of a copy in Venice. One of the most startling relics of Pompeii is the poster advertising gladiators. The oldest newspaper in the world, according to "L'Imprimière," is published at Pekin. It is printed on silk, and has appeared every week for a thousand years. Whatever the actual origin, however, it is natural to suppose that a gradual transition from oral to written, and thence to printed news, was the process by which the modern journal advanced towards its present completeness. It is remarkable that the retrograde movement essential to despotism in all interests, is obvious in the newspaper; — censorship driving free minds from written expression, as in the recent instance of Kossuth when advocating Hungarian progress.

A rigid and complete analytical history of the newspaper would perhaps afford the best illustration of the social and civic development of the civilized world.

* "News-letters were written by enterprising individuals in the metropolis and sent to rich persons who subscribed for them; and then circulated from family to family, and doubtless enjoyed a privilege which has not descended to their printed contemporary — the newspaper — of never becoming stale. Their authors compiled them from materials picked up in the gossip of the coffee-houses." — *Draper's History of the Intellectual Development of Europe*, p. 509.

Commencing with a mere official announcement of national events, such as the ancient Romans daily promulgated in writing, we find the next precursor of the public journal in that systematic correspondence of the scholars of the Middle Ages, whereby erudite, philosophical, or æsthetic ideas were regularly interchanged and diffused. From this to the written circular distributed among the English aristocracy, the transition was a natural result of economical and social necessity; and the historian of the subject in Great Britain, finds in the popularity of the ballad a still further development of the same instinct and want expressing itself among the people. As their vital interest in civic questions enlarged, pamphlets began to be written and circulated on the current topics of the day; then a periodical sheet was issued containing foreign intelligence, among the earliest specimens whereof is, "The Weekly Newes from Italy and Germanie," which first appeared in 1622. It is a characteristic fact that the first two special newspaper organs that were published in England were devoted to sporting * and medical intelligence. But it was reserved for the last century to expand these germinal experiments into what we now justly consider a great civilizing institution. When Burke † began to apply

* *Jockey's Intelligencer*, 1683.

† Burke's influence upon journalism was still more direct. While preparing for Dodsley "An Account of the European Settlements in America," he was led by his researches to suggest a periodical which should chronicle the important literary, political, and social facts of the year. Such was the origin of the "Annual Registers." The first volume appeared in 1759. For several years it was edited by Burke, is still regularly published, and has been imitated in similar publications elsewhere, having finally initiated and established the historical element of journalism.

philosophy to politics, and Junius to set the example of memorable anonymous writing on public questions, and Wilkes to battle for the liberty of the press, new and powerful intellectual and moral elements were infused into journalism; to these, vast mechanical improvements gave new diffusion; discussion gave birth to systems, invention to new industrial interests, social culture to original phases and forms of popular literary taste and talent. In England, Hazlitt's psychological criticisms, Jerrold's local wit, Thackeray's incisive satire, the descriptive talent of scores of travelling reporters, and the dramatic genius of such observers as Charles Dickens, blended their versatile attractions with the vivid chronicle of daily news and the elaborate treatise of political essayists; while in France, from Rousseau, Grimm, and Mirabeau, to Thiers and St. Beuve, the journal represented the sternest political and the most finished literary ability; from the old "Journal Étranger," devoted to scandal, to Marat's "Ami du Peuple," the vicissitudes and the genius of France are enrolled in her journalism.

The French papers have the largest subscription, those of London the most complete establishments, and in America they are far more numerous than in other countries; over three thousand are now published, and their price is about one seventh that of the English. The tone of the American press is usually less dignified and intellectual than that of France and England. It has also the peculiarity of being maintained, in a great degree, by advertisements; thus the commercial as well as the party element, both dangerous to the elevation of the press, enter largely into its character here. It has been said of penny-a-liners that they are to the newspaper corps what Cossacks are to a regular army, and the activity of journalism in Great Britain, and the detail of its enterprise, are signally evidenced by such a class of writers, as well by the fact that in 1826, when Canning sent British troops to Portugal, newspaper reporters went with the army, a custom which in the Crimean, East India, and recent American war, has given birth to such memorable correspondence. The shipping intelligence of United States journals is more minute, the philosophical eloquence of those of Paris more striking, and the details of court gossip and criminal jurisprudence more full in those of London, — characteristics which respectively mirror national traits and the existent state of society in each latitude. The shareholders of the London "Times" have occasionally divided a net profit of one hundred and twenty thousand pounds — the well-earned recompense for the complete arrangement and efficient exercise of this greatest of modern instruments. It is not surprising that the most renowned of writers have availed themselves of a medium so direct and universal. Chateaubriand wrote in the "Journal des Debats" against Polignac; Malte-Brun contributed geographical articles to the same print; Benjamin Constant's views were unfolded in the "Minerve Française"; Lafitte's opinions found expression in the "Journal du Commerce." Lamartine's ideal of a journal is one which has "assez de raison pour convenir aux hommes sérieux, assez de témerité pour plaire aux hommes légeres, assez d' excentricité pour plaire aux aventereux." With all the restrictions to which despotism in France has subjected the press, its history as a whole is as Protean as Paris life, and reflects the tendencies of national character.

As early as 1650, there was a "Gazette de Burlesque," soon after a "Mercury Galant"; the "Journal des Debats" is devoted to facts and its own dignity, the "Siècle" represents mercantile interests, "La Presse" is full of ideas, and has been well described as partaking of the nature of a torrent which "*Se grossit par la resistance.*"* Napoleon depended on the "Moniteur," and kept the press low because he feared its influence more than an army. The proprietors of the "Constitutionel" often pay a hundred and fifty francs for a single column. William Livingston wrote effectively in 1752, in the "Independent Reflector," of New York, against Episcopal encroachments. Freedom of the press, in America, was established by the trial of the printer Zenger. Kossuth was a journalist while at the head of a nation. Cavour began his public career in the same capacity, and Heine was the admirable correspondent of leading German journals for many years. Centralization vastly increases the influence of journalism in Paris, and its history there is a perfect index of the successive revolutions. From Benjamin Franklin to Walter Savage Landor, and from Junius to Jack Downing, these vehicles of ideas have enshrined memorable individualities as well as phases of general opinion. Jefferson, Hamilton, Rufus King, De Witt Clinton, and Everett, — all our statesmen, — have been newspaper writers.

* The following return of the numbers daily printed by the principal Paris journals is taken from M. Didot's pamphlet on the fabrication of paper. It may be regarded as official: "Presse," 40,000; "Siècle," 35,000; "Constitutionel," 25,000; "Moniteur," 24,000; "Patrie," 18,000; "Pays," 14,000; "Débats," 9,000; "Assemblée Nationale," 5,000; "Univers," 3,500; "Union," 3,500; "Gazette de France," 2,500; "Gazettes de Tribunaux," 2,500. These journals are all printed in five offices, and the quantity of paper they annually consume amounts to more than four millions of pounds.

Specimens of recorded thought from the earliest to the present time, would aptly mark the history of civilization; the writings on stone, wax, bones, lead, palm-leaves, bark, linen, and parchment — inscribed by patient manual toil, denoting the era when knowledge was a mystery and its possessor a seer; illuminated chronicles and missals representing its cloistered years; — black-letter, the transition period when it began to expand, although still a luxury, and the newspaper illustrating its modern diffusion and universality. The scribe's vocation was at once superseded by the invention of printing, and the scholar's monopoly broken up; hence the scarcity and value of books prior to the times of Faust and Caxton, can scarcely be appreciated by this generation. Wonderful indeed is the contrast to the American traveller, as he muses beside the Anapus at Syracuse, over the papyrus vegetating in its waters, — between the scrolls of antiquity engrossed on this material, and the twenty thousand closely printed sheets thrown off in an hour by one of the mammoth daily presses of his native country. This rapidity of production, however, is almost as oblivious in its tendency as the limited copies produced by the pen and transmitted in manuscript. It may be said of exclusive newspaper writers and readers, with a few memorable exceptions, that their intellectual triumphs are "writ in water"; and melancholy is that fate which condemns a man of real genius to the labors of a newspaper editor; fragmentary and fugitive, though incessant, are his labors, — usually destructive of style, and without permanent memorials; when of a political nature they often enlist bitter feelings and promote a knowledge of the world calculated to indurate as well as expand the mind. A veteran French writer for the press, describes the editor's life as always "*troublée et militante.*" An American poet,* whose divine art is a safeguard against the worst evils of journalism, in a recent history of his paper, thus speaks of the influence of the employment upon character: —

"It is a vocation which gives an insight into men's motives, and reveals by what influences masses of men are moved, but it shows the dark, rather than the bright side of human nature, and one who is not disposed to make due allowances for the peculiar circumstances in which he is placed, is apt to be led by it into the mistake, that the large majority of mankind are knaves. It fills the mind with a variety of knowledge relating to the events of the day, but that knowledge is apt to be superficial; since the necessity of attending to many subjects prevents the journalist from thoroughly investigating any. In this way it begets desultory habits of thought, disposing the mind to be satisfied with mere glances at difficult questions, and to delight in passing lightly from one thing to another. The style gains in clearness and fluency, but is apt to become, in consequence of much and hasty writing, loose, diffuse, and stuffed with local barbarisms and the cant phrases of the day. Its worst effect is the strong temptation which it sets before men, to betray the cause of truth to public opinion, and to fall in with what are supposed to be the views held by a contemporaneous majority, which are sometimes perfectly right and sometimes grossly wrong."

In regard to the influence of newspapers on style, it has been noted that since their cheap issue, colloquial simplicity has vanished. "A single number of a London morning paper," observes a writer in Blackwood, "(which in half a century, has expanded from the size of a dinner napkin to that of a breakfast tablecloth, from that to a carpet, and will soon be forced by the

* Bryant.

expansion of public business into something resembling the mainsail of a frigate,) already is equal in printed matter to a very large octavo volume. Every old woman in the nation now reads daily a vast miscellany, in one volume royal octavo; thus the whole artificial dialect of books has come into play as the dialect of ordinary life. This is one form of the evil impressed upon style by journalism; a dire monotony of bookish idiom has stiffened all freedom of expression."* As to its effect on the *morale*, when pursued exclusively as a material interest, one of the most acute and observant of modern French writers says:—"Le journal, au lieu d' être un sacerdoce, est devenu un moyen pour les partis; de moyen, il s'est fait commerce; et comme tous les commerces, il est sans foi ni loi;" and in allusion to the French, bitterly adds, "nous verrons les journaux, dirigés d' abord par des hommes d' honneur, tomber plus tard sons le gouvernement de plus médiocre, qui auront la patience et la lâcheté de gomme elastique qui manquent aux beaux genies, ou à des epiciers qui auront de l'argent pour acheter des plumes." Macaulay, says a French critic, "a conservè dans l'histoire, les habitudes qu' il avait gagnées dans les journaux." Journalism has proved an effective discipline for statesmen; the late prime minister of Sardinia first dealt with public questions in the columns of a political journal.

But whatever facility of expression and tact in the popular exposition of political science may be acquired by the statesman or annalist, in the practice of journalism, there is no doubt that the worst perversions of "English undefiled" have originated in, and been confirmed by, newspapers. On this subject, an American

* *Blackwood's Magazine*, Vol. xxviii., p. 8.

writer at once philosophical, erudite, and liberal, who has treated of the history and influence of the English language with remarkable insight and eloquence, emphatically testifies to the verbal corruptions and consequent moral degradation of the newspaper press. "The dialect of personal vituperation," says Marsh, "the rhetoric of malice in all its modifications, the Billingsgate of vulgar hate, the art of damning with faint praise, the sneer of contemptuous irony, have been sedulously cultivated; and, combined with a certain flippancy of expression and ready command of a tolerably extensive vocabulary, are enough to make the fortune of any sharp, shallow, and unprincipled journalist who is content with the fame and the pelf."

The interest which belongs to newspapers as arenas for discussion and records of fact, is greatly marred by the abuses of the press. No more humiliating exhibition of human passion can be imagined than printed scurrility; and no meaner and more contemptible evidence of skulking treachery than anonymous libels. By what anomaly base spirits enact and endure insult in this form, which public opinion and the faintest self-respect compel them to resent when orally uttered, we have never been able to explain. It is, however, a satire on the alleged freedom we enjoy in this country, that any malicious poltroon who has the means to purchase types, may defame the character, and thereby injure the prosperity, of any one towards whom he entertains a grudge, with comparative impunity. Indeed, if a man comes before the public in any shape, even in that of a benefactor, he is liable to gross personal attacks from the press; here the shafts of envy, of party hatred, of blackguardism and of detraction, find a covert whence they may be sped with deadly aim and little or no chance of punishment. To realize, at once, the moral grandeur and the degrading abuse of which the press is capable, one should read Milton's discourse on the "Liberty of Unlicensed Printing," and then a history of cases under the law of libel. The choice of weapons is allowed his enemy even by the inveterate duelist; but there is this essential dishonor in the attacks of the practiced writer — that he adroitly uses an instrument which his antagonist often cannot wield. Thus the laws of honorable warfare are basely set aside; and cowardice often wins an ostensible triumph. The meanest threat we ever heard was that of a popular author towards a spirited and generous but uneducated farmer with whom he was in altercation, and who proposed a resort to arms: — "I hold a pen that shall point the world's finger of scorn at you!" The cheapest abuse is that which can be poured out in newspapers; and besides the comparatively defenceless position of the assailed, if he have no skill in pen-craft, it is the more contemptible because premeditated; the insulting word may be uttered in the heat of rage, but the slanderous paragraph goes through the process of writing and printing; — it is therefore, the result of a deliberate act. The "scar of wrath" left on the heart by the partisan combats of the press, is seldom honorable, and the records of duels, persecutions, and street-fights originating in libels, is one of the most degrading to all concerned, of any in social history. Vituperation and invective, Billingsgate and the cant nicknames of newspaper controversy, belong to the most unredeemed species of blackguardism. No wounds rankle in the human bosom like those inflicted by the press; and no agent of redress should be used with such thorough observance of the golden rule. "The French," says Matthew Arnold, "talk of the 'brutalité des journaux Anglais.' What strikes them comes from the necessary inherent tendencies of newspaper writing not being checked in England by any centre of intelligent and urbane spirit, but rather stimulated by coming in contact with a provincial spirit."

From these various capabilities and liabilities of journalism we may infer what are the requisites of an editor. It is obvious that his intellectual equipment should be more versatile and complete than that demanded by any other profession. He is to interpret the events of the day, and must, of course, be versed in the history of the past; he is to speak a universal language, and the gifts of expression must be his chief endowment; he exercises a mighty influence, and, therefore, judgment, self-respect, a recognition of rights and duties, and a benevolent impulse are essential. The *juste milieu* between moral courage and respect for public sentiment, should be his goal. It is a significant fact, that, in this country, where there are more readers than in any other, and, at the same time, entire freedom of the press, journals have not attained to the intellectual standard of the best of foreign origin, nor has the profession of an editor reached the rank it has in Europe. With a few exceptions, the vocation has been adopted, as school-keeping used to be, as the most available resource. Cleverness has usually been the substitute for acquirement; loyalty to some dogma for philosophy, and glib phrases and cant terms for style. In some memorable cases, where the London system of a division of labor is resorted to, and the French practice of careful rhetoric and reasoning applied to current topics, the result has approximated to what a leading journal should be. Such names as Franklin, Russell, Thomas, Duane, Buckingham, Walsh, Gales, Noah, King, Hoffman, and the eminent contemporary editors of America, bear, it must be remembered, but a very small proportion to the sum total of newspapers published in this country; and it is the average ability and character of editors to which we refer. Yet familiarity alone blinds us to the "extraordinary talent" exhibited in the journalism of our times. "I 'll be shot," says Christopher North, to the shepherd, "if Junius, were he alive now, would set the world on the rave as he did some half century ago."

The rarest and most needful moral quality in an editor is magnanimity. Of all vocations this is the one with which narrow motives and exclusive points of view are most incompatible. It is true that the office is self-imposed; but, in its very nature, is included a comprehensive tone of mind and feeling; the editor, therefore, who pronounces judgment upon a book, a work of art, a public man or popular subject, according to his personal animosities or selfish interests, annuls his own claim to the position he occupies. If the pulpit, the medical chair, the justice's bench, or the authority of elective office is exclusively used by an individual for direct personal ends, for the exclusive emolument of friends, or the gratification of private revenge, the perversion is resented at once and indignantly by public opinion; and the same violation of a general principle for a particular end, is equally unjustifiable in the press. Yet how many journals serve but as channels for the prejudices, the likes and dislikes, the plans and whims of their editors, so that, at last, we recognize them, not as broad and reliable expositors of great questions and critical taste, but as mouthpieces for the spite, the flattery, and the ambition of a single vain mortal! For such evils Milton's arguments for patient toleration of all kinds of printed ideas, are the best remedy: "Punishing wits," he says, "enhances their authority; errors known, read, and collated, are of main service toward the speedy attainment of what is truest; and, though all the winds of doctrine were let loose to play upon the earth, so truth be in the field, we do injuriously by licensing and prohibiting to misdoubt her strength." With all its defects, therefore, the emanations of a free press are the best expositors of the immediate in taste, opinion, and affairs; and copies of the "Times," the "Court Journal," and "Bell's Life in London," deposited under the corner-stone of a modern English edifice, are as authentic memorials of the country and people as they exist to-day, as the styles of Grecian architecture, or the characteristics of Italian painting, of epochs in the history of art, and far more detailed, minute, and elaborate. The complex state of society, the multitudinous aspect of life, the progress of science and its influence on social economy, can indeed only be designated by such a versatile record. The miserable little gazzettas issued in the south of Europe, containing only the diluted news of the French journals; the spirited *feuilletons* of the cleverest authors of the day that appear in the latter, the enormous advertising sheets in this country, and the able rhetoric and argument of the daily press in Great Britain, are so many landmarks and gauges of the civic life, the mental recreations, the prosperity and the political intelligence of these different countries. Although Fanny Kemble snubbed the press-gang, ironically so called, — perhaps in this age there is no office capable of a higher ideal standard and a more practical efficiency combined, as that of the public writer. Let us suppose such a man endowed with the greatest faculty of expression, learned in history and the arts, with philosophic insight and poetical sensibility, chivalric in tone, uniting the principles of conservatism and reform, devoted to humanity, generous, heroic, independent and "clear in his great office;" and thus furnished and inspired, waging the battle of honest opinion, a stanch advocate of truth, stripping the mask from fanaticism and dishonesty, and shedding pure intellectual light on the common mind; — no more noble function can be imagined. Seldom, however, is the ideal of an editor even approached; and hence the wisdom of an eclectic system and a division of labor; concentrating upon the same journal, the humor of one, the statistical researches of another, the learning of a third, and the rhetoric of a fourth, until all the needful elements are brought into action for a common result.

In periods of war, emigration, or catastrophes of any kind, the newspaper becomes a chart of destiny to the heart, and is seized with overwhelming anxiety to learn the fate of the absent and the loved; and in times of peace and comfort, it is the readiest pastime. What traveller does not remember with zest the intervals of leisure he has spent, under the trees of the Palais Royal, over a fresh gazette; or the eagerness with which, in an Italian *café*, he has devoured "Galignani" with his breakfast? It is difficult to imagine how the social reforms that distinguish the age could have been realized without the aid of newspapers; or by what other means popular sympathy could be kindled simultaneously on both sides of the globe. In view of such offices, we must regard the editor as a species of modern *improvisatore* who gathers from clubs, theatres, legislative halls, private society, and the streets, the idea and the elemental spirit of the hour, the topic of the day, the moral influence born of passing events, and then concentrates and elaborates it to give forth its vital principles and absolute significance.

As a medium of controversy, the advantages of the newspaper are signal. In 1685, the discussion of popery in England was carried on by means of tracts issued from the presses of Oxford, Cambridge, and London; and some of the pamphlets of De Foe, Steele, and other popular writers, had a large sale; but the circulation of these vehicles of argument was limited compared to the daily journals of our day; and in order to reach the people, controversialist and agreeable essayists from the times of "Sir Roger L'Estrange" to that of "O. P. Q.," have wisely availed themselves of newspapers. That they now aid rather than form public opinion, however, is quite obvious. The implicit faith once bestowed upon editors has departed; and no class are more pertinacious in asserting the right of private judgment than habitual readers of journals; they derive from them materials of discussion rather than positive inferences. Yet there are two qualities that in Great Britain and America gain an editor permanent admirers — good-sense and an individual style. The thunder, as Carlyle calls it, of Edward Sterling in the London "Times," and the plain words of Cobbett, are instances. In fact, the same qualities insure consideration for a newspaper as for an individual; tone, manliness, grace or vigor, full and free knowledge, wit and fancy, and the sincerity or geniality of the editor's character, are not less recognized in his paragraphs than in his behavior. But as a general rule, as before suggested, in the United States, the press is the expositor, not the herald, of opinion; the newspapers simply mark the level of popular feeling; their criticism seldom transcends the existent taste, and their tone is rarely elevated above that of the majority. Between the radical and the conservative, there appears no medium; and newspapers symbolize these two extremes. In our large cities, there is always one newspaper which has a name for respectability of which its editors are extremely jealous; it never startles, offends, or inspires, but pursues an even, unexceptionable course, is praised by old people who have taken it for years, and desire that it shall contain their obituary; its news, however, is usually stale, its opinions timid, and its spirit behind the age. To represent the opposite element, there is always a vigorous, speculative, and fresh-toned newspaper, which continually utters startling things, and suggests glorious impossibilities; it is the exponent of reform, a harbinger of better times, and appeals to hope and fancy, rather than to memory and reflection. Now the experienced reader will at once perceive that an editor, worthy the name, should be an eclectic, and combine in his own mind and work, the expression of both these extremes of opinion and sentiment; but it is found, by experiment, that a hobby is the means of temporary success, — that a catholic temper is unappreciated, and that, in a republic, combativeness and self-esteem are the organs to be most profitably addressed.

There is a very large class whose reading is confined to newspapers, and they manifest the wisdom of Pope's maxim about the danger of a little learning. Adopting the cant and slang phrases of the hour, and satisfied with the hasty conjectures and partial glimpses of truth that diurnal journals usually contain, they are at once superficial and dogmatic, full of fragmentary ideas and oracular common-place. If such is the natural effect upon an undisciplined mind of exclusive newspaper reading, even the scholar, the thinker, and the man of refined taste is exposed to mental dissipation from the same cause. A celebrated French philosopher, recently deceased, remarkable for severe and efficient mental labor, told an American friend that he had not read a newspaper for four years. It is incalculable what productiveness of mind and freshness of conception is lost to the cultivated intellect by the habit of beginning the day with newspapers. The brain, refreshed by sleep, is prepared to act genially in the morning hours; and a statistical table, prepared by an able physiologist, shows that those authors who give this period to labor, most frequently attain longevity. Scott is a memorable example of the healthfulness and efficiency attending the practice. If, therefore, the student, the man of science, or the author dissipates his mental vigor, and the nervous energy induced by a night's repose, in skimming over the countless topics of a newspaper, he is too much in relation with things in general to concentrate easily his thoughts; his mind has been diverted, and his sympathies too variously excited, to readily gather around a special theme. Those intent upon self-culture, or intellectual results, should, therefore, make this kind of reading a pastime, and resort to it in the intervals of more consecutive thought. There is no element of civilization that debauches the mind of our age more than the indiscriminate and exclusive perusal of newspapers. Only by consulting history, by disciplining the reasoning powers in the study of philosophy, and cherishing a true sense of the beautiful by communion with the poets, — in a word, only by habitual reference to standard literature, can we justly estimate the record of the hour. There must be great examples in the mind, great principles of judgment and taste, or the immediate appeal to these qualities is ignorantly answered; whereas, the thoughtful, intelligent comments of an educated reader of journals upon the questions they discuss, the precedents he brings in view, and the facts of the past to which he refers, place the immediate in relation with the universal, and enable us to seize upon essential truth. To depend for mental recreation upon newspapers, is a desperate resource; not to consult them is to linger behind the age. De Tocqueville has shown that devotion to the immediate is characteristic of republics; and this tendency is manifest in the prevalence of newspapers in the United States. They, in a great measure, supersede the demand for a more permanent native literature; they foster a taste for ephemeral topics and modes of thought, and lamentably absorb, in casual efforts, gifts and graces of mind which, under a different order of things, would have attained not only a higher, but a lasting development. The comparative importance of newspapers among us, as materials of history, is evidenced by the fact that the constant reference to their files has induced the historical societies to propose an elaborate index to facilitate the labors of inquirers, which has been felicitously called a diving-bell for the sea of print. A list of the various journals now in existence would be found to include not only every political party and religious sect in the country, but every theory of life, every science, profession, and taste, from phrenology to dietetics, and from medicine, war, and odd-fellowship, to literature, catholicism, and sporting. Tribunals and punsters, not less than fashion and chess-players, have their printed organ. What was a subordinate element, has become an exclusive feature. "In those days," writes Lamb, "every morning-paper, as an essential retainer to its establishment, kept an author who was bound to furnish daily a quantum of witty paragraphs at sixpence a joke." Now "Punch" and "Charivari" monopolize the fun, and grave and gay are separately embodied. The cosmopolitan nature of the people would as obviously appear in the number of journals issued in foreign languages, each nation and tribe having its newspaper organ; and an analysis of the contents, even of one popular journal for a single year, would be found to touch the entire circle of human knowledge and vicissitude, without penetrating to a vital cause, or expanding to a comprehensive principle, yet affording a boundless horizon; — astronomical phenomena, *causes célèbres*, earthquakes, the advent of a great *cantatrice*, shipwrecks and revolutions, battles and bankruptcies, freshets and fires, *émeutes* and hail-storms, gold discoveries, anniversaries, executions, Arctic expeditions, World's Fairs, the utterance of patriots, and the acts of usurpers; — all the materials of history, the suggestions of philosophy, and the visions of poetry, in their chaotic, elemental, and actual state. It is evident that more excitement than truth, more food for curiosity than aid to reflection, more vague knowledge than actual wisdom, is thus promulgated and preserved. The harvest of the immediate is comparatively barren; and life only proves the truth of Dr. Johnson's association of intellectual dignity with the past and future. The individual, to be true to himself, must take a firm stand against the encroachments of this restless, temporary, and absorbing life of the moment represented by the newspaper; he must cleave to Memory and Hope; he must look before and after, or his mind will be superficial in its activity, and fruitless in its growth.

There is no mechanical invention around which cluster such interesting associations as that of printing; the indirect agency of the press and of journalism is remarkable; and this is owing to the relation they bear to the world at large, and to personal improvement. The newspaper office has always been a nucleus for wits, politicians, and literati, a nursery of local genius, and a school for knowledge of the world, and criticism. In Franklin's autobiography, the natural effect of even a mechanical connection with the press is memorably unfolded; and scarcely a great name in modern history is unallied with some incident or activity connected with the daily press. Otis, Adams, Hancock, and Warren, used to meet at the office of the "Boston Gazette," and write essays on colonial rights in its columns. Talleyrand and Louis Philippe frequented the sanctum of an editor in the same town, to read the "Moniteur," and discuss news. Chateaubriand first heard of the king's flight from a stray newspaper picked up in a log hut in the backwoods of America; and it sent him back at once to the army of the Princes. Horne Tooke's "Diversions of Purley" were written to beguile his imprisonment occasioned by a libel; and his trial resulted in making parliamentary reports legal. Hunt's prison-life, for which he was indebted to his comments on the Prince-Regent in the "Examiner," is the most charming episode in his memoirs; and some of the noblest flights of Erskine's eloquence arose from the defence of those prosecuted for constructive treason based on the free expression of opinion in regard to public questions. Jefferson thought Freneau's paper "prevented the Constitution from galloping into a monarchy"; and it was in the columns of a daily journal that Hamilton defended the proclamation of neutrality. It has been said that the most reliable history of the French revolution, and wars of the republic, could be gleaned from the pages of an American journal of the day, conducted by a man of political knowledge and military aptitude, who combined from various prejudiced foreign papers what he deemed an authentic narrative of each act in the drama; and it is certain that the best account of the massacre and the destruction of the tea — from which dates our Revolution, — are to be found in the contemporary newspapers. Never was contemporary history so copiously and minutely written as in the newspaper annals of the war for the Union. In fact, the best history thereof has been compiled by an assiduous collator from current journalism. The history of censorship in Europe in modern times is the history of opinion, of freedom, and of society. We felt the despotism of the King of Naples in all its baseness, only when a writer of genius told us, with a sigh, that he had been driven to natural history as the only subject upon which he could expatiate in print without impediment. Thus we see how the fate of nations and the experience of individuals are associated with the press; and how its influence touches the whole circle of life, — evoking genius, kindling nations, informing fugitives, and alarming kings.

PREACHERS.

"It is neither the vote nor the laying on of hands that gives men the right to preach. One's own heart is authority. If he cannot preach to edification, he is not authorized, though all the ministers of Christendom ordain him."

THUS writes a popular preacher of the conservative sect in theology: recognizing a spiritual fact and conviction which tempts us to analyze and define, as a subject of natural history, the function and fame of the preacher. The term by its derivation is the most generic word to indicate clerical vocation; "to say before," to proclaim, inculcate, preach; in other words, to be the herald and representative of truth, right, faith, and immortal hope, — such is the basis and logical claim of the preacher's authority, under whatever form, creed, or character. They may be divided into the inspired, the ascetic, the jovial, the belligerent, the finical, the shrewd, and the ingenuous. The "oily man of God" described by Pope, Scott's Covenanter, and Friar Tuck, the disinterested Vicar of Fielding, Shakspeare's good friars and ambitious cardinals, Mawworm, Mrs. Inchbald's Dorimel, the gentle hero of the Sexton's Daughter, Manzoni's Prelate and Capuchin, and Mrs. Radcliffe's Monks, are genuine and permanent types, only modified by circumstances. All that is subtle in artifice, all that is relentless in the love of power, all that is exalted in spiritual graces, all that is base in cunning, glorious in self-sacrifice, beautiful in compassion, and noble in allegiance, has been and is manifest in the priest. His great distinction is based upon the fact that "the church, rightly ministered, is the vestibule to an immortal life." He is at once the author of the worst tyranny and the grandest amenities of social life. The traveller on Alpine summits blesses the name of St. Bernard, and descends to Geneva to shudder at the bigoted ferocity of Calvin. The picture of the good pastor in the "Deserted Village," and Ranke's "Lives of the Popes," give us the two extremes of the character. The spiritual heroism of Luther, the religious gloom of Cowper, and the cheerful devotion of Watts, are but varied expressions of one feeling, which, according to the frail conditions of humanity, has its healthy and its morbid phase, its authentic and its spurious exposition, and is no more to be confounded in its original essence, with its imperfect development and representatives, than the pure light of heaven with the accidental mediums which color and distort its rays.

The *prestige* of the clerical office is greatly diminished because many of its prerogatives are no longer exclusive. "When ecclesiasticism became so weak as to be unable to regulate international affairs, and was supplanted by diplomacy, in the castle the physician was more than a rival for the confessor, in the town the mayor was a greater man than the abbot." * The clergy, at a former period, were the chief scholars; learning was not less their distinction than sanctity.

* Draper's *Intellectual Development of Europe.*

In every intelligent community, this source of influence is now shared with men of letters; and even the once peculiar office of public instruction, is now filled by the lecturer, who takes an evening from the avocations of business or professional life, to claim intellectual sympathy or impart individual opinions. But the great agent in breaking up the monopoly of the pulpit has been the press. Written has in a great measure superseded oral thought. Half the world are readers, and the necessity of hearing no longer exists to those desirous of knowledge. The sermons of the old English divines abound with classical learning and comments on the times, such as are now sought in periodical literature. In Latimer, Andrews, and Donne, we find such hints of the prevailing manners as subsequently were revealed by "The Spectator." The philosophy of antiquity and the morals of courts, the facts of distant climes, all that we now seek in popular books and the best journals, came to the minds of our ancestors through the discourses of preachers. American ministers, prior to and at the era of the Revolution, were the expositors of political as well as religious sentiments. Independent of the priestly rites, therefore, a clergyman, in past times, represented social transitions, and ministered to intellectual wants, for which we of this age have adequate provision otherwise; so that the most zealous advocate of reform, doctrine, or ethical philosophy, is no longer obliged to have recourse to the sacerdotal office, in order to reach the public mind. This apparent diminution of the privileges of the order, however, does not invalidate but rather simplifies its claims. In this as in so many other functions of the social economy, progress has the effect of reducing to its original elements the duties and the influence of the profession. Education, once their special responsibility, and popular enlightenment on the questions of the hour, being assumed by others, the preacher is free to concentrate his abilities on theology and the religious sentiment. Division of labor gives him a better opportunity to be "clear in his great office." It is reduced to its normal state. Except in isolated and newly-settled communities, there is not that incessant appeal to his benevolence and erudition: to heal the sick, reconcile litigants, argue civic questions, teach the elements of science, promote charities; in a word, to be the village orator and social oracle, are not the indispensable requisites of a clergyman's duty which they were before the Newspaper and the Lyceum existed. He is, therefore, at liberty to imitate the apostles of Christianity and the fathers of the Church, and bring all his power to awaken devotion and faith, and all his learning to the defence of sacred truth. That the time and capacity of the profession is diffused, and the sympathy of its members enlisted in behalf of other than these aims, is, indeed, true; but this is a voluntary and not an inevitable result, and only proves that the spirit of the age overlays instead of being penetrated and ruled by the priestly office.

"Civilization," says Lamartine, "was of the sanctuary. Kings were only concerned with acts; ideas belonged to the priest." And, by a singular contradiction, with the general progress of society, the same class as a whole, have proved the most antagonistic to innovation even in the form of genius, whose erratic manifestations are jealously regarded as inconsistent with professional decorum. Hence Byron, in one of his splenetic moods, exclaimed to Trelawney: "When did parsons patronize genius? If one of their black band dares to think for himself, he is drummed out or cast aside like Sterne and Swift." On the other hand, venerable physicians say that the clergy are the most efficient promoters of medical innovations; and that quackery owes its social *prestige* in no small degree to their countenance.

After the Reformation, this office as such lost its speciality; the right to exercise it was no longer peculiar; and in all societies and epochs, when a great activity of the religious sentiment, or an earnest discussion of questions of faith prevailed, men prayed, sermonized, commented on Scripture, and mingled all the duties of the clerical vocation with their own pursuits. Thus the English statesmen of Cromwell's time were versed in divinity, exhorted, and published tracts in behalf of their creeds. Theology was a popular study; and the kingdom swarmed with lay-preachers. Sects, too, repudiated official leaders; and even among the Pilgrim Fathers of New England, ministers betrayed a jealousy of encroachments on the part of their unconsecrated brethren. Many Christians also recognized spiritual gifts as the exclusive credentials of a priesthood. Church not less than State prerogatives were challenged by republican zeal; and the historical authority of the order being thus openly invaded, a new and more rational test was soon applied, and preachers, like kings, were made amenable to the tribunal of public opinion, and obliged to rest their claims on other than traditional or educational authority. "On conserva," says Rochambeau, writing of American society at the period of the Revolution, "au ministre du culte le première place dans les repas publics; il bénissoit le repas; mais ses prérogatives ne s'entendoient pas plus loin dans la société.* Cet exposé," he adds, evidently in view of priestly corruption in France, "doit amener naturellement des mœurs simples et pures." † "They," says the historian of preachers at the time of the Revolutionary war, "dealt in no high-sounding phrases of liberty and equality; they went to the very foundations of society, showed what the rights of man were, and how those rights became modified when men gathered into communities. The profound thought and unanswerable arguments, found in these sermons, show that the clergy were not a whit behind the ablest statesmen of the day in their knowledge of the great science of human government. In reading them, one gets at the true pulse of the people, and can trace the steady progress of the public sentiment. The rebellion in New England rested on the pulpit, received its strongest impulse, indeed, its moral character, from it; the teachings of the pulpit of Lexington caused the first blow to be struck for American independence."

The tendency of all the so-called liberal professions is to limit and pervert the development of character, by giving to knowledge a technical shape, and to thought a prescriptive action. Conformity to a specific method is unfavorable to original results, and organization often does injustice to its subjects. Only the strong men, the

* Dr. Sprague's "Annals of the American Pulpit," is full of delineations and anecdotes of prominent preachers. Their energy, zeal, and courage, are viewed in connection with their racy individual peculiarities. What some of the Methodists had and have to endure and suffer, is indicated by a direction from a circuit, in want of a preacher, to the Western Conference: "Be sure you send us a good swimmer," — it being the duty of the minister in that region frequently to swim wide and bridgeless streams to keep his appointments.

† *Mémoires de Rochambeau.*

brave and the highly endowed, rise above such restrictions. It is a kind of social necessity alone which reconciles the man of scientific genius to seek the passport of a medical diploma, — the logician to exert his mind exclusively before a legal tribunal, and the votary of religious truth to sign a creed and become responsible to a congregation. How constantly each breaks away from his respective sphere to expatiate in the broad kingdom of letters! Would Humboldt have written the Cosmos had his life been confined to a laboratory, or a round of medical practice? Would Burke have theorized in so comprehensive a range, if chained to an attorney's desk, or Sir Henry Vane's martyrdom acquired a holier sanction from the mere title of priest?

At the first glance, so distinct are the phases of the office that it is difficult to realize its identity. The ideal of a village pastor like Oberlin, self-devoted, in a secluded district, to the most pure and benevolent enterprise, — the life of a Jesuit missionary in Canada or Peru, who seems to incarnate the fiery zeal of the Church he represents, — the complacent bishop of the Establishment, listlessly going through a prescribed form, and his very person embodying worldly prosperity; and the inelegant but earnest Methodist swaying the multitude at a camp-meeting in the wilds of America, — consider the vast contrast of the pictures: the dark robe, lonely existence, and subtle eye of the Catholic; the simple, friendly, conscientious toil of the poor vicar; the scholarship and good dinners of the English bishop; the cathedral decked with the trophies of art, and fields lit up by watch-fires; the silence of the Quaker assembly, and the loud harangue and frantic moans of the "revival;" the solemn refinement of the Episcopal, the intellectual zeal of the Unitarian, and the gorgeous rites of the Roman worship; and an uninformed spectator, to whom each was a novelty, would imagine that a totally diverse principle was at work. To the philosophic eye, the ceremonies, organization, costume, rites, and even creeds of Christian sects, are but the varied manifestations of a common instinct, more or less mingled with other human qualities, and influenced in its development by time and place. Traced back to its source, and separated from incidental association, we find a natural sentiment of religion which is represented in social economy by the preacher. Simple as was the original relation between the two, however, in the process of time it has become so complicated that it now requires no ordinary analytical power to divest the idea of the priest from history, and that of religion from the Church, so as to perceive both as facts of human nature instead of parts of the machinery of civilized life. To do this, indeed, we look inward, and derive from consciousness the great idea of a religious sentiment; and then ask ourselves how far it is justly represented in the institutions of the Church and the persons of her ministers. Let this process be tried by a man of high endowments, genuine aspirations, and noble sympathies, and what is the result? "Milton," says Dr. Johnson, in his life of that poet, "grew old without any visible worship," a phrase which, considering the superstition of the writer, and the exalted devotional sentiment of the subject, has, to our minds, a most pathetic significance. It tacitly admits that Milton worshipped his Maker; it brings him before us in a venerable aspect, at the time when he was blind, proscribed, and indigent; we recall his image at the organ, and seem to catch the symphonies of "Paradise Lost" and the "Hymn on the Nativity;" and yet we are told by the greatest votary of religious forms and profession among English literary men — one who was oppressed by the sense of religious truth, and a slave to Church requirements, that, in his old age, the reverential bard had no "visible worship." It is an admission of great moment; it is a fact infinitely suggestive Why did not Milton practically recognize any organized church, or publicly enact any prescribed form? Not altogether because he had tasted of persecution, and been driven, by the force of individual opinion, away from popular rites; but also, and to a far greater degree, because he had so fully experienced within himself, the force and scope of the religious sentiment, and found in its prevalent representation, not an incitement, but a hindrance to its exercise.

In the patriarchal age, the head of a family was its priest; and, in all ages, the true and complete man feels a personal interest and responsibility, a direct and entire relation to his Creator, that will not suffer interference any more than genuine conjugal or parental ties. The so-called progress of society has rendered its functions more complex, and broken up this simple and natural identity between the offices of devotion and those of paternity. It has not only made the priestly office distinct and apart from domestic life, but shorn it of glory by the cumbrous details of a hierarchy and badges of exclusiveness; and lessened its sanctity by changing the grand and holy function of a spiritual medium and expositor into a professional business and special pleading. What are conventional preachers but the employées of a sect? And so regarded, how is it possible to rejoice "in the plain presence of their dignity"? Called upon by a thoroughly earnest soul in its deep perplexity and agonizing bewilderment, what can they do but repeat the common-places of their office? How instantly are they reduced to the level of other men, when brought into contact with a human reality! The voice of true sympathy, though from ignorant lips, the grasp of honest affection, though from unconsecrated hands, yield more of the balm of consolation in such an hour, because they are real, human, and therefore nearer to God, than the technical representative of His truth. The essential mistake is, that instead of regarding the man as something divine in essence and relation, a perverse theology assigns that quality to the office. It is what is grafted upon, not what is essential to, humanity, that is thus made the nucleus of reverence and hope, whereas priesthood and manhood are identical. The authority of the former is derived from the latter; by virtue of being men we become priests, that is, servants of the Most High; and not through any miraculous anointing, laying on of hands, courses of divinity, or rites of ordination. "How," says Carlyle, "did Christianity arise and spread abroad among men? Was it by institutions and establishments and well-arranged systems of mechanism? Not so. On the contrary, in all past and existing institutions for those ends, its divine spirit has invariably been found to languish and decay. It arose in the mystic deeps of man's soul; and spread abroad by the 'preaching of the word,' by simple, altogether natural, and individual efforts; and flew like hallowed fire from heart to heart, till all were purified and illuminated by it." Accordingly, if merely professional representatives of the

Church, as such, hold a less influential position now than formerly, it is not because the instinct of worship has died out in the human heart, nor because men feel less than before the need of interpreters of the true, the holy, and the beautiful; it is not that the mysteries of life are less impressive, or its vicissitudes less constant, or its origin and end less enveloped in sacred obscurity; but it is because more legitimate priests have been found out of the Church than in it; because that institution and its ministers fail to meet adequately the wants of the religious sentiment; and it has been discovered that the Invisible Spirit is more easily found by the lonely seashore than in the magnificent cathedral; that the mountain-top is an altar nearer to His throne than a chancel; and that the rustle of forest-leaves and the moaning of the sea less disturb the idea of His presence in the devout heart, than the monotonous chant of the choir, or the conventional words of the preacher. We have but to glance at the pictures of clerical life, so thickly scattered through the memoirs and novels of the day, to realize the necessity of an eclectic spirit in estimating the clerical character — whose highest manifestations and most patent abuses seem entirely irrespective of sect. A Scotch clergyman, writing in 1763, of the society at Harrowgate, "made up of half-pay officers and clergymen," thus describes the latter: "They are in general — I mean the lower order — divided into bucks and prigs; of which the first, though inconceivably ignorant, and sometimes indecent in their morals, yet I held them to be most tolerable, because they were unassuming, and had no other affectation but that of behaving themselves like gentlemen. The other division of them, the prigs, are truly not to be endured, for they are but half-learned, are ignorant of the world, narrow-minded, pedantic, and overbearing." * Contrast with this estimate of a class Victor Hugo's portrait of an individual in his "Provincial Bishop" — "Monseigneur Bienvenu," so called, instinctively, by the people: "The formidable spectacle of created things developed a tenderness in him; he was always busy in finding for himself and inspiring others with the best way of sympathizing and solacing. The universe appeared to him like disease. He auscultated suffering everywhere. The whole world was to this good and rare priest a permanent subject of sadness seeking to be consoled."

The absolute need of separating in our minds the idea of the clerical man as a natural development of humanity — a normal phase of character — from the historical idea of the same personage, is at once evinced by the immense distance between the lives, influence, and traits of the men who have conspicuously borne the office of public religious teachers and administrators in different sects, ages, and countries; as for instance, Ximenes, Wolsey, Richelieu, Whitfield, Channing, George Herbert, and Dr. Arnold; in position, habits, and relations to the world, how great the contrast! And yet each represented to society, in a professional way, the same principle; the former with all the pomp of hierarchal magnificence, and all the influence of executive power, and the latter by the force of patient usefulness, earnest simplicity, and individual moral energy. Between Puritan and Pope what infinite grades; between Jewish rabbi and Scotch elder how diverse is the traditional sanction; and how little would a novice imagine that the bare walls and plain costume

* Rev. Archibald Carlyle's *Autobiography*.

of a Friends' meeting had the least of a common origin with the gorgeous decorations of a Minster! Thus do the passions, the tastes, and the very blood of races and individuals modify the expression of the same instinct; worship is as Protean in its forms as labor, diversion, hygiene, or any other human need and activity. Philosophy reconciles us to the apparent incongruity, and reveals beneath surplice, drab-coat, and silken robe, hearts that pulsate to an identical measure.

The best writers have recognized the clerical tone of manners as significant of the social condition of each period. Burnett thought more highly of his "Pastoral Care" than of his History; and Baxter's "Reformed Pastor" is an indirect but keen testimony to the decadence of the clergy. Macaulay cites Fielding's parson. Sir Roger's chaplain in the "Spectator," Cowper's rebuke of the "cassocked huntsmen," the Stiggins of Dickens, and Honeyman of Thackeray, are but a popular reflex of that deep sense of the abuse of a profession which is the highest evidence of its normal estimation. And the types of the vocation seem permanent. Every era has its Whateley, its Lammenais, and its Spurgeon — or men in the church whose gifts, tone, and mission essentially correspond with these. When George Herbert abandoned court for clerical aspirations, a friend protested against his choice "as too mean an employment"; and yet so truly did he illustrate the spiritual grandeur of his office that the chime which called to prayer from the humble belfry of Bemerton, was recognized by the country people as the "saint's bell." It was his holiness, and not his attachment to the ritual year, that inspired his example while living, and embalmed his memory; lowly kindnesses were "music to him at midnight" ; charity was "his only perfume" ; to teach the ignorant in his estimation "the greatest alms" ; and a day well spent, "the bridal of the earth and sky" ; his humanity spiritualized by Christian faith and practice, so essentially constituted him a priest that "about Salisbury," writes his brother, "where he lived beneficed for many years, he was little less than sainted." He drew an ideal from his own soul, and for his own guidance, in the "Country Parson."

To the reverent mind that dares to exercise freely the prerogative of thought, the constant blending of human infirmity with the method of worship is painfully evident: the instinct itself, the sentiment — highest in man — is thus "sicklied o'er with the pale cast of thought;" what is beautiful and true in the ceremonial or the emblem, arrays itself to his consciousness so as to intercept the holy beams that he would draw from the altar. Let him obey the waves of accident, and pause at shrines by the wayside ; and according to circumstances will be the inspiration they yield. Thus turning from the gay Parisian thoroughfare, at noonday, he may pace the chaste aisles of the Madeleine, and feel his devotion stirred by the solemn quietude, the few kneeling figures — perhaps by the dark catafalque awaiting the dead in the centre of the spacious floor ; and then what to him is the doctrine of transubstantiation? Religious architecture is speaking to his heart. The voices of the choristers at St. George's Chapel, at Windsor, may touch his pious sensibility, but if his thoughts revert to the ruddy dean, his good dinners, and indulgent life, and the poor, toilsome vicars, which make the Establishment a reflection of the world's diversity of condition — the pampered and the drudged ;

or, if he notes the prayer that the Queen may be preserved "in health and *wealth*," how sanctity ceases to invest the priest and the ritual, thus typical of human vanity and selfishness! "We know not," wrote Jerrold, "and we say it with grief, but with profound conviction of the necessity of every man giving fullest utterance to his thoughts—we know not, in this world of ours, in this social, out-of-door masquerade, a more dreary short-coming, a greater disappointment to the business and bosoms of men than the Established Church. Its essence is self-denial; its foundations are in humility and poverty; its practice is self-aggrandizement and money-getting." Nor is the reverse of the picture, the contrast between the high and low clergy, less inauspicious. "A Christian bishop," writes Sydney Smith, "proposes in cold blood, to create a thousand livings of one hundred and thirty pounds each,—to call into existence a thousand of the most unhappy men on the face of the earth—the sons of the poor, without hope, without the assistance of private fortune, chained to the soil, ashamed to live with their inferiors, unfit for the society of the better classes, and dragging about the English curse of poverty, without the smallest hope that they can ever shake it off. Can any man of common sense say that all these outward circumstances of the ministers of religion, have no bearing on religion itself?" On the other hand, what divine significance to the pious soul, "as through a zodiac moves the ritual year,"—in the altar, the font, the choral service, the venerable liturgy, the holy emblems and hallowed forms whereby this Church is consecrated to the hearts of her devout children, and the reverence of sympathetic intelligence.

Buckle, drawing broad inference from extensive and

acute research, unmodified by sympathetic observation, wrote an historical treatise rich in knowledge and philosophy, to prove that Spain and Scotland owe whatever is hopeless and hampered in their intellectual development to the tyranny of priests and preachers. It was a special plea, but it serves to illustrate, with comprehensive emphasis, the antagonism between Ecclesiasticism and Christianity; for viewed individually, as a social phenomenon, and not the mere exponent of an organization, the preacher or teacher of the right, advocate of the true, representative of faith, becomes a distinct and personal character, and is identified with humanity. It is when the man and the function coalesce, and the former transcends and spiritualizes the latter, that in history and in life, all that is great and gracious in the vocation, is memorably vindicated. Under this genuine aspect, Rousseau found his ideal of happiness in the life of a village curé, Chateaubriand renewed the heartfelt claims of religion in eloquently describing its primitive and legitimate benignities. Medieval ecclesiasticism commenced its purifying though inadequate ordeal through the heroism of Savonarola at Florence and Sarpi at Venice. Current literature, indeed, continually and clearly states the problem; and illustrates the question with a frequency and a talent which indicates how largely it occupies the popular mind. To discriminate between the preacher's conventional office and his spiritual endowment, — between Christianity as a sentiment and a dogma, between the religious and the temporal authority, between the Church as an institution and a faith, is an emphatic mission of artist and author in our age. Witness the salient discussions of the "Roman question," the pleas and protests of Gallican and Ultramontane, the conservative zeal of the Puseyite, and liberal encroachments of the progressive clergy, and the picturesque or psychological fictions which instruct and beguile modern readers.* Both literature and life in modern times, while they attest the official decadence of the clergy, as a political and theological organization, still more significantly vindicate their normal influence as a social power. "Not as in the old times," says a philosophical historian, in allusion to the clergy of America, "does the layman look upon them as the cormorants and curses of society; they are his faithful advisers, his honored friends, under whose suggestion and supervision are instituted educational establishments, colleges, hospitals, whatever can be of benefit to men in this life, or secure to them happiness in the life to come." †

There are types of character that prophesy vocation, and we occasionally see in families a gentle being, so disinterested, thoughtful, and above the world in natural disposition, that he seems born to wear a surplice, as one we can behold officiating at the altar by virtue of a certain innate adaptation; and so there are men of strong affections, early bereft, and thereby alienated from personal motives, and thus peculiarly able to give an undivided heart to God and humanity; or, through a singular moral experience, initiated more deeply than their fellows into the arcana of truth, and hence justified in becoming her expositors. In cases like these, a more than conventional reason for the faith that is in

* The "Warden," "Barchester Towers," and "Framley Parsonage," by A. Trollope; "Vincenzo," by Ruffini; "Madamoiselle La Quintinie," par Geo. Sand; "La Maudit," par L'Abbe ——; "Adam Bede"; "Chronicles of Carlingford," etc.

† Dr. J. W. Draper.

them, causes them to speak and act with an authority which is its own sanction, and hence springs what is vital both in the life and the literature of the visible Church. Sacerdotal biography, the achievements of the true reformer, the literary bequests of the genuine pulpit orator, and the results of efficient parochial genius, attest the reality of such characters; they are of Nature's ordaining, and sectarianism itself is lost sight of in their universal and grateful recognition — as witness St. Augustine, Fenelon, Luther, Wesley, Fox, and Frederick Robertson. Landmarks in the history of our race, oases in the desert of theological controversy, flowers in the garland of humanity, they "vindicate the ways of God to man," and are the redeeming facts of ecclesiastical life. Above the system they illustrate, beyond the limits they designate, and providential exceptions to a general rule, we instinctively accept them as holding a relation to the religious sentiment and the highest interests of the world that only a profane imagination can associate with the pretensions of the thousands who claim their fraternity. This idea of asserting the human as consecrated and not usurped by the priestly, has ever distinguished the veritable ecclesiastical heroes. Lammenais, when a mere youth, was arrested for his eloquent advocacy of freedom and faith; "we will show them," he said of the civil tribunals, "what kind of a *man* a priest is."

Dupuytren, the most celebrated French surgeon of his day, was destitute of faith, and by his powerful mind and brusque hardihood, overcame the individuality of almost every one who approached him. One day a poor *curé* from some village near Paris called upon the great surgeon. Dupuytren was struck with his manly beauty and noble presence, but examined, with his usual nonchalance, the patient's neck, disfigured by a horrible cancer. "*Avec cela, il faut mourir*," said the surgeon. "So I thought," calmly replied the priest; "I expected the disease was fatal, and only came to you to please my parishioners." He then unfolded a bit of paper and took from it a five-franc piece, which he handed to Dupuytren, saying: "Pardon, sir, the little fee, for we are poor." The serene dignity and holy self-possession of this man, about to die in the prime of his life, impressed the stoical surgeon in spite of himself, though his manner betrayed neither surprise nor interest. Before the *curé* had descended half the staircase, he was called back by a servant. "If you choose to try an operation," said Dupuytren, "go to the Hotel Dieu, I will see you to-morrow." "It is my duty to make use of all means of recovery," replied the *curé*, "I will go." The next day, the surgeon cut away remorselessly at the priest's neck, laying bare tendons and arteries. It was before the days of chloroform, and, unsustained by any opiate, the poor *curé* suffered with uncomplaining heroism. He did not even wince. Dupuytren respected his courage; and every day lingered longer at his bedside, when making the rounds of the hospital. In a few weeks the *curé* recovered. A year after the operation, he made his appearance in the *salon* of the great professor with a neat basket containing pears and chickens. "Monsieur," he said, "it is the anniversary of the day when your skill saved my life; accept this humble gift; the pears and chickens are better than you can find in Paris; they are of my own raising." Each succeeding year, on the same day of the month, the honest priest brought his grateful offering. At length Dupuytren was taken ill, and the physicians declared his heart diseased. He shut himself up with his favorite nephew and refused to see his friends. One day he wrote on a slip of paper, "*Le medécin a besoin du curé,*" and sent it to the village priest, who quickly obeyed the summons. He remained for hours in the dying surgeon's chamber; and when he came forth, tears were in his eyes, and Dupuytren was no more. How easy for the imagination to fill up this outline, which is all that was vouchsafed to Parisian gossip.

Whoever has gone from Roman church or palace — his soul yet warm with the radiant figures and divine expression of saints and martyrs as depicted by the inspired hands of the Christian artists of the fifteenth century — into the gloomy and damp catacombs, where the early disciples met in order to enjoy "freedom to worship God," must have felt at once the solemn reality and the beautiful triumph of faith, in its unperverted glow — on the one hand nerving the believer to cheerful endurance, and on the other kindling genius to noble toil; and, before this fresh conviction, how vain appeared to him the mechanical rite and the cold response of conventional worship! The truth is that the history of religion is like the history of love; a natural and divine sentiment has been wrested into illegitimate service; ambitious pretenders, like the wanton and the coquette, abuse to selfish ends what should either be honorably let alone or sacredly cherished. This process, at once so habitual and so intricate — working through formulas, tradition, appeals to fear, the power of custom, the imperative needs and the ignorant credulity of the multitude — has gradually built up a partition between heaven and earth, obscured spiritual facts, made vague and mystical the primitive relation of the soul to the fatherhood of God, and thus induced either open scepticism or artificial conformity. In painting, in music, in literature, in the wonders of the universe, in the mysteries of life, and in human consciousness, the sentiment asserts itself forever; but to the genuine man of to-day is allotted the ceaseless duty of keeping it apart from the incrustations of form, the perversion of office, and the base uses of ambition and avarice.

The lionism of the pulpit is another desecration. London and New York must have their fashionable preachers as well as favorite *prima donnas*, and the phenomena attending each are the same. Intellectual amusement, exclusiveness, the *mode*, thus become identical with that which is their essential opposite, and the meekness and sublimity of the religious function is utterly lost in a frivolous glare and soulless vanity. The pew itself is a satire on existent Christianity; the very organ-airs played in the fashionable churches, by recalling the ball-room and the theatre, are ironical; and to these how often the elegantly-worded common-place of the preacher is a fit accompaniment — so well likened, by a thoughtful writer, to shovelling sand with a pitch-fork! Thank heaven, we have perpetually the Vicar of Wakefield and Parson Adams to keep green the memories of that genial simplicity and honest warmth of which modern refinement has deprived the clerical man. They, at least, were not effigies. Heroism as embodied in Knox, scholarship in Barrow, zeal in Doddridge, holy idealism in Taylor, sacred eloquence in Hall and Chalmers, earnest aspiration in Channing and Robertson, — these and like instances of a fine manly endowment, give vitality to the preacher and significance to his ministrations.

In a recent farce that had a run at Paris, and caricatures English life, the curtain rises on a deserted street, hushed and gloomy, through which two figures at last slowly walk on tiptoe: as they approach, and one begins to address the other, the latter, raising his finger to his lips, whispers "*C'est Soonday*," and both disappear: the comedy ends, however, with a prodigious dinner of beef and beer. Absurd as such pictures of a London Sabbath are, they yet indicate a suggestive truth, which is, that the extreme outward observance in Protestant countries, of one day in seven, by repudiating all pastime, is the best proof of a conscious defect in the social representation of the religious instinct, exactly as the festivity of continental people, on the same day, illustrates the opposite extreme of indifference to appearances. It is probable that neither affords a just index of the state of feeling; for domestic enjoyments in the one case, and attendance at mass, by sincere devotees, in the other, are facts that modify the apparent truth. It is highly probable, also, that in this age of free inquiry and general intelligence, what has been lost in public observance has been gained in individual sincerity. There is not the same dependence on the preacher. Devotional sentiment is fed from other sources. It has come to be felt and understood as never before, that man is personally responsible, and must seek light for himself, and repose on his own faith. Accordingly, he is comparatively unallied to institutions, and will no longer trust for spiritual insight to a mortal as frail and ignorant as himself. The redeeming fact is to be sought in the existence of the sentiment itself. The sensuality of a Borgia makes more impressive the sanctity of Fenelon; because of the artificial funeral eulogies of Bossuet, we are more sensible to the practical efficiency of Father Matthew; Calvin's intolerance heightens the glory of Luther's vindication of spiritual freedom; the fanaticism of the Methodist, the subtlety of the Jesuit, the cold rationalism of the Unitarian, the dark bigotry of the Presbyterian, the monotonous tone of the Quaker, the refined conservatism of the Episcopalian, and other characteristics of sects, philosophically considered, are but the excess of a tendency which also manifests its benign and desirable influence as an element of Christian society. What liberal mind can reflect upon the agency of the English Church, pregnant of abuses as it is, without feeling that she has greatly contributed to preserve a wholesome equilibrium amid conflicting agencies, to keep intact the dignity and hallowed associations of worship, to calm the feverish impulses and prolong a law of order amid chaotic tendencies? What just observer will hesitate to award to Dissenters the honor of imparting a vital spirit to the listless body of the Church, renewing the sentiment of religion which had become dormant through conventionalism and oppressive institutions, and making its divine reality once more a conscious motive and solace to the world? How much have the eminent preachers of liberal Christianity, in New England, done toward enlarging the charity of sects, elevating the standard of pulpit eloquence, and giving to the priestly office moral dignity and intellectual force! Who that has witnessed the life-devotion of the Sisters of Charity, in a season of pestilence, seen the tears on the bronze cheeks of hardy mariners at the Bethel, or heard the bold protest of the educated divine, above the voice of public opinion, at a social crisis, pleading for principle against expediency, and has not, for the moment at least, forgotten dogmas in grateful appreciation of the general benefits resulting from the direct inspiration of that sentiment, which the preacher, of whatever creed, is ordained to illustrate? Truly has it been said, that "it is the spirit of the soul's natural piety to alight on whatever is beautiful and touching in every faith, and take thence its secret draught of spiritual refreshment." Even popular literature enforces the argument. The lives of Fox, Wesley, Fenelon, Arnold, Chalmers, and Channing, illustrate the same truth, that the man can sanction the priest, the soul vindicate the office, and the reality of a sentiment reconcile or sublimate discordant creeds.

That good maxim of the brave English lexicographer, "Clear your mind of cant;" and the noble appeal of Campbell's chivalric muse, who asks —

——— "has Earth a clod
Where man, the image of his God,
Unscourged by Superstition's rod,
Should bend the knee?

have an eternal significance. We are called upon to resist formalism by as potential reasons as those which impel to sincere devotion. It is evidenced in the best writings of the day, that the highest in man's nature may be linked with the most ferocious and abject. Balfour of Burley is but the fanciful embodiment of an actual union between religious zeal and a thirst for blood. Blanco White's memoirs indicate the possible variations of speculative belief in an honest and ardent mind; and true observation induced John Foster to write his able treatise on "The Objections of Men of Taste to Evangelical Religion." "There is no denying," says a popular reviewer, "that there is a certain stiff, tough, clayish, agricultural, English nature, on which the *aggressive divine* produces a visible and good effect." Father Marquette's adventurous martyrdom, Pascal's metaphysical acuteness, the rude courage of John Knox, the witch-chronicle of Mather, the magnetic power of Edward Irving, the wit that scintillated from Sydney Smith, the poetry of Heber, the ideal beauty of Buckminster's style, and the virtuous charm of Berkeley, prove how the expositors of religion blend with professional life the essential characteristics of man, and how impossible it is to divide the office we are considering, from those qualities and conditions which belong essentially to the race. In the face of such diversity, before such acknowledged facts, how irrational is it to exempt the preacher from any law either of life or character; how unphilosophical and untrue to regard him in any other light than that of experience; and how unjust to imagine there is any occult virtue in ceremonial systems of faith, or the accident of vocation, whereby he derives any special authority unsustained by personal gifts and rectitude.

The problem we have suggested, of an antagonism between the theological profession, the office of priest, artificially held, and the manly instincts, has recently been illustrated by the criticisms on Carlyle's "Life of Sterling." In that work, it is lamented that the mental freedom and just development of a gifted, ingenuous and aspiring soul were restrained and baffled by the vocation of priest; and to this view Churchmen indignantly protest, and accuse the biographer of infidelity. It is evident, however, that it was not religion but its formula, not truth but an institution, which he thought hampered and narrowed the legitimate spirit of his friend. There is that which commands profound respect in Carlyle's recoil from the conventional; there is justice in his indignation at the attempt to link a true, loving, brave, and progressive mind to any wheel of social machinery. To keep apart from an organized mode of action is the instinct of the best natures, — not from pride, but self-respect. Of modern writers few have a better right to claim for literature an agency more effective. The press has, indeed, in a measure, superseded the pulpit. No intelligent observer of the signs of the times can fail to perceive that as a means of influence, the two are at least equal. In the pages of journals, in the verses of poets, in the favorite books of the hour, we have homilies that teach charity and faith more eloquently than the conventional Sunday's discourse; they come nearer to experience; they are more the offspring of earnest conviction, and therefore enlist popular sympathy. When we turn from such genuine pleadings and pictures to those offered by the unspiritual preacher, — how unreal do the last appear! It was once remarked by an auditor of a genial man, who gave a prescriptive emphasis to his sermons, quite foreign to his frank nature, that he seemed to feel that what he uttered was "important if true"; and such is the impression not a few preachers leave on the listener's mind. If we carefully note those within the sphere of our acquaintance, we find that many are either visibly oppressed or rendered artificial by their profession. It seldom harmoniously blends with their nature.

They seem painfully conscious of a false relation to society, or manfully, and, it may be recklessly, put aside the character, as if it were indeed a masquerade. Either course is a proof of incongruity; and in those cases where our confidence and affection are spontaneously yielded, is it not the qualities of the man that win and hold them? — his spiritual aptitude to, and not the fact of his vocation?

In no profession do we find so many instances of a mistaken choice, and this even when its duties are respectably fulfilled. The candid preacher, when arrived at maturity, will not seldom confess with pain, that the logical skill of the advocate, the love of representing nature of the artist, the scientific skill of the physician, or the practical industry of the man of affairs, constituted the natural basis of his usefulness; and proved inadequate endowments in his actual vocation. Perhaps the great error is in prematurely deciding on a step so responsible. To bind a youth's interests, reputation, and opinions to the priesthood, as is often done by the undue exercise of authority and influence, at an impressible age, by Protestant not less than Catholic families, is a positive wrong; and the moral courage which repudiates what was unjustly assumed, is more deserving of honor than blame. Inefficiency, in such cases, is proverbial: "He talks like a parson," said Lord Carteret, of Sherlock, "and consequently is used to talk to people that do not mind him." A clergyman in conversing with a gifted layman used the phrase "*born* preacher." "I do not believe there is such a thing," replied the former, "for it implies a born hearer, which is a being whose existence is incompatible with my idea of the goodness of the Creator." Occasionally we see delightful exceptions to such an erroneous choice; men of firm yet gentle souls, deep convictions, and sustained elevation, whose talents not less than the spirit they are of, whose natural demeanor, habitual temper, and constitutional sympathies, designate them for the sacred office. We listen to their ministrations without misgiving, accept their counsel, rise on the wings of their prayer, respond to their appeals, and rejoice in their holiness — as a true and a blest incentive and consolation. We ordain them with our hearts, for the idea of the preacher is lost in that of the brother.

In these instances, the normal conditions of the office are realized, the boundaries of sect forgotten, and the legitimate idea of a minister to the religious sympathies practically made apparent. Such a preacher was Fenelon, in whose life, aspect, and writings the love of God and man were exhibited with such pure consistency that his name is a spell which invokes all that is sacred in the associations of humanity. The blandishments of a court, the rudeness of soldiers, the ignorance of peasants, were alike chastened by his presence. Neither persecution, high culture, nor the gifts of fortune, for a moment, disturbed his holy self-possession. He disarmed prejudice, envy, intrigue, and violence, by the tranquil influence of the spirit he was of. Ecclesiastical power, ceremony, tradition, and literary fame were but the incidental accessories of his career. The principles of Christianity and the temper of its genuine disciple so predominated in his actions, speech, manners, writings, and in his very tones and expression of countenance, that every heart, by the instinct of its best affections, recognized his spiritual authority. The man thoroughly vindicated the office; therefore the courtier at Versailles and the rustic of Cambray held him in equal reverence.

In Madame Guyon, Anne Hutcheson, and Hannah More, we see the religious sentiment and the instinct of proselytism in connection with the idiosyncrasies of female character, rendered more affecting by its tenderness, or losing in efficient dignity by the weakness of the sex. A beautiful example of the natural preacher, unmodified by the paraphernalia of the office, is given in Wirt's description of the Blind Preacher, while its original identity with scholarship and philosophy is singularly illustrated in the career of Abelard; and Molière's "Tartuffe" is but the dramatic embodiment of its extreme actual perversion at those periods when the form, by a gradual process of social corruption, has completely superseded the reality, and cant and hypocrisy are allowed to pass for truth and emotion. All that is peculiar in the *modus operandi* of sects testifies to the constant adaptation of the office to occasion: thus the itinerant episcopacy of the Methodists, the attractive temples of the Catholics, the time-hallowed liturgy of the Church of England, the immersing fonts of the Baptists, the plain language and prescriptive uniformity of the Quakers, and the literary culture of the Unitarians, appeal to certain tastes, feelings, or associations, which, although independent of the religious sentiment, greatly tend to the impressiveness of its outward manifestation upon different classes of persons. A spiritual tendency is characteristic of Swedenborgians; an absence of the sense of beauty is observable in the Friends; the superstitious element is the usual trait of Romanists; conservatism prevails among Episcopalians; and a progressive spirit and broad sympathies usually distinguish liberal Christians. To a bigot this diversity is offensive; to a philosopher it is the result of an inevitable and beneficent law. An American poet has aptly described the scene which a Protestant city presents on a Sabbath morning, when its streets are filled with the diverging streams of a population, each moving toward its respective place of worship, in obedience to this law of individual faith.

The word "skeleton" as applied to the outline of sermons is very significant, for this is the only feature they have in common when vital; and yet how different the manner in which they are clothed with life! Sometimes it is logic, sometimes enthusiasm; now the eloquence of the heart, and now the ingenuity of the head that creates the animating principle; in one instance the beauty of style, and in another the force of conviction or the glow of sympathy; and there are cases where only grace of manner, melody of voice, and the magnetism of the preacher's temperament and delivery impart to his words their effect; for every grade of rhetorical power, from the refinements of artificial study to the gush of irresistible feeling, has scope in the pulpit; there is no sacred charm in that rostrum except what its occupant brings; its possible scale includes elocutionary tricks and the most disinterested and unconscious utterance; mediocrity lisps there its commonplace truisms, and devotional genius breathes its holy oracles; it is the medium of complacent formulas as well as of inspired truth.

The ancient philosophers and the modern essayists often apply wisdom to life in the manner of the best sermonizers; and as Christianity has infused its spirit into literature, this has become more apparent. Seneca and Epictetus as moralists, and Plato in psychological speculation, anticipated many of the sentiments that now have a religious authority. Rousseau, in as far as he was true to humanity, Montaigne to the extent he justly interprets the world, Bacon in the degree he indicates the approaches to universal truth, Saint Pierre when awaking the sentiment of beauty as revealed in Nature, Shakspeare by the memorable development of the laws of character, Dante as the picturesque limner of the material faith of the Middle Ages, Richter in his beautiful exposition of human sentiment,—all exhibit a phase or element of the preacher, and in the writings of Milton and Chateaubriand it breaks forth with a still more direct emphasis. Carlyle aud Coleridge, Isaac Taylor, Wordsworth, Lamb, and many other effective modern writers, are among the most influential of lay preachers. And this unprofessional teaching, this priesthood of nature, has multiplied with the progress of society, so that every community has its father confessors, its sisters of charity, its gifted interpreters and eloquent advocates; while literature, even in forms the most profane, continually emulates the sacred function, yielding great lessons, exciting holy sentiment, and demonstrating pure faith. Indeed, it is characteristic of the age, that the technical is becoming merged in the æsthetic; as culture extends, the distinctive in pursuit and office loses its prominence. Lamb jocosely told Coleridge he never heard him do anything but preach; and there is scarcely a favorite among the authors of the day that, in some way, does not hallow his genius by consecrating it to an interpretation or sentiment which, in its last analysis, is religious.

In these considerations may be found a partial explanation of that diminution of individual agency in the priesthood to which we have referred. The modern religious teachers also, as we have seen, have not the same extent of ignorance to vanquish as the old divines. The line of demarcation between ecclesiastical polity and Christian truth is more evident to the multitude; and it is now felt as never before, that "a heart of deep sympathies solves all theological questions in the flame of its love and justice." Hence the comparative indifference to controversy; and the recognition of the primal fact — so truly stated by the same reflective writer — that "spiritual insight, moral elevation, rich sympathies, are the tokens whereby the divinely ordained are signalized." *

The practical inference is, that never before was the obligation of personal responsibility in spiritual interests, on the part of the laity, so apparent, nor that of a thorough integrity in the preacher. To be "clear in his great office" — to rely on absolute gifts and essentials of character — to cleave to simplicity and truth, and keep within the line of honest conviction, is now his only guarantee, not only of self-respect, but of usefulness and honor. Organization, form, tact, theological acquirement, the *prestige* of traditional importance, are of little efficacy. The scientific era — the reaction to first causes — the universal and intense demand for the real — the exposure of delusions — the test of wide intelligence and fearless inquiry — the jealousy of mental freedom — the multiplied sources of devotional sentiment — the earnestness of the age — all invoke him to repudiate the machinery, the historical badge, the

* Calvert's *Scenes and Thoughts in Europe.*

conventional resources of his title — nay, to lose, if possible, his title itself — and incarnate only the everlasting principles, laws, and sentiments, by virtue of which alone he may hope for inspiration or claim authority.

STATUES.

> "And if it be Prometheus stole from Heaven
> The fire which we endure, it was repaid
> By him to whom the energy was given,
> Which this poetic marble hath arrayed,
> With an eternal glory."
>
> BYRON.

HERE is as absolute an instinct in the human mind for the definite, the palpable, and the emphatic, as there is for the mysterious, the versatile, and the elusive. With some, method is a law, and taste severe in affairs, costume, exercise, social intercourse, and faith. The simplicity, directness, uniformity, and pure emphasis or grace of Sculpture have analogies in literature and character; the terse despatch of a brave soldier, the concentrated dialogue of Alfieri, some proverbs, aphorisms, and poetic lines, that have become household words, puritanic consistency, silent fortitude, are but so many vigorous outlines, and impress us by virtue of the same colorless intensity as a masterpiece of the statuary. How sculpturesque is Dante, even in metaphor, as when he writes, —

> "Ella non ci diceva alcuna cosa;
> Ma lasciavane gir, solo guardando,
> A guisa di leon quando si posa."

Nature, too, hints the art, when her landscape tints are covered with snow, and the forms of tree, rock, and mountain are clearly defined by the universal whiteness.

Death, in its pale, still, fixed image, — always solemn, sometimes beautiful, — would have inspired primeval humanity to mould and chisel the lineaments of clay. Even New Zealanders elaborately carve their war-clubs; and from the "graven images" prohibited by the Decalogue as objects of worship, through the mysterious granite effigies of ancient Egypt, the brutal anomalies in Chinese porcelain, the gay and gilded figures on a ship's prow, — whether emblems of rude ingenuity, tasteless caprice, retrospective sentiment, or embodiments of the highest physical and mental culture, as in the Greek statues, — there is no art whose origin is more instructive and progress more historically significant. The vases of Etruria are the best evidence of her degree of civilization; the designs of Flaxman on Wedgwood ware redeem the economical art of England; the Bears at Berne and the Wolf in the Roman Capitol, are the most venerable local insignia; the carvings of Gibbons, in old English manor-houses, outrival all the luxurious charms of modern upholstery; Phidias is a more familiar element in Grecian history than Pericles; the moral energy of the old Italian republics is more impressively shadowed forth and conserved in the bold and vigorous creations of Michael Angelo than in the political annals of Macchiavelli; and it is the massive, uncouth sculptures, half buried in sylvan vegetation, which mythically transmit the ancient people of Central America.

We confess a faith in, and a love for, the "testimony of the rocks," — not only as interpreted by the sagacious Scotchman, as he excavated the "old red sandstone," but as shaped into forms of truth, beauty, and power by the hand of man through all generations. We love to catch a glimpse of these silent memorials of our race, whether as Nymphs half-shaded at noon-day with summer foliage in a garden, or as Heroes gleaming with startling distinctness in the moonlit city-square; as the similitudes of illustrious men gathered in the halls of nations and crowned with a benignant fame, or as prone effigies on sepulchres, forever proclaiming the calm without the respiration of slumber, so as to tempt us to exclaim, with the enamored gazer on the Egyptian queen, when the asp had done its work, —

> "She looks like sleep,
> As she would catch another Antony
> In her *strong toil of grace.*"

Although Dr. Johnson undervalued sculpture, partly because of an inadequate sense of the beautiful, and partly from ignorance of its greatest trophies, he expressed unqualified assent to its awe-inspiring influence in "the monumental caves of death," as described by Congreve. Sir Joshua truly declares that "all arts address themselves to the sensibility and imagination"; and no one thus alive to the appeal of sculpture, will marvel that the infuriated mob spared the statues of the Tuileries at the bloody climax of the French Revolution; that a "love of the antique" knit in bonds of life-long friendship Winckelmann and Cardinal Albani; that among the most salient of childhood's memories should be Memnon's image and the Colossus of Rhodes; that an imaginative girl of exalted temperament died of love for the Apollo Belvidere, and that Carrara should win many a pilgrimage because its quarries have peopled earth with grace.

To a sympathetic eye there are few more pleasing tableaux than a gifted sculptor engaged in his work.

How absorbed he is! — standing erect by the mass of clay, — with graduated touch, moulding into delicate undulations or expressive lines the inert mass, now stepping back to see the effect, now bending forward, almost lovingly, to add a master indentation or detach a thin layer; and so, hour after hour, working on, every muscle in action, each perception active, oblivious of time, happy in the gradual approximation, under patient and thoughtful manipulation, of what was a dense heap of earth, to a form of vital expression or beauty.

Much has been said and written of the limits of sculpture; but it is the sphere, rather than the art itself, which is thus bounded; and one of its most glorious distinctions, like that of the human form and face, which are its highest subject, is the vast possible variety within what seems, at first thought, to be so narrow a field. That the same number and kind of limbs and features should, under the plastic touch of genius, have given birth to so many and totally diverse forms, memorable for ages, and endeared to humanity, is in itself an infinite marvel, which vindicates, as a beautiful wonder, the statuary's art from the more Protean rivalry of pictorial skill. If we call to mind even a few of the sculptured creations which are "a joy forever," even to retrospection, haunting by their pure individuality the temple of memory, permanently enshrined in heartfelt admiration as illustrations of what is noble in man and woman, significant in history, powerful in expression, or irresistible in grace, — we feel what a world of varied interest is hinted by the very name of Sculpture. Through it the most just and clear idea of Grecian culture is revealed. The solemn mystery of Egyptian, and the grand scale of Assyrian, civilization are best attested by the same trophies. How a Sphinx typifies the land of the Pyramids and all its associations, mythological, scientific, natural, and sacred, — its reverence for the dead, and its dim and portentous traditions! and what a reflex of Nineveh's palmy days are the winged lions exhumed by Layard! What more authentic tokens of mediæval piety and patience exist than the elaborate and grotesque carvings of Albert Dürer's day? The colossal Brahma in the temple of Elephanta, near Bombay, is the visible acme of Asiatic superstition. And can an illustration of the revival of art, in the fifteenth century, so exuberant, aspiring, and sublime, be imagined, to surpass the Day and Night, the Moses, and other statues of Angelo? But such general inferences are less impressive than the personal experience of every European traveller with the least passion for the beautiful or reverence for genius. Is there any sphere of observation and enjoyment to such a one, more prolific of individual suggestions than this so-called limited art? From the soulful glow of expression in the inspired countenance of the Apollo, to the womanly contours, so exquisite, in the armless figure of the Venus de Milo, — from the aërial posture of John of Bologna's Mercury, to the inimitable and firm dignity in the attitude of Aristides in the Museum of Naples, — from the delicate lines which teach how grace can chasten nudity in the Goddess of the Tribune at Florence, to the embodied melancholy of Hamlet in the brooding Lorenzo of the Medici Chapel, — from the stone despair, the frozen tears, as it were, of all bereaved maternity, in the very bend of Niobe's body and yearning gesture, to the *abandon* gleaming from every muscle of the Dancing Faun, — from the stern brow of the

Knife-grinder, and the bleeding frame of the Gladiator, whereon are written forever the inhumanities of ancient civilization, to the triumphant beauty, and firm, light, enjoyable aspect of Dannecker's Ariadne, — from the unutterable joy of Cupid and Psyche's embrace, to the grand authority of Moses, — how many separate phases of human emotion "live in stone"! What greater contrast to eye or imagination, in our knowledge of facts, and in our consciousness of sentiment, can be exemplified, than those so distinctly, memorably, and gracefully moulded in the apostolic figures of Thorwaldsen, the Hero and Leander of Steinhaüser, the lovely funereal monument, inspired by gratitude, which Rauch reared to Louise of Prussia, Chantrey's Sleeping Children, Canova's Lions in St. Peter's, the bas-reliefs of Ghiberti on the Baptistery doors at Florence, and Gibson's Horses of the Sun?

The last time Heine went out of doors, before succumbing to his fearful malady, he says: "With difficulty I dragged myself to the Louvre, and almost sank down as I entered that magnificent hall where the ever-blessed goddess of beauty, our beloved Lady of Milo, stands on her pedestal. At her feet I lay long and wept so bitterly that a stone must have pitied me. The goddess looked compassionately on me, but at the same time disconsolately, as if she would say: Dost thou not see that I have no arms, and thus cannot help thee?"

Have you ever strolled from the inn at Lucerne, on a pleasant afternoon, along the Zurich road, to the old General's garden, where stands the colossal lion designed by Thorwaldsen, to keep fresh the brave renown of the Swiss guard who perished in defence of the royal family of France during the massacre of the Revolution? Carved from the massive sandstone, the majestic animal, with the fatal spear in his side, yet loyal in his vigil over the royal shield, is a grand image of fidelity unto death. The stillness, the isolation, the vivid creepers festooning the rocks, the clear mirror of the basin, into which trickle pellucid streams, reflecting the vast proportions of the enormous lion, the veteran Swiss, who acts as *cicerone*, the adjacent chapel with its altar-cloth wrought by one of the fair descendants of the Bourbon king and queen for whom these victims perished, the hour, the memories, the admixture of Nature and Art, convey a unique impression, in absolute contrast with such white effigies, for instance, as in the dusky precincts of Santa Croce droop over the sepulchre of Alfieri, or with the famous bronze boar in the Mercato Nuovo of Florence, or the ethereal loveliness of that sweet scion of the English nobility, moulded by Chantrey in all the soft and lithe grace of childhood, holding a contented dove to her bosom.

Even as the subject of taste, independently of historical diversities, sculpture presents every degree of the meretricious, the grotesque, and the beautiful, — more emphatically, because more palpably, than is observable in painting. The inimitable Grecian standard is an immortal precedent; the mediæval carvings embody the rude Teutonic truthfulness; where Canova provoked comparison with the antique, as in the Perseus and Venus, his more gross ideal is painfully evident. How artificial seems Bernini in contrast with Angelo! How minutely expressive are the terra-cotta images of Spain! What a climax of absurdity teases the eye in the monstrosities in stone which draw travellers in Sicily to the eccentric nobleman's villa, near Palermo! Who does not shrink from the French allegory, and horrible melodrama, of Roubillac's monument to Miss Nightingale, in Westminster Abbey? How like Horace Walpole to dote on Ann Conway's canine groups! We actually feel sleepy, as we examine the little black marble Somnus of the Florence Gallery, and electrified with the first sight of the Apollo, and won to sweet emotion in the presence of Nymphs, Graces, and the Goddess of Beauty, when, shaped by the hand of genius, they seem the ethereal types of that

> ——— " common clay ta'en from the common earth,
> Moulded by God and tempered by the tears
> Of angels to the perfect form of woman."

Calm and fixed as is the natural language of Sculpture, it is the artistic illustration of life's normal activity and character in the economy not less than in the ideal and heroic phase. "Our statues," says one of the quaint personages of Richter's "Titan," "are no idle, dawdling citizens, but all drive a trade. Such as are caryates hold up houses; and heathen water-gods labor at the public fountains, and pour out water into the pitchers of the maidens. Such as are angels bear up baptismal vessels."

Yet the distinctive element in the pleasure afforded by sculpture is tranquillity, — a quiet, contemplative delight; somewhat of awe chastens admiration; a feeling of peace hallows sympathy; and we echo the poet's sentiment, —

> " I feel a mighty calmness creep
> Over my heart, which can no longer borrow
> Its hues from chance or change, — those children of to-morrow."

It is this fixedness and placidity, conveying the impression of fate, death, repose, or immortality, which render sculpture so congenial as commemorative of the departed. Even quaint wooden effigies, like those in St. Mary's Church at Chester, with the obsolete peaked beards, ruffs, and broadswords, accord with the venerable associations of a mediæval tomb; while marble figures, typifying Grief, Poetry, Fame, or Hope, brooding over the lineaments of the illustrious dead, seem, of all sepulchral decorations, the most apt and impressive. We remember, after exploring the plain of Ravenna on an autumn day, and rehearsing the famous battle in which the brave young Gaston de Foix fell, how the associations of the scene and story were defined and deepened as we gazed on the sculptured form of a recumbent knight in armor, preserved in the academy of the old city; it seemed to bring back and stamp with brave renown forever the gallant soldier who so long ago perished there in battle. In Cathedral and Parthenon, under the dome of the Invalides, in the sequestered parish church, or the rural cemetery, what image so accords with the sad reality and the serene hope of humanity, as the adequate marble personification on sarcophagus and beneath shrine, in mausoleum or on turf-mound?

> "His palms enfolded on his breast,
> There is no other thought express'd
> But long disquiet merged in rest."

In truth, it is for want of comprehensive perception that we take so readily for granted the limited scope of this glorious art. There is in the Grecian mythology alone a remarkable variety of character and expression, as perpetuated by the statuary; and when to her deities, we add the athletes, charioteers, and marble portraits, a realm of diverse creations is opened. Indeed, to the average modern mind, it is the statues of Grecian divinities that constitute the poetic charm of her history; abstractly, we regard them with the poet: —

> 'Their gods? what were their gods?
> There 's Mars, all bloody-haired; and Hercules,
> Whose soul was in his sinews; Pluto, blacker
> Than his own hell; Vulcan, who shook his horns
> At every limp he took; great Bacchus rode
> Upon a barrel; and in a cockle-shell
> Neptune kept state; then Mercury was a thief;
> Juno a shrew; Pallas a prude, at best;
> And Venus walked the clouds in search of lovers;
> Only great Jove, the lord and thunderer,
> Sat in the circle of his starry power
> And frowned 'I will!' to all."

Not in their marble beauty do they thus ignobly impress us, — but calm, fair, strong, and immortal. "They seem," wrote Hazlitt, "to have no sympathy with us, and not to want our admiration. In their faultless excellence, they appear sufficient to themselves."

In the sculptor's art, more than on the historian's page, lives the most glorious memory of the classic past. A visit to the Vatican by torchlight endears even these poor traditional deities forever.

> On lofty ceilings vivid frescoes glow,
> Auroras beam,
> The steeds of Neptune through the waters go,
> Or Sibyls dream.
>
> As in the flickering torchlight shadows weaved
> Illusions wild,
> Methought Apollo's bosom slightly heaved
> And Juno smiled.
>
> Aërial Mercuries in bronze upspring,
> Dianas fly,
> And marble Cupids to the Psyches cling
> Without a sigh.

The absence of complexity in the language and intent of sculpture is always obvious in the expositions of its votaries. In no class of men have we found such distinct and scientific views of Art. One lovely evening in spring we stood with Bartolini beside the corpse of a beautiful child. Bereavement in a foreign land has a desolation of its own, and the afflicted mother desired to carry home a statue of her loved and lost. We conducted the sculptor to the chamber of death, that he might superintend the casts from the body. No sooner did his eyes fall upon it, than they glowed with admiration and filled with tears. He waved the assistants aside, clasped his hands, and gazed spell-bound upon the dead child. Its brow was ideal in contour, the hair of wavy gold, the cheeks of angelic outline. "How beautiful!" exclaimed Bartolini; and drawing us to the bedside, with a mingled awe and intelligence, he pointed out how the rigidity of death coincided, in this fair young creature, with the standard of Art; — the very hands, he declared, had stiffened into lines of beauty; and over the beautiful clay we thus learned from the lips of a venerable sculptor how intimate and minute is the cognizance this noble art takes of the language of the human form. Greenough would unfold by the hour the exquisite relation between function and beauty, organization and use, tracing therein a profound law and an illimitable truth. No more genial spectacle greeted us in Rome than Thorwaldsen at his Sunday-noon receptions; — his white hair, kindly smile, urbane manners, and unpretending simplicity, gave an added charm to the wise and liberal sentiments he expressed on Art, reminding us, in his frank eclecticism, of the spirit in which Humboldt cultivated science, and Sismondi history. Nor less indicative of this clear apprehension was the thorough solution we have heard Powers give, over the mask taken from a dead face, of the problem, how its living aspect was to modify its sculptured reproduction; or the original views expressed by Palmer as to the treatment of the eyes and hair in marble.

Appropriate and inspiring as are statues as memorials of character, in no department of art is there more need of a pure and just sense of the appropriate than in the choice of subject, locality, and treatment in statuary embellishment. Many greatly endeared human benefactors cannot thus be wisely or genially celebrated. Of late years there has been a mania on the subject; and even popular sentiment recognized the impropriety of setting up a statue in the market-place, of pious, retiring Izaak Walton.

Shelley used to say that a Roman peasant is as good a judge of sculpture as the best academician or anatomist. It is this direct appeal, this elemental simplicity, which constitutes the great distinction and charm of the art. There is nothing evasive and mysterious; in dealing with form and expression through features and attitude, average observation is a reliable test. The same English poet was right in declaring that the Greek sculptors did not find their inspiration in the dissecting-room; yet upon no subject has criticism displayed greater insight on the one hand and pedantry on the other, than in the discussion of these very *chefs-d'œuvres* of antiquity. While Michel Angelo, who was at Rome when the Laocoön was discovered, hailed it as "the wonder of Art," and scholars identified the group with a famous one described by Pliny, Canova thought that the right arm of the father was not in its right position, and the other restorations in the work have all been objected to. Goethe recognized a profound sagacity in the artist. "If," he wrote, "we try to place the bite in some different position, the whole action is changed, and we find it impossible to conceive one more fitting; the situation of the bite renders necessary the whole action of the limbs." And another critic says, "In the group of the Laocoön, the breast is expanded and the throat contracted to show that the agonies that convulse the frame are borne in silence." In striking contrast with such testimonies to the scientific truth to Nature in Grecian Art, was the objection I once heard an American backwoods mechanic make to this celebrated work. He asked why the figures were seated in a row on a dry-goods box, and declared that the serpent was not of a size to coil round so small an arm as the child's without breaking its vertebræ. So disgusted was Titian with the critical pedantry elicited by this group, that, in ridicule thereof, he painted a caricature, — three monkeys writhing in the folds of a little snake.

Few statues at Rome excite the imagination apart from intrinsic beauty, like that of Pompey, at whose base tradition says "great Cæsar fell." It was discovered lying across the boundary line of two estates, and claimed by both proprietors. Shrewd Cardinal Spada decided the head belonged to one and the body to another. It was decapitated, and sold in fragments for a small sum, and by this device was added to his famous collection, by the wily churchman.

Yet, despite the jargon of connoisseurship, against which Byron, while contemplating the Venus de Medici, utters so eloquent an invective, sculpture is a grand, serene, and intelligible art, — more so than architecture and painting,—and, as such, justly consecrated to the heroic and the beautiful in man and history. It is pre-eminently commemorative. How the old cities of Europe are peopled to the imagination, as well as the eye, by the statues of their traditional rulers or illustrious children, keeping, as it were, a warning sign, or a sublime vigil, silent, yet expressive, in the heart of busy life and through the lapse of ages! We could never pass Duke Cosmo's imposing effigy in the old square of Florence, without the magnificent patronage and the despotic perfidy of the Medicean family being revived to memory with intense local association,—nor note the ugly mitred and cloaked papal figures, with hands extended, in the mockery of benediction, over the beggars in the piazzas of Romagna, without Ranke's frightful picture of Church abuses reappearing, as if to crown these brazen forms with infamy. There was always a gleam of poetry — however sad — on the most foggy day, in the glimpse afforded from our window, in Trafalgar Square, of that patient horseman, Charles the Martyr. How alive old Neptune sometimes looked, by moonlight, in Rome, as we passed his plashing fountain. And those German poets,—Goethe, Schiller, and Jean Paul,—what to modern eyes were Frankfort, Stuttgart, and Baireuth, unconsecrated by their endeared forms? The most pleasant association Versailles yielded us of the Bourbon dynasty was that inspired by Jeanne d'Arc, graceful in her marble sleep, as sculptured by Marie d'Orléans; and the most impressive token of Napoleon's downfall we saw in Europe was his colossal image intended for the square of Leghorn, but thrown permanently on the sculptor's hands by the waning of his proud star. The statue of Heber, to Christian vision, hallows Calcutta. The Perseus of Cellini breathes of the months of artistic suspense, inspiration, and experiment, so graphically described in that clever egotist's memoirs. One feels like blessing the grief-bowed figures at the tomb of Princess Charlotte, so truly do their attitudes express our sympathy with the love and the sorrow her name excites. Would not Sterne have felt a thrill of complacency, had he beheld his tableau of the Widow Wadman and Uncle Toby so genially embodied by Ball Hughes? What more spirited symbol of prosperous conquest can be imagined than the gilded horses of St. Mark's? How natural was Michel Angelo's exclamation, "March!" as he gazed on Donatello's San Giorgio, in the Church of San Michele,—one mailed hand on a shield, bare head, complete armor, and the foot advanced,—like a sentinel who hears the challenge, or a knight listening for the charge! Tenerani's "Descent from the Cross," in the Torlonia Chapel, outlives in remembrance the brilliant assemblies of that financial house. The outlines of Flaxman, essentially statuesque, seem alone adequate to illustrate to the eye the great mediæval poet, whose verse seems often cut from stone in the quarries of infernal destiny. How grandly sleep the lions of Canova at Pope Clement's tomb!

A census of the statues of the world, past and present, would indicate an enormous marble population: in every Greek and Roman house, temple, public square, cemetery, these effigies abounded. According to Pliny the number of memorable statues in Athens exceeded three thousand; the number brought to Rome from conquered provinces was so great that the record seems incredible; add to these the countless statues we know to have been destroyed, the innumerable fragmentary images encountered in Italy, and the variety of modern works from those which people the cathedral roof to those which adorn private galleries and favorite studios, and the mind is bewildered by the extent not less than the beauty of the products of the chisel.

We have sometimes wondered that some æsthetic philosopher has not analyzed the vital relation of the arts to each other and given a popular exposition of their mutual dependence. Drawing from the antique has long been an acknowledged initiation for the limner, and Campbell, in his terse description of the histrionic art, says that therein "verse ceases to be airy thought, and sculpture to be dumb." How much of their peculiar effects did Talma, Kemble, and Rachel owe to the attitudes, gestures, and drapery of the Grecian statues! Kean adopted the "dying fall" of General Abercrombie's figure in St. Paul's as the model of his own. Some of the memorable scenes and votaries of the drama are directly associated with the sculptor's art, — as, for instance, the last act of "Don Giovanni," wherein the expressive music of Mozart breathes a pleasing terror in connection with the spectral nod of the marble horseman; and Shakspeare has availed himself of this art, with beautiful wisdom, in that melting scene where remorseful love pleads with the motionless heroine of the "Winter's Tale," —

> "Her natural posture!
> Chide me, dear stone, that I may say, indeed,
> Thou art Hermione; or rather thou art she,
> In thy not chiding: for she was as tender
> As infancy and grace."

Garrick imitated to the life, in "Abel Drugger," the vacant stare peculiar to Nollekens, the sculptor; and Colley Cibber's father was a devotee of the chisel, and adorned Chatsworth with free-stone Sea-Nymphs.

In view of the great historical value, comparative authenticity, and possible significance and beauty of busts, this department of sculpture has a peculiar interest and charm. The most distinct idea we have of the Roman emperors, even in regard to their individual characters, is derived from their busts at the Vatican and elsewhere. The benignity of Trajan, the animal development of Nero, and the classic vigor of young Augustus, are best apprehended through these memorable effigies which Time has spared and Art transmitted. And a similar permanence and distinctness of impression associate most of our illustrious moderns with their sculptured features; the ironical grimace of Voltaire is perpetuated by Houdon's bust; the sympathetic intellectuality of Schiller by Dannecker's; Handel's countenance is familiar through the elaborate chisel of Roubillac; Nollekens moulded Sterne's delicate and unimpassioned but keen physiognomy, and Chantrey the lofty cranium of Scott. Who has not blessed the rude but conscientious artist who carved the head of Shakspeare, preserved at Stratford? How quaintly appropriate to the old house in Nuremberg is Albert Dürer's bust over the door! Our best knowledge of Alexander Hamilton's aspect is obtained from the expressive marble head of him by that ardent republican sculptor, Ceracchi. It was appropriate for Mrs. Damer, the daughter of a gallant field-marshal, to portray in marble, as heroic idols, Fox, Nelson, and Napoleon. We were never more convinced of the intrinsic grace and solemnity of this form of "counterfeit presentment" than when exploring the Baciocchi *palazzo* at Bologna. In the centre of a circular room, lighted from above, and draped as well as carpeted with purple, stood on a simple pedestal the bust of Napoleon's sister, thus enshrined after death by her husband. The profound stillness, the relief of this isolated head against a mass of dark tints, and its consequent emphatic individuality, made the sequestered chamber seem a holy place, where communion with the departed, so spiritually represented by the exquisite image, appeared not only natural, but inevitable. Our countryman, Powers, has eminently illustrated the possible excellence of this branch of Art. In mathematical correctness of detail, unrivalled finish of texture, and with these, in many cases, the highest characterization, busts from his hand have an absolute artistic value, independent of likeness, like a portrait by Vandyck or Titian. When the subject is favorable, his achievements in this regard are memorable, and fill the eye and mind with ideas of beauty and meaning undreamed of by those who consider marble portraits as wholly imitative and mechanical. Was there ever a human face which so completely reflected inward experience and individual genius as the bust which haunts us throughout Italy, broods over the monument in Santa Croce, gazes pensively from library niche, seems to awe the more radiant images of boudoir and gallery, and sternly looks melancholy reproach from the Ravenna tomb?

"The lips, as Cumæ's cavern close,
The cheeks, with fast and sorrow thin,
The rigid front, almost morose,
But for the patient hope within,

> Declare a life whose course hath been
> Unsullied still, though still severe,
> Which, through the wavering days of sin,
> Kept itself icy chaste and clear."

National characters become, as it were, household gods through the sculptor's portrait; the duplicates of Canova's head of Napoleon seem as appropriate in the *salons* and shops of France, as the heads of Washington and Franklin in America, or the antique images of Scipio Africanus and Ceres in Sicily, and Wellington and Byron in London.

It is to us a source of noble delight, that with these permanent trophies of the sculptor's art may now be mingled our national fame. Twenty years ago, the address in Murray's Guide-Book, — *Crawford, an American Sculptor, Piazza Barberini,* — would have been unique; now that name is enrolled on the list of the world's benefactors in the patrimony of Art. Greenough, by his pen, his presence, and his chisel, gave an impulse to taste and knowledge in sculpture and architecture not destined soon to pass away; no more eloquent and original advocate of the beautiful and the true in the higher social economies has blest our day; his Cherubs and Medora overflow with the poetry of form; his essays are a valuable legacy of philosophic thought. The Greek Slave of Powers was invariably surrounded by visitors at the London World's Fair and the Manchester Exhibition. Story's Cleopatra was the nucleus of charmed observation at Sydenham. The Pearl Diver of Paul Akers is his own most beautiful monument. Palmer has sent forth from his isolated studio at Albany a series of ideal busts, of a pure type of original and exquisite beauty; and many others might be named who have honorably illustrated an American claim to distinction in an art eminently republican in its perpetuation of national worth and the identity of its highest achievements with social progress.

BRIDGES.

"I stood on the bridge at midnight,
As the clocks were striking the hour,
And the moon rose over the city,
Behind the dark church-tower.
And like those waters rushing
Among the wooden piers,
A flood of thoughts came o'er me,
That filled my eyes with tears."

LONGFELLOW.

NSTINCTIVELY, Treason, in this vast land, aimed its first blow at the Genius of Communication, — the benign and potent means and method of American civilization and nationality. The great problem Watt and Fulton, Clinton and Morse, so gloriously solved, a barbaric necessity thus reduced back to chaos; and not the least sad and significant of the bulletins whereby the most base of civic mutinies found current record is that entitled, "Destruction of the Bridges"; and (melancholy contrast!) simultaneously we hear of constructive energy in the same direction, on the Italian peninsula, — an engineer having submitted to Victor Emmanuel proposals for throwing a bridge across the Straits of Messina, "binding Scylla to Charybdis, and thus clinching Italian unity with bonds of iron."*

* Recent Italian journals speak of a project to construct a bridge over the Straits of Messina, to unite Sicily with the mainland. The bridge proposed will be a suspension one, on a new system, the chains being of cast-steel, and strong enough to support the weight of several railway trains.

Bonds of nationality, in more than a physical sense, indeed, are bridges; even cynical Heine found an endeared outlook to his native Rhine on the bastion of a familiar bridge. Tennyson makes one an essential feature of his English summer-picture, wherein forever glows the sweet image of the "Gardener's Daughter"; and Bunyan found no better similitude for Christian's passage from Time to Eternity than the "river where there is no bridge."

The primitive need, the possible genius, the science, and the sentiment of a bridge, endear its aspect and associations beyond those of any other economical structure. There is, indeed, something genially picturesque about a mill, as Constable's pencil and Tennyson's muse have aptly demonstrated; there is an artistic miracle possible in a sculptured gate, as those of Ghiberti so elaborately evidence; science, poetry, and human enterprise consecrate a light-house; sacred feelings hallow a spire, and mediæval towers stand forth in noble relief against the sunset sky; but around none of these familiar objects cluster the same thoroughly human associations which make a bridge attractive to the sight and memory. In its most remote suggestion it typifies man's primal relation to Nature, his first instinctive effort to circumvent or avail himself of her resources; indeed, he might take his hint of a bridge from Nature herself, — her fallen monarchs of the forest athwart a stream, "the testimony of the rocks," the curving shores, cavern roofs, and pendent branches, and the prismatic bow in the heavens, which a poet well calls "a bridge to tempt the angels down."

A bridge of the simplest kind is often charmingly effective as a landscape-accessory; there is a short plank one in a glen of the White Mountains, which, seen through a vista of woodland, makes out the picture so aptly that it is sketched by every artist who haunts the region. What lines of grace are added to the night-view of a great city by the lights on the bridges! What subtile principles enter into the building of such a bridge as the Britannia, where even the metallic contraction of the enormous tubes is provided for by supporting them on cannon-balls! How venerable seems the most graceful of Tuscan bridges, when we remember it was erected in the fifteenth century, — and the Rialto, when we think of Shylock and Portia; and how signal an instance is it of the progressive application of a true principle in science, that the contrivance whereby the South Americans bridge the gorges of their mountains, by a pendulous causeway of twisted osiers and bamboo, — one of which, crossed by Humboldt, was a hundred and twenty feet long, — is identical with that which sustains the magnificent structure over the Niagara River! The chasms and streams thus spanned by a rope of seven strands, have a fairy-like aspect. Artist and engineer alike delight in this feature of tropical scenery. In some cases the stone structures built by the Spaniards, and half destroyed by earthquakes, are repaired with bamboo, and often with an effective grace. In a bridge the arch is triumphal, both for practical and commemorative ends. Unknown to the Greeks and Egyptians, even the ancient Romans, it is said by modern architects, did not appreciate its true mechanical principle, but ascribed the marvellous strength thereof to the cement which kept intact their semicircle. In Cæsar's "Commentaries," the bridge transit and vigilance form no small part of military tactics, — boats and baskets serving the same purpose in ancient and modern warfare. The Church of old originated and consecrated bridges; religion, royalty, and art celebrate their advent; the opening of Waterloo Bridge is the subject of one of the best pictures of a modern English painter; and Cockney visitors to the peerless Bridge of Telford still ask the guide where the Queen stood at its inauguration. But it is when we turn from the historical and scientific to the familiar and personal that we realize the spontaneous interest attached to a bridge. It is as a feature of our native landscape, the goal of habitual excursions, the rendezvous, the observatory, the favorite haunt or transit, that it wins the gaze and the heart. There the musing angler sits content; there the echoes of the horse's hoofs rouse to expectancy the dozing traveller; there the glad lover dreams, and the despairing wretch seeks a watery grave, and the song of the poet finds a response in the universal heart, —

> "How often, oh, how often,
> In the days that have gone by,
> Have I stood on that bridge at midnight,
> And gazed on the wave and sky!"

One of the most primitive tokens of civilization is a bridge; and yet no artificial object is more picturesquely associated with its ultimate symbols. The fallen tree whereon the pioneer crosses a stream in the wilderness is not more significant of human isolation than the fragmentary arch in an ancient city of the vanished home of thousands. Thus, by its necessity and its survival, a bridge suggests the first exigency and the last relic of civilized life. The old explorers of our Western Continent record the savage expedients whereby watercourses were passed, — coils of grape-vine carried between the teeth of an aboriginal swimmer and attached to the opposite bank, a floating log, or, in shallow streams, a series of stepping-stones; and the most popular historian of England, when delineating to the eye of fancy the hour of her capital's venerable decay, can find no more impressive illustration than to make a broken arch of London Bridge the observatory of the speculative reminiscent.

The bridge is, accordingly, of all economical inventions, that which is most inevitable to humanity, signalizing the first steps of man amid the solitude of Nature, and accompanying his progress through every stage of civic life; its crude form makes the wanderer's heart beat in the lonely forest, as a sign of the vicinity or the track of his kind; and its massive remains excite the reverent curiosity of the archæologist, who seeks among the ruins of Art for trophies of a by-gone race. Few indications of Roman supremacy are more striking than the unexpected sight of one of those bridges of solid and symmetrical masonry which the traveller in Italy encounters, when emerging from a mountain-pass or a squalid town upon the ancient highway. The permanent method herein apparent suggests an energetic and pervasive race whose constructive instinct was imperial; such an evidence of their pathway over water is as suggestive of national power as the evanescent trail of the savage is of his casual domain. In the bridge, as in no other structure, use combines with beauty by an instinctive law; and the stone arch, more or less elaborate in detail, is as essential now to the function and the grace of a bridge, as when it was first thrown, invincible and harmonious, athwart the rivers Cæsar's legions crossed.

As I stood on the scattered planks which afford a precarious foothold amid the rapids of St. Anthony, methought these frail bridges of hewn timber accorded with the reminiscence of the missionary pioneer who discovered and named the picturesque waters, more than an elaborate and ancient causeway. Even those long, inelegant structures which lead the pedestrian over our own Charles River, or the broad inlets of the adjacent bay, have their peculiar charm as the scene of many a gorgeous autumnal sunset and many a patient "constitutional" walk. It is a homely, but significant proverb, "Never find fault with the bridge that carries you safe over." What beautiful shadows graceful bridges cast, when the twilight deepens and the waves are calm! How mysteriously sleep the moonbeams there! What a suggestive vocation is a toll-keeper's! Patriarchs in this calling will tell of methodical and eccentric characters known for years.

Bridges have their legends. There is one in Lombardy whence a jilted lover sprang with his faithless bride as she passed to church with her new lover; it is yet called the "Bridge of the Betrothed." On the mountain range, near Serravazza, in Tuscany, is a natural bridge which unites two of the lofty peaks; narrow and aerial, it is believed by the peasantry to have miraculously formed itself to give foothold to the Madonna as she passed over the mountains, and it bears her name. An old traveller, describing New York amusements, tells us of a favorite ride from the city to the suburban country, and says, — "In the way there is a bridge about three miles distant, which you always pass as you return, called the 'Kissing Bridge,' where it is part of the etiquette to salute the lady who has put herself under your protection." * A curious lawsuit was lately instituted by the proprietor of a menagerie who lost an elephant by a bridge giving way beneath his unaccustomed weight; the authorities protested against damages, as they never undertook to give safe passage to so large an animal.

The office of a bridge is prolific of metaphor, whereof an amusing instance is Boswell's comparison of himself, when translating Paoli's talk to Dr. Johnson, to a "narrow isthmus connecting two continents." It has been aptly said of Dante's great poem, that, in the world of letters, it is a mediæval bridge over that vast chasm which divides classical from modern times. All conciliating authors bridge select severed intelligences, and even national feeling: as Irving's writings brought more near to each other the alienated sympathies of England and America, and Carlyle made a trysting-place for British and German thought; as Sydney Smith's talk threw a suspension-bridge from Conservative to Refôrmer, and Lord Bacon's (in the hour of bitter alienation between Crown and Commons) "reconciling genius spanned the dividing stream of party."

How quaint, yet effective, Jean Paul's illustration of an alienated state of human feeling, "the *drawbridge of countenances*, whereupon once the two souls met, stood suddenly raised, high in air." Nor less significant is a modern historian's definition of an Englishman as "an island surrounded by a misty and tumultuous sea of prejudices and hatreds, generally unapproachable, and, at all times, *utterly repudiative of a bridge.*" Pontifex Maximus has long ceased to wear the great spirit-

* *Travels through the Middle Settlements of North America in* 1759–60. By Rev. Andrew Burnaby.

ual title whose unchallenged attribute was to bridge the chasm between earth and heaven. What humor may be evolved from a nose-bridge Punch in his dealings with the great Duke, and Sterne in his record of Tristram Shandy's infancy, have notably chronicled; while the infinite delicacy of tension in the bridge of Paganini's violin, indicates the relation thereof to exquisite gradations of sound. "The Mahomedans," says Scott, "have a fanciful idea that the believer, in his passage to Paradise, is under the necessity of passing barefoot over a bridge composed of red-hot iron plates. All the pieces of paper which the Moslem has preserved during his life, lest some holy thing being written upon them might be profaned, arrange themselves between his feet and the burning metal, and so save him from injury." In the "Vision" of Mirza, a bridge is typical of human life. That was a ludicrous incident related of poor, obstinate, crazy George the Third,—that encountering some boys near a bridge early one morning, he asked them what bridge it was. "The Bridge of Kew," they replied; whereupon the king proposed and gave three vociferous cheers for the Bridge of Kew, as a newly-discovered wonder. Amusing, too, was the warm dispute of the two errant lake poets whether a certain acutely angular bridge in the Alps was called great A from its resemblance to that letter, or as the first of its kind.

How isolated and bewildered are villagers, when, after a tempest, the news spreads that a freshet has carried away the bridge! Every time we shake hands, we make a human bridge of courtesy or love; and that was a graceful fancy of one of our ingenious writers to give expression to his thoughts in "Letters from under a Bridge." With an eye and an ear for Nature's poetry, the gleam of lamps from a bridge, the figures that pass and repass thereon, the rush and the lull of waters beneath, the perspective of the arch, the weather-stains on the parapet, the sunshine and the cloud-shadows around, are phases and sounds fraught with meaning and mystery.

It is an acknowledged truth in the philosophy of Art, that Beauty is the handmaid of Use; and as the grace of the swan and the horse results from a conformation whose *rationale* is movement, so the pillar that supports the roof, and the arch that spans the current, by their serviceable fitness, wed grace of form to wise utility. The laws of architecture illustrate this principle copiously; but in no single and familiar product of human skill is it more striking than in bridges; if lightness, symmetry, elegance, proportion, charm the ideal sense, not less are the economy and adaptation of the structure impressive to the eye of science. Perhaps the ideas of use and beauty, of convenience and taste, in no instance, coalesce more obviously; and therefore, of all human inventions, the bridge lends the most undisputed charm to the landscape. It is one of those symbols of humanity which spring from and are not grafted upon Nature; it proclaims her affinity with man, and links her spontaneous benefits with his invention and his needs; it seems to celebrate the stream over which it rises, and to wed the wayward waters to the order and the mystery of life. There is no hint of superfluity or impertinence in a bridge; it blends with the wildest and the most cultivated scene with singular aptitude, and is a feature of both rural and metropolitan landscape that strikes the mind as essential. A striking confirmation of this idea offers itself in a recent critic's definition of a classic style of writing: "A bridge," he says, "*completes* river landscape; it *stiffens* the scenery which was before too soft, too delicate, too vegetable. Just such is the effect of pure style in literary art." * The most usual form has its counterpart in those rocky arches which flood and fire have excavated or penned up in many picturesque regions, — the segments of caverns, or the ribs of strata, — so that, without the instinctive suggestion of the mind itself, Nature furnishes complete models of a bridge whereon neither Art nor Science can improve. Herein the most advanced and the most rude peoples own a common skill; bridges, of some kind, and all adapted to their respective countries, being the familiar invention of savage necessity and architectural genius. The explorer finds them in Africa as well as the artist in Rome; swung, like huge hammocks of ox-hide, over the rapid streams of South America; spanning in fragile cane-platforms the gorges of the Andes; crossing vast chasms of the Alleghanies with the slender iron viaduct of the American railways; and jutting, a crumbling segment of the ancient world, over the yellow Tiber: as familiar on the Chinese tea-caddy as on Canaletto's canvas; as traditional a local feature of London as of Florence; as significant of the onward march of civilization in Wales to-day as in Liguria during the Middle Ages. Where men dwell and wander, and water flows, these beautiful and enduring, or curious and casual expedients are found, as memorable triumphs of architecture, crowned with historical associations, or as primitive inventions that unconsciously mark the first faltering steps of humanity in the course of empire; for, on this continent, where the

* Bagehot.

French missionary crossed the narrow log supported by his Indian convert in the midst of a wilderness, massive stone arches shadow broad streams that flow through populous cities; and the history of civilization may be traced from the loose stones whereon the lone settler fords the watercourse, to such grand, graceful, and permanent monuments of human prosperity as the elaborate and ancient stone bridges of European capitals.

When we look forth upon a grand or lovely scene of Nature, — mountain, river, meadow, and forest, — what a fine central object, what an harmonious artificial feature of the picture, is a bridge, whether rustic and simple, a mere rude passage-way over a brook, or a curve of gray stone throwing broad shadows upon the bright surface of a river! Nor less effective is the same object amid the crowded walls, spires, streets, and chimney-stacks of a city. There the bridge is the least conventional structure, the suggestive point, the favorite locality; it seems to reunite the working-day world with the freedom of Nature; it is, perhaps, the one spot in the dense array of edifices and thoroughfares which "gives us pause." There, if anywhere, our gaze and our feet linger; people have a relief against the sky, as they pass over it; artists look patiently thither; lovers, the sad, the humorous, and the meditative, stop there to observe and to muse; they lean over the parapet and watch the flowing tide; they look thence around as from a pleasant vantage-ground. The bridge, in populous old towns, is the rendezvous, the familiar landmark, the traditional nucleus of the place, and perhaps the only picturesque framework in all those marts and homes, more free, open, and suggestive of a common lot than temple, square, or palace; for there pass and repass noble and peasant, regal equipage and humble caravan; children plead to stay, and veterans moralize there; the privileged beggar finds a standing-place for charity to bless; a shrine hallows or a sentry guards, history consecrates or Art glorifies, and trade, pleasure, or battle, perchance, lend to it the spell of fame. The dearest associations of a life are described in one of Jean Ingelow's most elaborate poems, as revolving around and identified with "Four Bridges":

> "Our brattling river tumbles through the one;
> The second spans a shallow, weedy brook;
> Beneath the others, and beneath the sun,
> Lie two long stilly pools, and on their breasts
> Picture their wooden piles, encased in swallows' nests.
> And round about them grows a fringe of weeds,
> And then a floating crown of lily flowers,
> And yet within small silver-budded weeds;
> But each clear centre evermore embowers
> A deeper sky, where stooping, you may see
> The little minnows twirling restlessly."

In the neighborhood of Aberdeen, the picturesque bridge over the Don, with its adjacent rocks, trees, and deep, dark stream, is known as the "brig of Balgownie." Thomas the Rhymer uttered many prophecies about "Balgownie's brig black wa'"; and it figures among the scenes of Byron's boyhood. Let any one recall his sojourn in a foreign city, and conjure to his mind's eye the scenes, and prominent to his fancy, distinct to his memory, will be the bridge. He will think of Florence as intersected by the Arno, and with the very name of that river reappears the peerless grace of the Ponte Santa Trinità with its moss-grown escutcheons and aërial curves. He will recall the Pont du Gard with the vicinage of Nismes; the Pont Neuf, at Paris, with its soldiers and priests, its boot-blacks and grisettes, the gay streets on one side, and the studious quarter on the other, typifies and concentrates for him the associations of the French capital; and what a complete symbol of Venice — its canals, its marbles, its mysterious polity, its romance of glory and woe, — is a good photograph of the Bridge of Sighs! Her history is, indeed, singularly identified with bridges. One, as her exchange, is permanently associated with the palmiest days of mediæval commerce; another with the darker records of her criminal law; while on one of her bridges, Sarpi, the "terrible friar" Paolo was waylaid and nearly killed by Papal assassins, whence dates the most efficient protest against ecclesiastical tyranny.

The history of Rome is written on her bridges. The Ponte Rotto is Art's favorite trophy of her decay; two thirds of it has disappeared; and the last Pope has ineffectively repaired it, by a platform sustained by iron wire: yet who that has stood thereon in the sunset, and looked from the dome of St. Peter's to the islands projected at that hour so distinctly from the river's surface, glanced along the flushed dwellings upon its bank, with their intervals of green terraces, or gazed, in the other direction, upon the Cloaca of Tarquin, Vesta's dome, and the Aventine Hill, with its palaces, convents, vineyards, and gardens, has not felt that the Ponte Rotto was the most suggestive observatory in the Eternal City? The Ponte Molle brings back Constantine and his vision of the Cross; and the statues on Sant' Angelo mutely attest the vicissitudes of ecclesiastical eras.

England boasts no monument of her modern victories so impressive as the bridge named for the most memorable of them. The best view of Prague and its people is from the long series of stone arches which span the Moldau. The solitude and serenity of genius are rarely better realized than by musing of Klopstock and Gessner, Lavater and Zimmermann, on the Bridge of Rapperschwyl on the Lake of Zurich, where they dwelt and wrote or died. From the Bridge of St. Martin we have the first view of Mont Blanc. The Suspension Bridge at Niagara is an artificial wonder as great, in its degree, as the natural miracle of the mighty cataract which thunders forever at its side; while no triumph of inventive economy could more aptly lead the imaginative stranger into the picturesque beauties of Wales than the extraordinary tubular bridge across the Menai Strait. The aqueduct-bridge at Lisbon, the long causeway over Cayuga Lake in our own country, and the bridge over the Loire at Orléans, are memorable in every traveller's retrospect.

But the economical and the artistic interest of bridges is often surpassed by their historical suggestions, almost every vocation and sentiment of humanity being intimately associated therewith. The Rialto at Venice and the Ponte Vecchio at Florence, are identified with the financial enterprise of the one city and the goldsmith's skill of the other: one was long the Exchange of the " City of the Sea," and still revives the image of Shylock and the rendezvous of Antonio; while the other continues to represent mediæval trade in the quaint little shops of jewellers and lapidaries. One of the characteristic religious orders of that era is identified with the ancient bridge which crosses the Rhone at Avignon, erected by the " Brethren of the Bridge," a fraternity instituted in an age of anarchy expressly to protect travellers from the bandits, whose favorite place of attack was at the passage of rivers. The builder of the old London Bridge, Peter Colechurch, is believed to have been attached to this same order; he died in 1176, and was buried in a crypt of the little chapel on the second pier, according to the habit of the fraternity. For many years a market was held on this bridge; it was often the scene of war; it stayed the progress of Canute's fleet; at one time destroyed by fire, and at another carried away by ice; half ruined in one era by the bastard Faulconbridge, and, at another, the watchword of civil war, when the cry resounded, "Cade hath gotten London Bridge," and Wat Tyler's rebels convened there. Elizabeth and her peerless courtiers have floated, in luxurious barges and splendid attire, by its old piers, and the heads of traitors rotted in the sun upon its venerable battlements. Only sixty years ago a portion of the original structure remained;* it was once covered with houses; Peter the Dutchman's famous water-wheels plashed at its side; from the dark street and projecting gables noted tavern-signs vibrated in the wind. The exclusive thoroughfare from the city to Kent and Surrey, what ceremonial and scenes has it not witnessed,—royal entrances and greetings, rites under the low brown arches of the old chapel, revelry in the convenient hostels, traffic in the crowded mart, chimes from the quaint belfry, the tragic triumph of vindictive law in the gory heads upon spikes! The veritable and minute history of London Bridge would illustrate the civic and social annals of England; and romance could scarce invent a more effective background for the varied scenes and personages such a

* Sir Astley Cooper's nephew presented to Dr. Valentine Mott, the late eminent New York surgeon, an elegantly wrought case of amputating instruments, the handles of which are made of the wood and the blades of iron from old London Bridge, whose oak timbers were laid in 1176.

chronicle would exhibit than the dim local perspective, when, ere any bridge stood there, the ferryman's daughter founded, with the tolls, a House of Sisters, subsequently transformed into a college of priests. By a law of Nature, thus do the elements of civilization cluster around the place of transit; thus do the courses of the water indicate the direction and nucleus of emigration, —from the vast lakes and mighty rivers of America, whereby an immense continent is made available to human intercourse, and therefore to material unity, to the point where the Thames was earliest crossed and spanned. More special historical and social facts may be found attached to every old bridge. In war, especially, heroic achievement and desperate valor have often consecrated these narrow defiles and exclusive means of advance and retreat: —

"When the goodman mends his armor
And trims his helmet's plume,
When the goodwife's shuttle merrily
Goes flashing through the loom,
With weeping and with laughter
Still is the story told
How well Horatius kept the bridge
In the good old days of old."

The bridge of Darius spanned the Bosphorus, — of Xerxes, the Hellespont, — of Cæsar, the Rhine, — and of Trajan, the Danube; while the victorious march of Napoleon has left few traces so unexceptionably memorable as the massive causeways of the Simplon. Cicero arrested the bearer of letters to Catiline on the Pons Milonis, built in the time of Sylla on the ancient Via Flaminia; and by virtue of the blazing cross which he saw in the sky from the Ponte Molle the Christian emperor Constantine conquered Maxentius. The Pont du Gard near Nismes, and the St. Esprit near Lyons, were originally of Roman construction. During the war of freedom, so admirably described by our countryman, whereby rose the Dutch Republic, the Huguenots, at the siege of Valenciennes, we are told, "made forays upon the monasteries for the purpose of procuring supplies, and the broken statues of the dismantled churches were used to build a bridge across an arm of the river, which was called, in derision, the Bridge of Idols."

But a more memorable historical bridge is admirably described in another military episode of this favorite historian,—that which Alexander of Parma built across the Scheldt, whereby Antwerp was finally won for Philip of Spain. Its construction was a miracle of science and courage; and it became the scene of one of the most terrible tragedies and the most fantastic festivals which signalize the history of that age, and illustrate the extraordinary and momentous struggle for religious liberty in the Netherlands. Its piers extended five hundred feet into the stream,—connected with the shore by boats, defended by palisades, fortified parapets, and spiked rafts; cleft and partially destroyed by the volcanic fire-ship of Gianebelli, a Mantuan chemist and engineer, whereby a thousand of the best troops of the Spanish army were instantly killed, and their brave chief stunned,—when the hour of victory came to the besiegers, it was the scene of a floral procession and Arcadian banquet, and "the whole extent of its surface from the Flemish to the Brabant shore" was alive with "war-bronzed figures crowned with flowers." "This magnificent undertaking has been favorably compared with the celebrated Rhine bridge of Julius Cæsar. When it is remembered, however, that the Roman work was performed in summer, across a river only half as broad as the Scheldt, free from the disturbing action of the tides, and flowing through an unresisting country, while the whole character of the structure, intended only to serve for the single passage of an army, was far inferior to the massive solidity of Parma's bridge, it seems not unreasonable to assign the superiority to the general who had surmounted all the obstacles of a northern winter, vehement ebb and flow from the sea, and enterprising and desperate enemies at every point." *

It was at the bridge of Pinos, where the Moors and Christians had so fiercely battled, that Columbus, after pleading his cause in vain at the court, hastening away with despondent steps, was overtaken by the queen's messenger; recalled and provided with the substantial aid that led to his momentous discovery. It was in a pavilion in the middle of the bridge across the Seine at Montereau, that the Dauphin, afterwards Charles the Seventh, invited the Duke of Burgundy to meet him in colloquy; and there the latter met his death. The Bridge of Lodi is one of the great landmarks of Napoleon's career; and the Bridge of Concord no insignificant landmark of the American Revolutionary War. Over the Melos at Smyrna is a bridge which is a rendezvous for camels, and has been justly called "the central point of the commerce of Asia Minor."

We have a memorable illustration of the historic interest of bridges, in the elaborate annals of the Pont Neuf. † Although in importance it has long since been superseded by other elegant causeways, for centuries it

* *History of the Netherlands*, Vol. I. p. 182.

† *Histoire du Pont Neuf*, par Edouard Fournier.

was the centre of Paris life, — of the trade and pastime, of the scandal and the violences, of the shows and *émeutes*, so that the record of what occurred there is an epitome of political and social history. It was the rendezvous of dog-clippers and ballad-singers, of *bravi* and gallants, of the quack and the courtesan, of student, soldier, artist, and gossip. "The heart of Paris beat there," says the historian of the Pont Neuf, "from the seventeenth century;" the statue of Henry IV. alone made it the nucleus of political associations; it was alike the scene of Cellini's adventure and Sterne's sentiment. Catherine de Medicis laid its first stone. Henry IV. completed it; guillotines, *cafés*, and altars have signalized its extremities or parapets. La Fronde was there inaugurated; there the discharge of cannon proclaimed the flight of the king in '91; its pavement was bloody with the massacres of September; the first Napoleon there first tried his hand against the revolution; it was the scene of an Englishman's famous bet and a parrot's famous lingo. Huguenot, royalist, priest, executioner, *gamin*, assassin, thief, dandy, nun, hero, and actress, — procession, tryst, ambush, faction, and farce, — murder, song, *bon-mot*, watchword, — the tragic, the holy and the hopeless in life, alternate in the story of the Pont Neuf. The Countess du Barri, as a child, "the pretty little angel," was a vendor there; and an old epigram identified her career with bridges, — her birth with the Pont au Choux, her childhood with the Pont Neuf, her triumph with the Pont Royale, and her end with the Pont aux Dames.

Even the fragile bridges of our own country, during the Revolution, have an historical importance in the story of war. The "Great Bridge" across the Elizabeth

River, nine miles from Norfolk in Virginia; the floating bridge at Ticonderoga; that which spanned Stony Brook in New Jersey; and many others, are identified with strife or stratagem. What an effective object in the distant landscape, to the *habitué* of the Central Park in New York, is the lofty bridge whereby the Croton aqueduct crosses the Harlaem River, with its fifteen arches, its fourteen hundred feet of length, and its span of nearly a thousand! How few of the multitude to whom King's Bridge is a daily goal or transit, are cognizant of its historical associations; yet the records of Manhattan Island declare that in 1692 "His Excellency the Governor, out of great favor and good to the city," proposed the building of this bridge, and soon ordered that "if Frederick Phillipse will undertake the same, he shall have the preference of their Majesties' grant, (5th of King William, and 3d of Queen Mary,) which was subsequently confirmed to the lord of the manor of Phillipsburgh"; whereon was born and lived Washington's first love — the beautiful Mary Phillipse. Here was the barrier of the British when they occupied New York Island in the Revolution; while as far north as the Croton River, extended the neutral ground, the scene of Cooper's first American romance, the heroine of which is this same fair but unresponsive enslaver of our peerless chief's young affections. Here in '75 Congress ordered a post established to protect New York by land; two years later occurred the sanguinary fight between the Continentals under Heath, and the Hessians under Knyphausen. The next year Cornwallis fixed his command at the same border causeway; and in '81, when our army came near the spot to give the French officers a view of the outposts, a brisk skirmish ensued, and a number of our men were killed at long shot. King's Bridge was long the rendezvous of freebooters in those unsettled times, and the rallying-point of the Cow-boys. Beautifully situated at the confluence of the Hudson and Harlaem rivers, surrounded by high rolling hills, then thickly wooded and crowned with forts, the region was originally selected as the site of New Amsterdam, on account of its secure position. When Manhattan Island was abandoned by the British in '76, Washington occupied King's Bridge as his head-quarters. Indeed, from Trenton to Lodi, military annals have few more fierce conflicts than those wherein the bridge of the battle-ground is disputed; to cross one is often a declaration of war, and Rubicons abound in history.

There is probably no single problem, wherein the laws of science and mechanical skill combine, which has so won the attention and challenged the powers of inventive minds as the construction of bridges. The various exigencies to be met, the possible triumphs to be achieved, the experiments as to form, material, security, and grace, have been prolific causes of inspiration and disappointment. In this branch of economy, the mechanic and the mathematician fairly meet; and it requires a rare union of ability in both vocations to arrive at original results in this sphere. To invent a bridge, through the application of a scientific principle by a novel method, is one of those projects which seem to fascinate philosophical minds; in few have theory and practice been more completely tested; and the history of bridges, scientifically written, would exhibit as remarkable conflicts of opinion, trials of inventive skill, decision of character, genius, folly, and fame, as any other chapter in the annals of progress. How to unite security with the least inconvenience, permanence with availability, strength with beauty, — how to adapt the structure to the location, climate, use, and risks, — are questions which often invoke all the science and skill of the architect, and which have increased in difficulty with the advance of other resources and requisitions of civilization. Whether a bridge is to cross a brook, a river, a strait, an inlet, an arm of the sea, a canal, or a valley, are so many diverse contingencies which modify the calculations and plans of the engineer. Here liability to sudden freshets, there to overwhelming tides, now to the enormous weight of railway-trains, and again to the corrosive influence of the elements, must be taken into consideration; the navigation of waters, the exigencies of war, the needs of a population, the respective uses of viaduct, aqueduct, and roadway, have often to be included in the problem. These considerations influence not only the method of construction, but the form adopted and the material, and have given birth to bridges of wood, brick, stone, iron, wire, and chain, — to bridges supported by piers, to floating, suspension, and tubular structures, many of which are among the remarkable trophies of modern science and the noblest fruits of the arts of peace. Railways have created an entirely new species of bridge, to enable a train to intersect a road, to cross canals in slanting directions, to turn amid jagged precipices, and to cross arms of the sea at a sufficient elevation not to interfere with the passage of ships, — objects not to be accomplished by suspension-bridges because of their oscillation, nor girder for lack of support, the desiderata being extensive span with rigid strength, so triumphantly realized in the tubular bridge. The day when the great Holyrood train passing over the Strait of Menai by this grand expedient, established the superiority of this principle of construction, became a memorable occasion in the annals of mechanical science, and immortalized the name of Stephenson.

We find great national significance in the history of bridges in different countries. Their costly and substantial grandeur in Britain accords with the solid qualities of the race, and their elegance on the Continent with the pervasive influence of Art in Europe. It is a curious illustration of the inferior economical and high intellectual development of Greece, that the "Athenians waded, when their temples were the most perfect models of architecture"; and equally an evidence of the practical energy of the old Romans, that their stone bridges often remain to this hour intact. Our own incomplete civilization is manifest in the marvellous number of bridges that annually break down, from negligent or unscientific construction; while the indomitable enterprise of the people is no less apparent in some of the longest, loftiest, most wonderfully constructed and sustained bridges in the world. We have only to cross the Suspension Bridge at Niagara, or gaze up to its ærial tracery from the river, or look forth upon wooded ravines and down precipitous and umbrageous glens from the Erie Railway, to feel that in this, as in all other branches of mechanical enterprise, our nation is as boldly dexterous as culpably reckless. In no other country would so hazardous an experiment have been ventured as that of an engineer on one of the most frequented lines of railroad in the land, who finding the bridge he was approaching on fire, bade the passengers keep their seats, and dashed boldly through the flames ere the main arch gave way! "The vast majority of bridges in this country," says a recent writer, "whether for railroads or for ordinary horse-travel, have these elemental points:—1. Fragility. 2. Unendurably hideous ugliness. 3. Great aptitude for catching fire. They are all built of wood, and must be constantly patched and mended, and will rot away in a very few years. They are enormous blots on the landscape, stretching as they do like long unpainted boxes across the stream; like huge Saurian monsters with ever-open jaws into which you rush, or walk, or drive, and are gobbled up from all sight or sense of beauty. The dry timber of which they are built will catch fire from the mere spark of a locomotive, as in the case a few years ago of that hideous bridge which had so long insulted the Hudson River at Troy; and which was not only burned itself, but spread the destroying flame to the best part of the town. These bridges deface all the valleys of our land. The Housatonic, the Mohawk, the Lehigh, the hundreds of small yet beautiful rivers which so delightfully diversify our country, one and all suffer by the vile wooden-bridge system which has nothing at all to plead in extenuation of its tasteless, expensive existence. Every bridge in this country should be deprived of its heavy roof; and if the exigencies of engineering required side-walls, they should be plentifully perforated with open spaces. The more recent railroad bridges are fortunately open bridges, or 'viaducts,' as it is fashionable to call them, and the traveller, as in the case of the Starucca viaduct on the Erie road, can both admire the engineering skill and enjoy the scenery. The Connecticut Valley is terribly disfigured by these bridges; and a traveller from New Haven to Memphremagog will be thoroughly impressed with this fact, which is the only drawback to the pleasure of the route." As an instance of ingenuity in this sphere, the bridge which crosses the Potomac Creek, near Washington, deserves notice. The hollow iron arches which support this bridge also serve as conduits to the aqueduct which supplies the city with water.

Amid the mass of prosaic structures in London, what a grand exception to the architectural monotony are her bridges! How effectually they have promoted her suburban growth! "The English," wrote Rose, from Italy, "are Hottentots in architecture except that of bridges." Canova thought the Waterloo Bridge the finest in Europe, and, by a strangely tragic coincidence, this noble and costly structure is the favorite scene of suicidal despair, wherewith the catastrophes of modern novels and the most pathetic of city lyrics are indissolubly associated. Westminster Bridge is as truly the Swiss Laboyle's monument of architectural genius, fortitude, and patience, as St. Paul's is that of Wren; there Crabbe, with his poems in his pocket, walked to and fro in a flutter of suspense the morning before his fortunate application to Burke; and our own Remington's bridge-enthusiasm involves a pathetic story. At Cordova, the bridge over the Guadalquiver is a grand relic of Moorish supremacy. The oldest bridge in England is that of Croyland in Lincolnshire; the largest crosses the Trent in Staffordshire. Tom Paine designed a cast-iron bridge, but the speculation failed, and the materials were subsequently used in the beautiful bridge over the River Wear, in Durham County. There is a segment of a circle six hundred feet in diameter in Palmer's

24

bridge which spans our own Piscataqua. It is said that the first edifice of the kind which the Romans built of stone was the Ponte Rotto, begun by the Censor Fulvius and finished by Scipio Africanus and Lucius Mummius. Popes Julius III. and Gregory XIV. repaired it; so that the fragment now so valued as a picturesque ruin symbolizes both Imperial and Ecclesiastical rule. In striking contrast with the reminiscences of valor, hinted by ancient Roman bridges, are the ostentatious Papal inscriptions which everywhere in the States of the Church, in elaborate Latin, announce that this Pontiff built, or that Pontiff repaired, these structures.

The mediæval castle-moat and drawbridge have, indeed, been transferred from the actual world to that of fiction, history, and art, except where preserved as memorials of antiquity; but the civil importance which from the dawn of civilization attached to the bridge is as patent to-day as when a Roman emperor, a feudal lord, or a monastic procession went forth to celebrate or consecrate its advent or completion; in evidence whereof, we have the appropriate function which made permanently memorable the late visit of Victoria's son to her American realms, in his inauguration of the magnificent bridge bearing her name, which is thrown across the St. Lawrence for a distance of only sixty yards less than two English miles, — the greatest tubular bridge in the world. When Prince Albert, amid the cheers of a multitude and the grand cadence of the national anthem, finished the Victoria Bridge by giving three blows with a mallet to the last rivet in the central tube, he celebrated one of the oldest, though vastly advanced, triumphs of the arts of peace, which ally the rights of the people and the good of human society to the representatives of law and polity.

One may recoil with a painful sense of material incongruity, as did Hawthorne, when contemplating the noisome suburban street where Burns lived; but all the humane and poetical associations connected with the long struggle sustained by him, of "the highest in man's soul against the lowest in man's destiny," recur in sight of the Bridge of Doon, and the two "briggs of Ayr," whose "imaginary conversations" he caught and recorded; or that other bridge which spans a glen on the Auchinleck estate, where the rustic bard first saw the Lass of Ballochmyle. The tender admiration which embalms the name of Keats is also blent with the idea of a bridge. The poem which commences his earliest published volume was suggested, according to Milnes, as he "loitered by the gate that leads from the battery on Hampstead Heath to the field by Caenwood"; and the young poet told his friend Clarke that the sweet passage, "Awhile upon some bending planks," came to him as he hung "over the rail of a foot-bridge that spanned a little brook in the last field upon entering Edmonton." One of Wordsworth's finest sonnets was composed on Westminster Bridge. To the meditative pedestrian, indeed, such places lure to quietude; the genial Country Parson, whose "Recreations" we have recently shared, unconsciously illustrates this, as he speaks of the privilege men like him enjoy, when free "to saunter forth with a delightful sense of leisure, and know that nothing will go wrong, although he should sit down on the mossy parapet of the little one-arched bridge that spans the brawling mountain-stream." On that Indian-summer day when Irving was buried, no object of the familiar landscape, through which, without formality, and in quiet grief, so many of the renowned and the humble followed his remains from the village-church to the rural graveyard, wore so pensive a fitness to the eye as the simple bridge over Sleepy-Hollow Creek, near to which Ichabod Crane encountered the headless horseman, — not only as typical of his genius, which thus gave a local charm to the scene, but because the country-people, in their heartfelt wish to do him honor, had hung wreaths of laurel upon the rude planks. There are few places in Europe where the picturesque and historical associations of a bridge more vividly impress the spectator than Sorrento; divided from the main land by a gorge two hundred feet deep and fifty wide, the chasm is spanned by a bridge which rests on double arches, built by the Romans; it is the popular rendezvous, and, beheld on coming from some adjacent orange-garden, resembles a picture, — the men with their crimson or brown caps, and the women with jetty hair and eyes, and enormous ear-rings, cluster there in the centre of the most exquisite scenery. There is a bridge across the Adige at Verona, which used to be opened but once a year, on account of the risk of injury — its span being prodigious; it was long called the "Holiday Bridge." In Paris the change in the names of bridges is historically significant: in 1817 "the bridge of Austerlitz abdicated its name," and became the bridge of the Jardin des Plantes. The lofty bridge of Carignano, at Genoa, owes its existence to a quarrel between two noblemen; and it is a favorite sacrificial spot to suicides who have repeatedly thrown themselves therefrom headlong into the Strada Servi.

"The Baltimore and Ohio railroad company lose two of their admirable bridges: one at Fairmount, over the Monongahela River, and the famous one over the Cheat

River," wrote a late reporter from the scene of war in Virginia. "The latter was one of the most beautiful structures in the United States, and, being placed amid scenery of unsurpassed grandeur, it had already become a classic spot in the guide-book of American art. It was vandalism fit for ingrates and traitors of the lowest type to destroy what was at once so beautiful and useful a monument of taste and science."

Another fine landscape effect produced by a bridge is at Spoleto, in the Roman States; the ten brick arches that so picturesquely span the romantic valley, have carried the water for centuries into the old city. The magnificent bridge by which Madrid is approached, is a grand feature in the adjacent landscape; and its striking photograph a noble souvenir of the Spanish capital. The most awful bridge imagination ever created, is that described by Milton, whereby Satan's "sea should find a shore":—

> "Sin and Death amain
> Following his track, such was the will of Heaven,
> Pav'd after him a broad and beaten way
> O'er the dark abyss, whose boiling gulf
> Tamely endured a bridge of wond'rous length,
> From hell continued, reaching th' utmost orb
> Of this frail world; by which the spirits perverse
> With easy intercourse pass to and fro
> To tempt and punish mortals."

Fragments, as well as entire roadways and arches of natural bridges, are more numerous in rocky, mountainous, and volcanic regions than is generally supposed; the action of the water in excavating cliffs, the segments of caverns, the accidental shapes of geological formations, often result in structures so adapted for the use and like the shape of bridges as to appear of artificial origin. In the States of Alabama and Kentucky, especially, we have notable instances of these remarkable freaks of Nature; there is one in Walker County, of the former State, which, as a local curiosity, is unsurpassed; and one in the romantic County of Christian, in the latter State, makes a span of seventy feet with an altitude of thirty; while the vicinity of the famous Alabaster Mountain of Arkansas boasts a very curious and interesting formation of this species. Two of these natural bridges are of such vast proportions and symmetrical structure that they rank among the wonders of the world, and have long been the goals of pilgrimage, the shrines of travel. Their structure would hint the requisites, and their forms the lines of beauty, desirable in architectural prototypes. Across Cedar Creek, in Rockbridge County, Virginia, a beautiful and gigantic arch, thrown by elemental forces and shaped by time, extends. It is a stratified arch, whence you gaze down two hundred feet upon the flowing water; its sides are rock, nearly perpendicular. Popular conjecture reasonably deems it the fragmentary arch of an immense limestone cave; its loftiness imparts an aspect of lightness, although at the centre it is nearly fifty feet thick, and so massive is the whole that over it passes a public road, so that by keeping in the middle one might cross unaware of the marvel. To realize its height it must be viewed from beneath; from the side of the creek it has a Gothic aspect; its immense walls, clad with forest-trees, its dizzy elevation, buttress-like masses, and aerial symmetry, make this sublime arch one of those objects which impress the imagination with grace and grandeur all the more impressive because the mysterious work of Nature,—eloquent of the ages, and instinct with the latent forces of the universe. Equally remarkable, but in a diverse style, is the Giant's Causeway, whose innumerable black stone columns rise from two to four hundred feet above the water's edge in the County of Antrim, on the north coast of Ireland. These basaltic pillars are for the most part pentagonal, whose five sides are closely united, not in one conglomerate mass, but articulated so aptly that to be traced the ball and socket must be disjointed.

The effect of statuary upon bridges is memorable; the Imperial statues which line that of Berlin form an impressive array; and whoever has seen the figures on the Bridge of Sant' Angelo at Rome, when illuminated on a Carnival night, or the statues upon Santa Trinità at Florence, bathed in moonlight, and their outline distinctly revealed against sky and water, cannot but realize how harmoniously sculpture may illustrate and heighten the architecture of the bridge. More quaint than appropriate is pictorial embellishment; a beautiful Madonna or local saint placed midway or at either end of a bridge, especially one of mediæval form and fashion, seems appropriate; but elaborate painting, such as one sees at Lucerne, strikes us as more curious than desirable. The bridge which divides the town and crosses the Reuss is covered, yet most of the pictures are weather-stained; as no vehicles are allowed, foot-passengers can examine them at ease. They are in triangular frames, ten feet apart, but few have any technical merit. One series illustrates Swiss history; and the Kapellbrücke has the pictorial life of the Saint of the town; while the Mile Bridge exhibits a quaint and rough copy of the famous "Dance of Death."

In Switzerland what fearful ravines and foaming cascades do bridges cross! sometimes so aerial, and overhanging such precipices, as to justify to the imagination the name superstitiously bestowed on more than one, of the Devil's Bridge; while from few is a more lovely effect of near water seen than the "arrowy Rhone," as we gaze down upon its "blue rushing" beneath the bridge at Geneva. Perhaps the varied pictorial effects of bridges, at least in a city, are nowhere more striking than at Venice, whose five hundred, with their mellow tint and association with palatial architecture and streets of water, especially when revealed by the soft and radiant hues of an Italian sunset, present outlines, shapes, colors, and contrasts so harmonious and beautiful as to warm and haunt the imagination while they charm the eye. It is remarkable, as an artistic fact, how graciously these structures adapt themselves to such diverse scenes, — equally, though variously, picturesque amid the sturdy foliage and wild gorges of the Alps, the bustle, fog, and mast-forest of the Thames, and the crystal atmosphere, Byzantine edifices, and silent canals of Venice.

Whoever has truly felt the aerial perspective of Turner has attained a delicate sense of the pictorial significance of the bridge; for, as we look through his floating mists, we descry, amid Nature's most evanescent phenomena, the span, the arch, the connecting lines or masses whereby this familiar image seems to identify itself not less with Nature than with Art. Among the drawings which Arctic voyagers have brought home, many a bridge of ice, enormous and symmetrical, seems to tempt adventurous feet and to reflect a like form of fleecy cloud-land; daguerreotyped by the frost in miniature, the same structures may be traced on the window-pane; printed on the fossil and the strata of rock, in the veins of bark and the lips of shells, or floating in sunbeams, an identical design appears; and, on a summer morning, as the eye carefully roams over a lawn, how often do the most perfect little suspension-bridges hang from spear to spear of herbage, their filmy span embossed with glittering dew-drops! *

* "The invention of the Suspension Bridge, by Sir Samuel Brown, sprung from the sight of a spider's web hanging across the path of the inventor, observed on a morning walk, when his mind was occupied with the idea of bridging the Tweed."

www.ingramcontent.com/pod-product-compliance
Lightning Source LLC
LaVergne TN
LVHW020124110826
845151LV00001B/265

* 9 7 8 1 4 2 5 5 4 1 2 2 4 *